Collins *gem* W9-ATX-050

SAS
Survival
Guide

John Wiseman

Collins
An Imprint of HarperCollins Publishers

ISBN-10: 0-00-718330-5
ISBN-13: 978-0-00-718330-2

ISBN-10: 0-06-084982-7 (in the United States)
ISBN-13: 978-0-06-084982-5
FIRST U.S. EDITION Published 2006

Text © John Wiseman 1986, 1993, 2004
Illustrations © HarperCollins Publishers, 1986, 1993
John Wiseman, a former SAS instructor, teaches and writes about survival techniques

Printed and bound in Italy by Amadeus
10 09 08
9 8 7 6 5 4

INTRODUCTION

For 26 years, as a professional soldier, I had the privilege to serve with the Special Air Service (SAS). This elite unit of the British Army is trained to carry out arduous operations in all parts of the world. They have to develop skills that enable them to survive anywhere and to handle every kind of situation. As the survival instructor to the SAS, it was my job to ensure that each and every member of the Regiment could apply these skills. Tested in training and operations, they form the basis of this book.

When I am teaching soldiers or civilians how to deal with survival situations, part of my job is to ensure their safety. I cannot do that for the reader of this book. I do know that what I have written has saved lives in the past and that I can save more in the future. In learning the skills described here, readers must be restrained by the need to conserve our environment and to avoid cruelty to animals, as well as the laws that some of these techniques may contravene. Remember, this is a handbook for the survival situation when self-preservation is paramount and risks may be involved that would otherwise be out of the question. Apply survival techniques with caution, as the consequences will be your responsibility and no one else's.

Although this is not an official publication, by sharing survival knowledge gained through my SAS experience, I aim to help you to be a survivor too.

J.W.
The Survival School, Hereford, England

WARNING

The survival techniques described in this publication are to be used in dire circumstances where the safety of individuals is at risk. As such the publishers cannot accept any responsibility for any prosecutions or proceedings that are brought or instituted against any person or body as a result of the use or misuse of any techniques described or any loss, injury, or damage thereby caused. In practicing and perfecting these survival techniques the rights of landowners and all relevant laws protecting certain species of animals and plants and controlling the use of firearms and other weapons must be regarded as paramount.

CONTENTS

CONTENTS

CONTENTS

CONTENTS

CONTENTS

CONTENTS

CONTENTS

CONTENTS

ESSENTIALS FOR SURVIVAL

Survival is the art of staying alive. Mental attitude is as important as physical endurance and knowledge. You must know how to take everything that is possible to find from nature and use it to its full potential, how to attract attention to yourself so that rescuers can find you, how to make your way across unknown territory and back to civilization if there is no hope of being rescued, navigating without a map or compass. You must know how to maintain a healthy physical condition, or if sick or wounded, how to heal yourself and others. You must be able to maintain your morale as well as that of others.

Any equipment you have must be considered a bonus. Lack of equipment should not mean that you are not equipped, since you will carry skills and experience with you, but those skills and experience must not be allowed to get rusty, and you must build up your knowledge all the time.

Think of survival skills as a pyramid that is built on the foundation of the will to survive. The next layer is knowledge. This builds confidence and dispels fears. The third layer is training: mastering and maintaining skills. Add your equipment to the top. Combine the instinct for survival with knowledge, training, and equipment and you will be ready for anything.

ESSENTIALS

BE PREPARED

The Boy Scouts' motto is the right one. Make sure that
you are physically and mentally prepared before you head
off and pack the appropriate gear for what you plan to do.

CHECKLIST

Before any journey or expedition ask yourself :

How long will I be away? How much food and water
do I need to carry?

Do I have the right clothing/footwear for the climate?
Should I take extras?

What special equipment do I need for the terrain?
What medical equipment is appropriate?

HEALTH CHECKUPS

Have thorough medical and dental checkups and ensure
that you have all the necessary injections for the territories
through which you intend to travel.

Pack a medical kit to cover all your likely needs, as
well as those of each member of your group.

GROUP EXPEDITIONS

Consider the ability of each member of your group to deal
with the challenges ahead: it may be necessary to drop
unfit members. Have frequent meetings to discuss plans
and responsibilities. Nominate a medic, a cook, a
mechanic, a driver, a navigator, etc. Ensure that everyone
is familiar with the equipment and that you carry spares.

RESEARCH

The more detailed knowledge you have of the place and
people, the better your chances for a successful

ESSENTIALS

expedition. Study your maps carefully, gain as much knowledge of the terrain as possible: climate; weather conditions; river directions and speed of flow; how high are the mountains/hills; what type of vegetation/animal life can you expect?

PLANNING

Divide the project into phases: entry, objective, and recovery. Clearly state the aim of each phase and work out a timescale. Plan for emergency procedures such as vehicle breakdown, sickness, and casualty evacuation.

Allow plenty of time when you are estimating the rate of progress. Pressure to stick to an overly ambitious schedule leads to exhaustion and errors in judgment.

The need to replenish water supplies from local sources should be a major factor in determining your route.

Make sure that someone knows where you are planning to go and of your times of departure and expected arrival. Keep them informed at prearranged stages so that failure to contact will set off alarm bells . Boats and aircraft are strictly controlled in this respect. If you are hiking in the hills, inform the police and local mountain rescue center of your proposed plan.

Contingency plans

Be prepared in case anything goes wrong. What will you do if your vehicle breaks down or if the weather conditions turn out to be more severe than you had anticipated? If in a group, how will you regroup if you are separated? What happens if someone gets sick?

ESSENTIALS

EQUIPMENT

Clothes should fit well but not be restrictive, giving
protection from the cold and rain while keeping the body
ventilated. Carry waterproof outerwear, a change of
clothes, and extra warm garments. Layer clothing in cold
climates. Synthetics such as Gore-tex™ and fleece are
versatile and useful. Wool is excellent in cold and wet
climates, while cotton works well in the tropics.

Sleeping bag

Down sleeping bags are light and give better insulation than
man-made fibers. When it is wet, however, down loses its
insulating properties and is difficult to dry out. If you don't
have a tent, a bivouac bag of "breathable" material will keep
you dry.

Backpack

Backpacks must be strong and waterproof, with tough,
adjustable webbing secured to the frame, and a
comfortable belt to hold the weight on your hips. External
frames are the best: although heavier and prone to snag on
branches, they can take awkward, heavy loads—and even
an injured person. The frame should allow air space
between the backpack and your back to reduce
perspiration. Zip-fastened side pockets are the best.

STOWING EQUIPMENT

Pack so that you know where everything is and the first
things you need are on the top. If it's wet, stow items in
polyethylene bags. Tent and heavy items go on top, but
don't make the pack too high as it will be hard to balance
in strong winds. Keep damageable food in containers.

ESSENTIALS

RADIO

Radios are a necessity for long, remote expeditions. Prearrange a plan of signals with twice-daily scheduled calls to your base giving your location and plans. Base can supply weather updates and other info and monitor the frequency for emergency calls, if necessary. Select frequencies that will work in the areas that you are going to. At least two group members should be able to operate the radio. An emergency plan will go into operation if you miss two consecutive calls to base. In this case, go to or stay at the last reported location and await contact.

GPS

A GPS (Global Positioning System) receives radio signals from satellites and can locate your current position anywhere in the world. They are relatively easy to use and have a 95% accuracy rate. However, the satellite transmission must not have any obstructions in its way, so be sure that you are standing still and out in the open when using your GPS. As with any battery-operated piece of equipment, do not use the GPS as a substitute for basic navigational skills, but instead as a way of confirming or correcting your navigation.

CELLULAR PHONES

Cell phones offer a helpful supplement to radio contact and can be a real lifesaver in emergency situations. Check your network coverage before an expedition. Conserve batteries and protect them from moisture. Remember, it takes less power to listen than it does to transmit.

ESSENTIALS

SURVIVAL KIT

The items shown on p. 19 can make all the difference in the fight for survival. They should be stored in a small container, such as a 2 oz. tobacco tin. Polish the inside of the lid to make a reflecting surface. Seal it with a strip of adhesive tape (a) that can easily be removed and replaced to make it waterproof. Pack the empty space with cotton wool (for lighting fires) to keep the contents from rattling.

Check the contents regularly, changing anything that deteriorates. Never leave the tin open or lying on the ground. Make a habit of always having it with you.

1 **MATCHES** Preferably waterproof, but nonsafety matches can be "shower proofed" by dipping their heads in melted candle fat. Snap off half to save space.

2 **CANDLE** Shave it square for packing. Tallow candles can be eaten in an emergency or used for frying, but are difficult to store in hot climates. Others are inedible.

3 **FLINT** Processed flint with a saw striker.

4 **MAGNIFYING GLASS** To start fire in sunlight.

5 **NEEDLES AND THREAD** Several needles, including at least one with a very large eye to fit sinew and coarse threads. Wrap a length of strong thread around the needles.

6 **FISHHOOKS AND LINE** Selection of hooks and split lead weights, plus as much line as possible.

7 **COMPASS** Liquid-filled compass with a luminous button is the best. Make sure it is in working order and that you know how to use it. The pointer is prone to rust: check that it is on its pivot and swings freely.

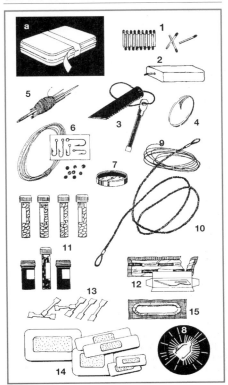

ESSENTIALS

8 **BETA LIGHT** A light-emitting crystal for reading maps at night and as a fishing lure.

9 **SNARE WIRE** Preferably brass. 2–3 feet (60–90 cm).

10 **FLEXIBLE SAW** Remove the handles and grease it before storing. To use it, fit wooden toggle handles.

11 **MEDICAL KIT** Pack medicines in airtight containers with cotton wool. Label them carefully with the full dosage instructions and expiry dates. Do not exceed recommended dosages or take with alcohol. The following items are only a guide:

Analgesic Pain reliever for mild/moderate pain.

Intestinal sedative For acute/chronic diarrhea.

Antibiotic For general infections. Carry enough for a full course.

Antihistamine For allergies, insect bites/stings.

Water sterilizing tablets Use when you cannot boil questionable water.

Antimalarial tablets Essential in areas where malaria is present.

Potassium permanganate Add to water and mix until pink to sterilize, until deeper pink to make antiseptic, and full red to treat fungal diseases, e.g. athlete's foot.

12 **SURGICAL BLADES** At least two scalpel blades of different sizes.

13 **BUTTERFLY SUTURES** To hold the edges of wounds together.

14 **BAND-AIDS** Waterproof, assorted sizes.

15 **CONDOM** Makes a good waterbag: holds 2 pints (1L).

SURVIVAL POUCH

In addition to your survival tin, pack a pouch and keep it handy for emergencies.

ESSENTIALS

POUCH Must be waterproof and large enough to take a mess kit, with a positive fastening that will not come undone and a strong loop to hold it onto your belt.

FUEL Solid fuel tablets in their own stove container (1). Use this sparingly when a wood fire is inconvenient. They make excellent fire lighters. Stove unfolds to form an adjustable pot stand (2).

SIGNAL FLARES (3) To attract attention. Carry red and green miniflares (4) and a discharger (5). Beware: these are explosives! Remove the discharger and screw it onto a flare (6). Withdraw the flare and point it skywards at arm's length. Pull the trigger to fire. Use with care; do not waste (see p. 281).

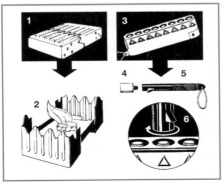

ESSENTIALS

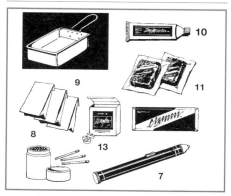

MESS KIT Aluminum cooking utensil. Pack kit inside.

PENCIL-SIZED FLASHLIGHT (7). Keep batteries reversed inside to avoid accidentally switching it on.

MARKER PANEL Fluorescent strip c. 1 x 5 feet (0.3 x 2 m) for signaling. (See p. 275.)

MATCHES (8) Pack in a waterproof container.

BREW KIT Tea powder, sachets of milk, and sugar (9).

FOOD Tube of butter (10). Dehydrated meat (11). Chocolate (12). Salt tablets (13) or electrolyte powder, which contains vitamins, salt, and other minerals.

SURVIVAL BAG Heat-insulated bag of 7 x 2 feet (200 x 60 cm) of reflective material that keeps you warm and free of condensation.

SURVIVAL LOG Written log of all events. It will become a valuable reference and training tool.

ESSENTIALS

KNIVES

A knife is an invaluable asset in a survival situation, but remember that knives are weapons and should be given to airline staff when you are traveling by air. Never display them in tense or awkward situations.

CHOOSING A KNIFE

A multibladed penknife is useful, but if you can only carry one knife, take something stronger—a general-purpose blade that will do all likely tasks efficiently and comfortably, from cutting trees to skinning animals and preparing food. Some have built-in compasses or hollow handles for carrying kit, but any advantages are offset by the fact that such handles may break or the compass may lose its accuracy.

FOLDING KNIVES: Should have a good locked position. A wooden handle is more comfortable to use.

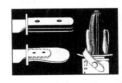

Handle (a) is ideal: a single, rounded piece of wood, the knife tang passing through it and fastened at the end. Handle (b) is riveted and would cause blisters, handle (c) could easily break. The sheath (d) must have a positive fastening and a tunnel belt loop.

ESSENTIALS

You are only as sharp as your knife. It must be sharp and ready for use. Don't misuse your knife by throwing it. Keep it clean, oiled, and in a sheath when not in use.

PARANG: A knife with a large, curved blade like a machete. Too large for everyday use, it is ideal in the wild for cutting down trees and building shelters and rafts. The ideal parang size is 12 inches (30 cm) overall blade length, with a blade that is 2 inches (5 cm) at its widest, and weighing no more than 1.5 lbs. (750 g). The end of the blade should be bolted into a wooden handle.

The parang blade has three different edges: (b) does the heavy work of chopping wood and bone; (a) is finer and used for skinning; (c) is for carving and delicate work. The curved blade enables the maximum effort to be applied when you are cutting timber and the blade arrives before the knuckles, offering protection.

The sheath must have positive fastenings to keep the parang secure, and a loop for attaching it to a belt. Some sheaths have a pocket on the front for a sharpening stone.

ESSENTIALS

 There is a danger that the cutting edge may come through the side of the sheath. NEVER hold the sheath on the same side as the cutting edge when drawing the parang. Always grip the side AWAY FROM THE CUTTING EDGE.

Sharpening a knife

Sandstone, quartz, and granite will sharpen tools. Rub two pieces together to make them smooth. A double-faced stone with a rough and smooth surface is ideal. Use the rough surface first to remove burrs then use the smooth surface to get a fine edge. The object is to get an edge that will last and not chip.

To sharpen the blade, hold the handle in your right hand. Use a clockwise, circular motion and apply steady pressure on the blade with the fingertips of your left hand as you push away. Keep the angle constant and the stone wet. Don't drag the blade toward you under pressure; this produces burrs. Reduce the pressure for a finer edge. Work counterclockwise on the other side.

Blade profile: (A) is too steep and will soon wear; (B) is good; and (C) is too fine and will chip.

Get in the habit of checking all your equipment regularly, especially after negotiating difficult terrain. A check of all your pockets and possessions should be second nature.

ESSENTIALS

FACING DISASTER

It is no use giving up. Only positive action can save you. People can survive almost impossible situations if they have the determination.

SURVIVAL STRESSES

A survival situation will put you under physical and mental pressure. You will have to overcome some or all of the following stresses:

Fear and anxiety

Pain, sickness, and injury

Cold and/or heat

Thirst, hunger, and fatigue

Sleep deprivation

Boredom

Loneliness and isolation

Can you cope? You have to.

Self-confidence is the product of good training and knowledge. These must be acquired before you face a survival situation. Confidence will help you overcome the mental stresses. Physical fitness will give you the resources to cope with fatigue and loss of sleep. The more fit you are, the better you will survive. Start training now.

Pain and fever draw attention to an injured body part and prevent you from using it. It is important to treat any injury as soon as possible, but pain may have to be overcome and controlled in order to seek help and avoid the risk of further injury or death.

ESSENTIALS

WATER

Ordering your priorities is one of the first steps for survival. Our basic needs are food, fire, shelter, and water. Their order of importance will depend on where you are, but water is always essential.

An adult can survive for three weeks without food but for only three days without water. Don't wait until you run out of water before you look for more. Conserve your supplies and seek a new source of fresh running water, although all water can be sterilized.

The human body loses 4–6 pints (2–3L) of water each day. Loss of liquids through respiration and perspiration increases with your work rate and temperature. Vomiting and diarrhea increase this loss even further. This must be replaced either by actual water or water contained in food.

HOW TO RETAIN FLUIDS

To keep fluid loss to a minimum, take the following precautions:

Avoid exertion. Just rest. Don't smoke.

Stay cool. Stay in the shade. If there isn't any, erect a cover to provide it.

Do not lie on hot ground or heated surfaces.

Don't eat, or eat as little as possible—digestion uses up fluids, increasing dehydration. Fat is especially hard to digest.

Never drink alcohol. This takes fluid from vital organs to break it down.

Don't talk. Breathe through your nose, not your mouth.

ESSENTIALS

FINDING WATER

Look in the bottoms of valleys where water naturally drains. If there is no stream or pool, look for patches of green vegetation and dig there.

Dig in gullies and dry streambeds.

In mountains look for water trapped in crevices.

On the coast dig above the high waterline, or look for lush vegetation in faults in cliffs: you may find a spring.

 Be suspicious of any pool with no green vegetation growing around it or animal bones present. It is likely to be polluted. Check the edge for minerals that might indicate alkaline conditions. Always boil water from pools. In the desert lakes with no outlets become salt lakes: their water must be distilled before drinking.

DEW AND RAIN COLLECTION: Use as big a catchment area as possible, running the water off into containers. A covered hole in the ground lined with clay will hold water. If you have no impermeable sheeting, use metal sheets or bark to catch water.

Use clothing to soak up water: tie clean clothes around your legs and ankles and walk through wet vegetation. These can be sucked or wrung out.

RATION YOUR SWEAT, NOT YOUR WATER!
If you have to ration water, take it in sips. After going without water for a long time, don't guzzle when you do find it. Only take sips at first. Large gulps will make a dehydrated person vomit, losing even more of the valuable liquid.

ANIMALS AS SIGNS OF WATER

Mammals

Most animals require water regularly. Grazing animals are usually never far from water since they need to drink at dawn and dusk. Converging game trails often lead to water; follow them downhill. Meat eaters are not good indicators—they get moisture from their prey.

Birds

Grain eaters, such as finches and pigeons, are never far from water and drink at dawn and dusk. When they fly straight and low, they are heading for water. When returning from water, they fly from tree to tree, resting frequently. Waterbirds and birds of prey do not drink frequently and are therefore not good indicators.

Insects

Bees are especially good indicators. At most they fly 4 miles (6.5 km) from their nests or hives. Ants are dependent on water. A column of ants marching up a tree is going to a small reservoir of trapped water. Such reservoirs are even found in arid areas. Most flies stay within 295 feet (90 m) of water.

Reptiles

Reptiles collect what little moisture they need from dew and their prey. They are not good indicators.

Humans

Tracks usually lead to a well, borehole, or soak. It may be covered with scrub or rocks to reduce evaporation. Always replace the cover.

ESSENTIALS

CONDENSATION

Trees can draw moisture from a water table that is 50 feet (15 m) or more below ground, too deep for you to dig. Let the tree pump it up for you by tying a plastic bag around a healthy, leafy branch or by placing a polyethylene tent over vegetation. Evaporation from the leaves will produce condensation in the bag.

Keep the opening of the bag at the top, with a corner hanging down to collect water.

Suspend a tent from the apex or support it with a padded stick. Avoid foliage touching the sides, or it will divert droplets from collecting in plastic-lined channels at the bottom.

Even cut vegetation will produe condensation when it is placed in a large plastic bag. *Keep foliage off the bottom with stones so that water collects below it and don't let it touch the sides. Keep the bag taut with stones. Support the top on a padded stick. Arrange the bag on a slight slope so that condensation runs down to the collecting point.*

ESSENTIALS

Solar still

Dig a hole that is approximately 36 inches (90 cm) across and 18 inches (45 cm) deep. Place a collecting can in the center, then cover the hole with a sheet of plastic that is formed into a cone. Roughen the underside of the sheet with a stone to ensure that droplets run down it. The sun raises the temperature of the air and soil below, producing vapor. Water condenses on the underside of the plastic, running down into the container. This is especially effective where it is hot during the day and cold at night. This type of still should collect at least 1 pint (550 ml) over a 24-hour period.

The still doubles as a trap. Insects and small snakes, attracted by the plastic, slide down into the cone or wriggle beneath it into the hole and cannot climb out.

A solar still can be used to distill pure water from poisonous or contaminated liquids.

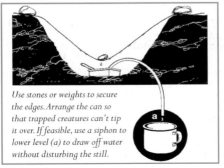

Use stones or weights to secure the edges. Arrange the can so that trapped creatures can't tip it over. If feasible, use a siphon to lower level (a) to draw off water without disturbing the still.

ESSENTIALS

 URINE AND SEAWATER.
Never drink either—ever. But both can
produce drinking water if they are distilled—
and seawater will provide you with a residue of salt.

DISTILLATION

Pass a tube into the top of a water-filled, covered container
that is placed over a fire, and the other end into a sealed
collecting tin that should be set inside another container
providing a jacket of cold water to cool the vapor as it
passes out of the tube. You can use any tubing, e.g. pack
frames. To avoid wasting water vapor, seal around the gaps
with mud or wet sand.

An easier method is a variation on the desert still.
Take a tube from a covered vessel in which polluted or
saltwater is to boil. Set the other end under a solar still. A
sheet of metal, bark, or a leaf weighted down will cover
the vessel and help direct the steam into the tube.

WATER FROM ICE AND SNOW

Ice produces twice as much water as snow for half the
heat. To heat snow, melt a little in a pot and gradually add
more. If you fill the pot with snow, a hollow will form at
the bottom as the snow melts, causing the pot to burn.
Surface snow yields less water than lower layers.

Sea ice is salt—of no use for drinking—until it has
aged. Old sea ice is bluish and has weathered, rounded
edges; the bluer it is, the better it is for drinking. New sea
ice is white and rough. But beware of even old ice that has
been exposed to spray from the sea.

WATER FROM PLANTS

WATER COLLECTORS: Plants often trap water in cavities. Old, hollow joints of bamboo fill up with water: shake them—if you hear water, cut a notch at the base of each joint and tip the water out.

Cup-shaped plants catch and hold water, which should be strained to remove insects and debris.

Bromeliads range from 2 inches–30 feet (5cm–9 m) high but most are 1–5 feet (30–150 cm). Some store water in their tissues, and all collect it in a reservoir formed by leaf bases.

VINES: Vines with rough bark and shoots around 2 inches (5 cm) thick can be a useful source of water. But beware: not all have drinkable water, and some yield a sticky, milky sap that is poisonous. Some vines cause skin irritation on contact, so collect the liquid in a container or let it drip into your mouth rather than put your mouth up to the stem. To obtain water from a vine, select a stem and trace it upward. Reach up as high as possible and cut a deep notch in the stem. Cut off the same stem close to the ground and let the water drip from it. When it ceases to drip, cut a section from the bottom and repeat this until the vine is drained. Do not cut the bottom of the vine first as this will cause the liquid to run up the vine through capillary action.

ESSENTIALS

ESSENTIALS

ROOTS: In Australia the water tree, desert oak, and bloodwood have their roots close to the surface. Pry the roots out and cut them up into 12 inches (30 cm) lengths. Remove the bark. Suck out the moisture or shave the root to a pulp and squeeze over the mouth.

PALMS: The buri, coconut, and nipa palms all contain a sugary fluid that is drinkable. To start it flowing, bend a flowering stalk downward and cut off its tip. If a thin slice is cut off the stalk every 12 hours, the flow will be renewed, making it possible to collect up to one quart each day. Nipa palms shoot out from the base so that you can work from ground level, but on grown trees of other species you may have to climb up to reach a flowering stalk.

Milk from ripe coconuts is a powerful laxative; drinking too much would make you lose more fluid.

CACTI: Water is stored in the fruit and bodies, but some cacti are very poisonous. Avoid contact with the spines, which can be difficult to remove and can cause festering sores.

The barrel cactus (see p. 97) can reach a height of 4 feet (120 cm) and is found in the southwestern United States through to South America. The spine-covered outer skin is very tough: the best method is to cut off the top and chop out pieces from the inside to suck, or smash the pulp within the plant and scoop out the watery sap. A 3.5 feet (100 cm) barrel cactus will yield around 2 pints (1 L) of milky juice, and this is an exception to the rule to avoid milky-sapped plants.

Saguaro cactus of Mexico and the U.S. grows to 17 feet (5 m) and holds lots of poisonous liquid. Collect this and place it in a solar still to evaporate and recondense overnight.

Prickly pears have big "ears" and produce oval fruits that ripen to red or gold. Their large spines are easy to avoid. Both fruit and "ears" are laden with moisture.

WATER FROM ANIMALS

Animal eyes contain water that can be extracted by sucking them.

All fish contain a drinkable fluid. Large fish, in particular, have a reservoir of freshwater along the spine. Tap it by gutting the fish and, keeping the fish flat, remove the backbone, being careful not to spill the liquid, and then drink it.

If water is very scarce, be careful not to suck up the other fish juices in the flesh, because they are rich in protein, and fluid will be taken from your vital organs to digest them.

Desert animals can also be a source of moisture. In northwestern Australia Aborigines dig for desert frogs that burrow in the ground. They store water in their bodies, and it can be squeezed out of them.

ESSENTIALS

SALT

Salt is another essential for human survival. A normal diet includes a daily intake of 0.5 ounces (10 g). The body loses salt in sweat and urine, and you need to replace that loss.

> The first symptoms of salt deficiency are muscle cramps, dizziness, nausea, and tiredness. The remedy is to take a pinch of salt in a pint of water. There are salt tablets in your survival kit. Break them up and dissolve them in an appropriate amount of water. Do not swallow them whole, as this can cause stomachaches and kidney damage.

If your supplies run out and you are close to the sea, saltwater contains around 0.75 ounces (15 g) of salt, but do not drink it as it is. Dilute it with plenty of freshwater to make it drinkable or evaporate it to get salt crystals.

Inland, salt can be obtained from some plants such as the roots of hickory trees in North America or of the nipa palm in southeastern Asia. Boil the roots until all the water evaporates and black salt crystals are left.

If no direct salt sources are available, then rely on getting it second hand through animal blood, which is a valuable source of minerals.

SURVIVAL LOG

Keep a record of all events, especially discoveries of edible plants and other resources. It becomes a valuable reference and making it helps keep up morale.

CLIMATE AND TERRAIN

This chapter cannot provide the worlds geography, it can only summarize types of climate and terrain. It is vital to research conditions in areas that you plan to visit, but a knowledge of climate zones will help if an accident throws you into unfamiliar territory.

Temperate climates cover much of the globe and offer the best chances for survival without special skills or knowledge. These territories are also the most heavily urbanized. Heavy winter conditions may call for polar skills.

CLIMATE ZONES

POLAR REGIONS: This includes latitudes higher than 60°33′north and south, but polar skills may be needed at very high altitudes everywhere. In addition, arctic conditions can occur in Alaksa, Canada, Greenland, Iceland, Scandinavia, and the former U.S.S.R.

TUNDRA: The treeless zone south of the polar cap. The subsoil is permanently frozen, and vegetation is stunted.

NORTHERN CONIFEROUS FOREST: Up to 800 miles (1300 km) deep, this lies between arctic tundra and temperate lands. The winters are long and severe. Trees and plants flourish along the great rivers that flow to the Arctic Ocean. Game, ranging from elks and bears to squirrels and birds, is plentiful. Melted snow creates swamps in the brief summer. Fallen trees and dense growth make the journey difficult, and mosquitoes can be a nuisance. Travel along rivers. Movement is easier in the winter.

CLIMATE AND TERRAIN

DECIDUOUS FORESTS: Oak, beech, maple, and hickory are the main species in America; oak, beech, chestnut, and lime in Eurasia. The rich soil supports many plants. Survival is easy, except in very high altitudes where tundra or snowfield conditions apply.

TEMPERATE GRASSLAND: These are found in the central continental areas of North America and Eurasia. Hot summers, cold winters, and moderate rainfall have made these the great food producing areas.

MEDITERRANEAN REGIONS: Lands bordering the Mediterranean are semiarid, with long, hot summers and short, dry winters. Trees are few, water is scarce.

TROPICAL FORESTS: Equatorial rain forests, subtropical rain forests, and montane forests all feature high rainfall and rugged mountains, which drain into large, swift-flowing rivers, with coastal and low-lying regions as swampland.

SAVANNAS: These are tropical grasslands found in Australia, Venezuela, Colombia, Brazil, and Africa. Grass grows up to 10 feet (3 m). Temperatures are high all year round. Water is scarce, but where it is found there will be lush vegetation and plenty of wildlife.

DESERTS: One fifth of the earth's land surface is desert, of which only small parts are sand; most is flat gravel cut by dried-up water courses (wadis). Very high temperatures occur during the day, falling to below freezing at night. Survival is difficult.

POLAR REGIONS

Winter temperatures are far below freezing and
hurricane-force winds can whip snow 100 feet (30 m) into
the air. A 20 mph (32 kmph) wind brings a 5 °F (-14 °C)
thermometer reading down to an actual temperature of
-30 °F (-34° C). Days vary from total darkness midwinter
to 24-hour daylight midsummer.

TRAVEL

Establish shelter as close to the aircraft or vehicle as
possible. Move only if rescue is improbable. Cold dulls the
mind—plan while you can still think clearly.

Navigation is difficult in featureless terrain, and the
journey is treacherous. Don't move in a blizzard. Sea ice
turns to slush in the summer, and the tundra is boggy.

Don't make shelter close to water, the habitat of black-
fly, mosquito, and deerfly. Cover your skin, wear a net
over your head, and burn green wood to keep them at bay.

Navigation

Compasses are unreliable near the poles, so be guided by
the constellations and travel at night. During the day use
the shadow stick method. (See p. 230.)

Do not use icebergs or distant landmarks to fix your
direction: ice floes move constantly, and relative positions
change. If breaking ice forces you to another floe, leap to a
spot at least 2 feet (60 cm) from the edge.

Avoid icebergs—they can turn over without warning,
especially with your added weight.
Avoid sailing close to ice cliffs—huge masses of ice
can break off without warning.

CLIMATE AND TERRAIN

Observe birds: in the thaw wildfowl fly to land; seabirds fly out to sea during the day, returning at night.

Clouds over open water, timber, or snow-free ground appear black below; over sea ice and snowfields, white. New ice produces grayish reflections, mottled ones indicate pack ice or drifted snow.

Follow rivers: travel downstream—by raft or on ice—except in N. Siberia, where rivers flow north. On frozen rivers stay on edges and along the outer curves on bends. Where rivers join, follow the outside edge or move to outer bank. If a river has many bends, move to land.

> ICE-COLD WATER IS A KILLER
> Falling into icy water knocks the breath out of you. The body loses muscular control, consciousness fades, and death follows in 15–20 minutes. Move quickly to land. Roll in snow to absorb water. Get to shelter and dry off at once.

CLOTHING

Severe cold freezes exposed flesh in minutes. Cover every part of the body. Wear a drawstring hood; a fur trim prevents breath from freezing on the face and injuring the skin. If clothing has no drawstrings, tie the sleeves above the cuffs, tuck your trousers in to prevent heat escaping. If you sweat, loosen your collar or cuffs or remove a layer.

Outer garments should be windproof, but not waterproof, which could trap water inside—animal skins are ideal. Inner layers should trap air for insulation. Wool is the best for inner garments. It does not absorb water and is warm even when it is damp. Cotton absorbs moisture and rapidly loses heat when it is wet.

CLIMATE AND TERRAIN

Footwear

Mukluks—waterproof canvas boots with rubber soles—are ideal. They should have an insulated liner.

Wear three pairs of socks, graded in size to fit over each other and not wrinkle. To improvize footwear, use layers of fabric. Canvas seat covers make good boots. (See trench foot, p. 328.)

Snowshoes: Skiing is fine for firm snow, but snowshoes are the best in soft snow. Lift each foot without angling it, keeping the shoe as flat to the ground as possible.

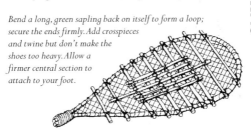

Bend a long, green sapling back on itself to form a loop; secure the ends firmly. Add crosspieces and twine but don't make the shoes too heavy. Allow a firmer central section to attach to your foot.

SHELTER

Get out of the wind! Look for natural shelter to improve on, but avoid sites where a snowdrift, avalanche, or rock fall might bury you. Avoid snow-laden trees (branches may fall) unless lower boughs are supported (see p. 168).

Don't block every hole against drafts. You must have ventilation, especially if your shelter has a fire.

CLIMATE AND TERRAIN

C.O.L.D.

The key to keeping WARM:

Keep it   **C**lean—Dirt and grease block air spaces!

Avoid   **O**verheating—Ventilate!

Wear it   **L**oose—Allow air to circulate!

Keep it   **D**ry—Outside and inside!

FIRE

Fuel sources are limited: driftwood, seal and bird fat, fuel from a wreckage—in extreme cold drain oil from the sump before it congeals. Can be used solid if drained onto ground. High octane fuel can be left in the tanks.

On the tundra willow, birch scrub, and juniper may be found. (See p. 177.)

Casiope is a low, spreading, heatherlike plant with tiny leaves and white, bell-shaped flowers. It contains so much resin that it burns when it is wet.

WATER

In the summer water is plentiful. Pond water may look brown and taste brackish, but vegetation growing in it keeps it fresh. If in doubt, boil it.

In the winter melt ice and snow. Do not eat crushed ice, it can injure your mouth and cause further dehydration. Thaw snow enough to mold it into a ball before sucking it.

Remember—if you are already cold and tired, eating snow will further chill your body.

FOOD

The best chances for survival are along coasts where food supplies—fish, seals, seabirds—are dependable.

ANTARCTIC: Lichens and mosses are the only plants here. Most birds migrate in the fall, but penguins stay. They are easiest to catch when they are nesting.

ARCTIC: Arctic foxes sometimes follow polar bears to scavenge their kills. Northern wildlife is migratory, and its availability depends on the season.

TUNDRA AND FORESTS: Plants and animals are available year-round. Tundra plants are small compared to temperate species (see p. 95).

> POISONOUS PLANTS
> The majority of arctic plants are edible, but avoid water hemlock, baneberry, and arctic buttercups. Other poisonous species include lupine, monkshood, larkspur, vetch, hellebore, and death camas. it's best to avoid fungi too—make sure you can distinguish lichens from them!

ANIMALS FOR FOOD

Caribou (reindeer), musk oxen, and elks (moose) inhabit the Arctic, as do wolves, beaverx, mink, wolverines, and weasels. Foxes, living in the tundra in the summer and open woodlands in the winter, are an indication of other, smaller prey—mountain hares, squirrels, and small burrowing rodents.

Bears and walrus are very dangerous. Leave them alone unless you are armed.

CLIMATE AND TERRAIN

Hunting and trapping

Tracks in the snow are easy to follow but make sure to leave a trail of bright flags to guide you back to base. Make them high enough that they are not covered by fresh snow.

Caribou can be lured by waving a cloth and moving on all fours. Ground squirrels and marmots may run to you if you are between them and their mounds. Kissing the back of your hand makes a sound like a wounded mouse or bird and attracts prey. Find a concealed, downwind position. Be patient. Keep trying.

If you have a projectile weapon (gun, bow, catapult) that can be fired from ground level, lie in ambush behind a screen of snow or make a screen of cloth.

Owls, ravens, and ptarmigans are relatively tame and easy prey in the winter. Many birds have a summer molt that makes them flightless. Eggs are edible at any stage of embryo development.

Seals provide food, clothing, and blubber. They are the most vulnerable on the ice with their pups (produced March to June). Newborn pups cannot swim. Out of the breeding season catch seals by their cone-shaped breathing holes (narrower on the upper surface of the ice). In thick ice flipper and tooth marks show where the seal has been keeping the hole open. Club the animal, then enlarge the hole to recover the carcass.

Polar bears feed on seals and fish. Most are curious and will come to you. Treat them with respect and caution.

Always cook meat: muscles carry the trichinosis worm. Never eat seal or polar bear liver, which can have lethal concentrations of vitamin A.

CLIMATE AND TERRAIN

Preparing meat

Bleed, gut, and skin while the carcass is warm. Roll hides before they freeze. Cut the meat into usable portions and freeze. Do not reheat meat—eat leftovers cold. Leave fat on all animals except for seals. Remove seal fat; render it down before it can turn rancid and spoil the meat.

> Rodents—squirrels, rabbits—carry tularemia, which can be caught from ticks or handling infected animals. Wear gloves when skinning them. Boil the meat.

ARCTIC HEALTH

Frostbite, hypothermia, and snow blindness are the main hazards. Efforts to exclude drafts in shelters can lead to a lack of oxygen and carbon monoxide poisoning.

Your thinking can become sluggish. Stay alert and active, but avoid fatigue and conserve energy for useful tasks. Sleep as much as possible—you won't freeze in your sleep unless you are so exhausted that you cannot regenerate the heat you lose to the air. Exercise your fingers and toes to improve circulation. Take precautions against frostbite (see pp. 327–328).

Avoid spilling gasoline on bare flesh, as it will freeze immediately and damage the skin.

Don't put off defecation—this can cause constipation. Try to time it conveniently before leaving your shelter so that you can take your waste out with you.

> The glare from snow can cause blindness. Protect the eyes with goggles or a strip of cloth or bark with narrow slits cut for your eyes. Blacken underneath the eye with charcoal to reduce glare even further.

ESSENTIALS

MOUNTAINS

Snow-covered peaks offer no food or shelter. Climbing and negotiating ice fields call for skills that must be learned in mountaineering training.

    If disaster strands you on a mountainside and rescue is unlikely, travel during the day to the valleys, where food and shelter are available. At night and in bad visibility this is too dangerous. Find shelter until visibility improves.

    Shelter yourself among rocks or wreckage (see p. 157). Salvage blankets from a crashed plane and cover up to prevent exposure. A plastic bag makes an improvised sleeping bag. On stony ground sleep on your stomach; on a slope sleep with your head uphill.

JUDGING TERRAIN

As you descend, it is difficult to see what is below you. Try moving along a spur for a better view. The far side of a valley will give you an idea of what's on your side. The ground can fall steeply between a distant slope and a foreground cliff. Scree slopes are deceptive, appearing continuous until you are very close to a cliff.

DESCENT

Negotiating cliffs without a rope is very dangerous. Never attempt a high cliff. In the event of a plane crash it is less risky to wait for rescue than to climb.

    On steep cliffs face the rock. For less steep rock faces with deep ledges, adopt a sideways position, using the inside of your hand for support. For easier crags descend facing outward with the body bent and, where possible, carry weight on the palms of the hands.

Descending by rope

With a rope it is possible to rappel (abseil) down sheer cliffs. Use a doubled-up rope, unless someone is left above to untie it or you are prepared to leave it behind, in which case use it undoubled-up for twice the descent.

RAPPELING: Loop rope around a firm anchor (test it with full body weight). Avoid sharp edges. Pass both ends of rope between legs from the front, bring around to left of body, over right shoulder and down across back. Hold rope in front with left hand and at back with right. Plant feet firmly against slope about 18 inches (45 cm) apart and lean back. Let the rope around body carry your weight. Do not try to support yourself with your upper hand. Step downward slowly. The lower hand controls rate of descent. Let the rope out one hand at a time.

Make sure that you are in a firm position before hauling the rope down and that you have planned your next move. Once the rope is down, you may have no way of retracing your steps.

Rappelling can be dangerous. If possible, pad out your shoulders and groin and use gloves to prevent damage from friction. Never attempt this unless accompanied by an expert or in a survival situation.

ASCENT

Climbing up, holds are easier to see, but it is safer to go around than over obstacles to avoid getting stuck. Plan a route from the bottom; keep body away from the rock, feet flat, and look up. Don't overstretch. Always keep three points of contact. Reach for a hold with one hand or foot, test it, and seek a hold for the next hand.

CLIMATE AND TERRAIN

CLIMATE AND TERRAIN

To ascend fissures, use the chimney technique. Place your back against one surface and wedge your legs across the gap to the other. Slowly move up.

Ascending with ropes

BELAYING: one person makes the ascent with a light line attached around the waist with a bowline knot, then hauls up the rope. At each stage of the ascent there must be a ledge to accommodate everyone and a tree or rock for an anchor. Secure the rope with a loop tied in a figure eight or an overhand knot.

The belayer ties on with a bight (loop) or two bights to steady himself and passes the climbing rope over the head and down to the hips, making a twist around the arm closest to the anchor and takes up any slack. The climber ties on with a bowline knot around waist and begins to mount. Belayer takes in rope to keep it taut. Anchor, belayer, and climber should be in a straight line.

To take up rope, pull in with right hand and push away with left so that it passes behind back. Slide right hand out for more rope. Bring hands together and hold both parts of rope in right hand, while the left slides in towards the body to take up slack. Be ready to halt the rope, in case climber falls. Bring the rope tight around body by bringing the hands together.

FALLING ROCK CAN KILL
On loose rock always test the holds gently
and never pull outward on a loose hold. Be
careful that your rope does not dislodge rocks. Even
small falling rocks can inflict serious injury. If you
knock a piece down, shout a warning to those below.

SNOW AND ICE FIELDS

If you are not equipped with an ice ax and crampons and
skilled in their use, try to steer clear of mountain ice.

On steep slopes climb in zigzags, using kicking steps
and driving a snow ax or stick in sideways for stability.
For gentle slopes dig in heels and use a walking stick. On
steep slopes descend backward, driving your stick into
the snow for support and as a brake if you slip. Never use
this method where there is any risk of an avalanche.

SECURITY ROPES: A party crossing a glacier should be tied
together at not less than 30 foot (9 m) intervals. The
leader should probe the snow with a stick for crevasses.
Ropes fixed to a firm anchor at both ends can prevent
falls: tie a short rope around the waist in a bowline knot
and tie onto the main rope with a prusik knot. This will
slide along to allow for descent but will arrest any falls.

If one of the group falls into a crevasse, he or she
must be hauled out with care: the pressure of a rope on
the chest can cause asphyxiation. Pass a looped rope
down to put a foot in to take the weight. If the faller is
unconscious, three people in manharness hitches will be
needed to pull them out. Speed is vital: temperatures in a
crevasse are very low, and the victim will rapidly weaken.

CLIMATE AND TERRAIN

CLIMATE AND TERRAIN

AVALANCHES

Avalanches are a serious hazard in all high mountain regions. They usually occur on slopes of 30°–45° within 24 hours of a snowfall. After a major snowfall of several hours' duration, wait a day for snow to settle. Rain or a rise in temperature after a snowfall increases the risk, as does heavy snow falling in low temperatures, because it does not have time to stabilize.

MAIN AREAS OF DANGER

Snow-covered convex slopes.

Lee slopes where snow has accumulated.

Deep snow-filled gullies.

PRECAUTIONS

Irregular or timbered slopes are the safest.

The sun's heat on snow can cause avalanches, so before noon travel in shaded areas, while after noon keep to slopes that have already been exposed to sun.

Avoid small gullies and valleys with steep side walls.

Stick to ridges and high ground above avalanche paths —you are more likely to trigger a slide but, if you do, you have a better chance of being on top of the debris or not being carried down at all.

When crossing dangerous ground, rope together and use belays, always staying at least 50 feet (15 m) apart.

Always look out for avalanche activity, even if you do not see it happening. Assess where avalanches started, their direction, and how long ago they took place. They will be a guide to where other avalanches are likely to occur.

CLIMATE AND TERRAIN

SEASHORES

Most seashores offer abundant sources of food and excellent prospects for survival.

SANDY BEACHES: Burrowing species—mollusks, crabs, worms—are left below the sand when the water recedes. They attract feeding birds.

It may be possible to find freshwater in the dunes and it is here that plants will grow. Dunes tend to be full of insects, so don't make camp there.

MUDDY SHORES AND ESTUARIES: Where a river joins the sea, it deposits sediment, forming large mudflats. These support many species of worms and mollusks and provide a feeding ground for birds and animals.

ROCKY SHORES: If the cliffs are not too sheer, rockpools may form—these teem with life. Rocks form an anchor for seaweed and sea urchins and crevices where octopus and other cephalopods can live.

Soft rocks, such as chalk, marl, and limestone, erode quickly and have smooth surfaces. Hard rocks fracture in chunks and provide good nesting sites for birds.

PEBBLE BEACHES: Continual movement of pebbles makes a difficult habitat for most plants and animals.

TIDES: Vary according to location and season.

HIGH-TIDE LEVEL INDICATORS
A line of debris along the beach.
Change in the texture of the sand.
Weeds, shells, and color changes on cliff faces.

CLIMATE AND TERRAIN

SHORE SAFETY

Time the tides and study their pattern to avoid being cut off by an incoming tide or swept out by the ebb.

Always check access from a beach or rocky shore. Keep an eye on the tide so you do not get cut off.

Look out for strong currents, especially off headlands. Sandbanks and submerged rocks are also dangerous. Where a beach falls steeply into deep water, there will be a strong undertow. If you enter the water, have a safety line around the waist and a firm anchor on shore.

SWIMMING

When fishing or swimming, stay within your depth and watch out for large waves that can knock you off your feet. If you get caught in the undertow of a large wave, push off the bottom and swim to the surface. Swim to the shore in the trough between waves. When the next wave comes, face it and submerge yourself. Let it pass and swim in the next trough shoreward.

If you are forced offshore by a strong current, do not fight it—swim across it, using sidestroke, and head for land farther along the coast. Sidestroke is not the strongest or fastest stroke, but it is the least tiring.

If you are being swept onto rocks, face land, adopt a sitting position, feet first to absorb the shock. Wear shoes.

A relaxed body floats the best, so stay calm. It is difficult to sink in saltwater. The main danger is in swallowing the water. Women are more buoyant than men and float naturally on their backs. Men float naturally facedown, but don't forget to lift your head out to breathe!

CLIMATE AND TERRAIN

WATER

Freshwater is best obtained from small river outlets—
large rivers tend to be polluted and full of silt.

Seek pools among dunes (see p. 28).

Freshwater rock pools can be identified by the growth
of green algae that is not grazed by mollusks
(saltwater mollusks cannot survive in freshwater).

Look for water trickling through rock, especially where
mosses and ferns grow—it will be drinkable.

If stranded on a rocky outcrop offshore, your only
source of water may be the sea. Never drink seawater
without distilling it. It can be used for cooking—but do
not eat until you have a supply of freshwater.

FOOD

Hunt for fish and mollusks in rock pools at low tide and
dig for mollusks and other creatures in the sand.

Only eat mollusks that have been collected alive.
Bivalves (oysters, mussels) should close tightly if tapped.
Gastropods, (periwinkles, whelks) have a trapdoor
entrance, which should close tightly if the shell is shaken.
Limpets and abalones are anchored to rocks. Prize them
off with a knife. If they are hard to dislodge, they are
good to eat—only sick or dead ones come off easily.

Bivalves can build up dangerous concentrations of
toxic chemicals in polluted areas. In tropical zones
mussels are poisonous in the summer, especially when
seas are reddish or phosphorescent. In the Arctic
black mussels are poisonous at any time of year.

CLIMATE AND TERRAIN

Don't expose yourself to parasites and pollutants: cook shellfish by boiling for at least five minutes.

On most coasts the best time to fish from the shore is around two hours after high tide. Make use of the tide by building fish traps (see pp. 151–152).

Hunt octopuses at night: attract them with a light, then spear them. To kill an octopus, turn it inside out: place your hand inside the fleshy hood, grab the innards, and pull hard—alternatively, stab it between the eyes or bang it against a rock. The flesh is tough but nourishing. Boil the body and roast the tentacles.

Seashore plants differ according to the climate. Gather these when the weather or tide prevent you from taking food from the sea (see p. 105).

 Seaweeds are a valuable contribution to your diet, but the blue-green algae that is often found on freshwater pools is very poisonous.

Sea cucumbers live on the seabed or in the sand. They look like warty, black cucumbers, up to 8 inches (20 cm) long. Boil them for five minutes. Sea urchins cling to rocks just below the low-water mark. Boil, split open, and eat the egglike inside, but avoid them if their spines don't move when touched or if they smell bad when they are opened.

You can also fish for seabirds by leaving baited hooks among offal on flat rocks or by throwing baited hooks into the air to be taken in flight. Hunt on the ground for eggs that are easy to collect before risking raiding cliff nests.

(See *Reptiles* and *Crustaceans* , p. 116 and p. 156.)

DANGERS

CLIMATE AND TERRAIN

Beware in water that is too murky to see through. Wear shoes when foraging to protect feet from spines, which can inflict a painful wound. If you get pricked and the spine breaks off, trying to squeeze it out may push it in deeper. Most will work their way out after a few days.

Well-camouflaged creatures like stingrays can lie hidden: prod the bottom with a stick and stir up sand and rocks in front of you as you go. Stingray wounds can be soothed with very hot water.

Don't put your hands into underwater crevices— you could get bitten.

Always approach a coral reef with caution. Both the reef and its inhabitants—e.g. cone snails, which shoot a poisonous barb—can present dangers.

Lagoon fish are often poisonous—even species that are edible in the open sea. Fish from the reef on the seaward side of the lagoon instead.

If you are stung by a jellyfish, do not pull the tentacles off or the slime wipe away with your hand— you will only get stung more. Use seaweed or a cloth or wipe the sting with sand.

Octopuses have a hard beak, and a few can give a poisonous bite, e.g. the blue-ringed octopus.

Shark attacks occur in very shallow water. Beware!

Stay clear of snakes in the water—they are highly poisonous. If they are found onshore, pin them with a forked stick—they make a good meal.

See pp. 350–356 for a more detailed guide to coastal perils.

CLIMATE AND TERRAIN

ISLANDS

Islands offer a special challenge, with acute isolation to be overcome. Explore the island and establish a daily routine. If it has been inhabited in the past, remains of buildings will offer shelter. If you find caves, make sure that they are not tidal and won't be flooded or cut off by spring tides, which are higher than normal.

On a barren outcrop shelter may simply mean finding a place out of the wind. Food will be whatever clings to the rocks and what you can haul from the sea.

RESOURCES

Be careful not to overexploit limited resources. Lack of water is the reason that many islands are uninhabited. Catch and store rainwater and distill seawater. Lush vegetation is a sign of springs and streams.

Distilling seawater takes lots of fuel, e.g. driftwood, dried seaweeds, or seal blubber. Have a fire only when it is necessary. Search beaches after every tide for flotsam.

Coconut palms

Tropical islands are rarely desert islands—they usually offer plenty to eat. Coconut palms grow throughout the tropics and subtropics, providing fronds for shelter, husks for ropes, and milk and meat.

To remove the husk, force it over a sharpened stake or split it with a hand ax. Extract the milk by piercing one of the dark eyes of the nut before smashing it open to get at the meat. Coconut milk is safe and refreshing—a large nut may hold 2 pints (1 L). Do not drink from young (green) or old (dark brown) nuts, as there is a risk of diarrhea. The meat is indigestible in large amounts: eat a little at a time. Extract the oil by exposing chopped white meat to heat—sun or fire—and collecting oil as it runs off, or by boiling and skimming the oil as it rises to the surface. Rub it on to protect against sunburn and chafing from saltwater, to repel insects, as a salve for sores and blisters, or, mixed with wood ash, as soap.

CLIMBING PALMS: If you need to climb to reach nuts, tie a strap of strong cloth and slip it around your ankles. Adjust it to hold your feet close to the trunk and press the soles of your feet inward to grip the tree.

> ATTRACTING RESCUE
>
> Lay out signals by arranging rocks, seaweed, or anything that contrasts with the surroundings.
>
> Polish metal with sand to make signaling mirrors.
>
> If you see a ship, try to make contact on a VHF radio.

MOVING ON

In a group of islands you may be able to move on when resources are exhausted on the first island. If land is in sight, study tides and currents. Float something you can observe and make a note of its progress. It may be possible to swim, but use a flotation aid, e.g. an empty box or coconuts. Time your swim so that the ebb takes you out from your island and the high tide takes you to the new island. Build a raft in cold climates—from fall to spring seal carcasses will float; lash several together to support your weight.

CLIMATE AND TERRAIN

CLIMATE AND TERRAIN

ARID REGIONS

To survive, you must make the most of any available shade, create protection from the sun, cut moisture loss, and restrict activity during the heat of the day.

   Where great temperature differences occur between night and day, condensation is a source of water.

   When rain does come—years can pass with none at all —it may be in torrential downpours that create flash floods, before quickly being absorbed.

   Dust storms or sandstorms reduce visibility. Protection is needed against sand entering every orifice.

WATER

Water is vital. If you have it, ration it immediately. If you are stranded due to a mechanical failure during a desert crossing, you will have planned your route with an awareness of oases, wells, and waterholes. Wells may require a container lowered down on a line to reach water. Small water holes in wadi (watercourse) bottoms are often seasonal. They are usually covered with a stone or brushwood.

   Away from known water holes, dig at the lowest point of the outside bend of a dry streambed or at the lowest point between dunes. Do not dig in the heat of the day— you'll sweat liquid you may not be able to replace. Always balance fluid loss against possible gain (see p. 27).

   Life expectancy depends on the water that is available and your ability to minimize perspiration. Without water you will last 2 days at 120 °F (48 °C) if you rest in the shade and do nothing. If you must walk to safety, the distance you cover will relate to the water available. With none, at a temperature of 120°F (48 °C), walking at night and resting during the day, you could cover 25 miles (40 km). Walking by day, you would cover 5 miles (8 km) before you collapsed. At 120°F (48 °C) with 4 pints (2 L) of water you might cover 35 miles (56 km) and last 3 days.

Drink 3 pints (1.5 L) for every 4 lost (3:4 pints). Less fluid will not result in less sweat. If more fluid is drunk than is needed, it will be excreted and serve no purpose.

SHELTER AND FIRE

Find immediate shade. In the cool of the evening build a shelter. Do not stay in a metal vehicle or plane. Use it to support a shelter or make use of the shadow beneath an aircraft's wing. Pile up rocks to make a windbreak and make use of wadi walls (except when flash floods seem likely). Use the double-layer technique to aid cooling (see p.161). If you are using fabrics, leave bottom edges lifted and loosen them by day to increase air circulation. Weight them down with rocks at night. Avoid lying directly on hot ground: air can circulate under a raised bed.

You will need fire for warmth at night and for boiling water. Smoke is useful for signaling. Desert scrub burns easily. If the land is barren, vehicle fuel and oil mixed with sand in a container will burn. Animal dung is also flammable.

CLOTHING

Clothing helps reduce fluid loss and gives protection from sunburn and insect bites. Clothes should be light and loose fitting, with air space between the garments and the body. Copy the flowing, layered garments of the Arab

CLIMATE AND TERRAIN

CLIMATE AND TERRAIN

world. Pants give more protection from insects and guard against serious sunburn on the legs. Cover the head and feet.

> Stay covered! Aside from risking severe sunburn, an uncovered body will lose sweat by evaporation. Keep clothing loose with a layer of insulating air. Sweating will then cool you more efficiently.

HEADGEAR: A hat with a piece of cloth attached to the back will protect you but, even better, copy Arab headwear: make a handkerchief into a wad on top of the head, diagonally fold a piece of cloth about 4 feet (120 cm) square, place it over the handkerchief, with the long edge forward, and secure it with a cord tied around head. This traps pockets of air and protects from sand. Wrap it around the face for warmth at night.

EYE PROTECTION: Sunglasses may not be enough. Soot from the fire smeared below the eyes will reduce glare. Shield the eyes from glare and windborne sand with a strip of material. Cut narrow slits to see through.

FOOTWEAR: Do not walk barefoot until your feet have hardened, or they will burn and blister. Do not leave the tops of your feet exposed. Puttees keep sand out of boots; wrap them around the feet over open sandals.

FOOD

Heat causes loss of appetite—don't force yourself to eat. Protein foods increase metabolic heat and water loss. If water is scarce, keep eating to a minimum and try to eat only moisture-containing foods, e.g. fruits and vegetables. Food spoils quickly in the desert. Once it is open, eat your supplies immediately or keep them covered and shaded.

Vegetation is scarce (see p. 97), but deserts often support some animal life. Insects, reptiles, rodents and some small mammals burrow or hide during the day. Large mammals are an indication that there is water close at hand.

HEALTH

Most desert illnesses are caused by excessive exposure to sun and heat. They can be avoided by keeping the head and body covered and remaining in the shade.

Constipation and pain in passing urine are common, and salt deficiency can lead to cramps.

Heavy sweating paired with garments that rub can block the sweat glands and result in an uncomfortable skin irritation known as prickly heat.

Heat cramps, leading to heat exhaustion, heatstroke and serious sunburn are all dangers. A gradual increase in activity and daily exposure to the sun will build up a defense, provided that plenty of drinking water is available.

Keep moist areas of the body—crevices of armpits, groin and toes—clean and dry to prevent infection.

 DESERT SORES
Even the most minor wound will become infected if it is not dealt with right away. Pull out thorns as soon as possible. Where the skin is broken, a large and painful sore may develop that could prevent walking. Bandage all cuts with clean dressings and use whatever medical aids are available.

CLIMATE AND TERRAIN

CLIMATE AND TERRAIN

TROPICAL REGIONS

Everything in the jungle thrives, including diseases and parasites. Even if it is saturated by perspiration, clothing offers protection from stings and bites.

Except at high altitudes, equatorial and subtropical regions are characterized by high temperatures, heavy rainfall, and oppressive humidity. Violent storms may occur toward the end of summer. When choosing camp-sites, make sure that you are above potential flooding.

EQUATORIAL RAIN FORESTS: Temperatures range from 68° F to 86° F (20° C to 30° C) at night. Trees rise from buttress roots to 200 feet (60 m). In this primary jungle the canopy prevents light from reaching the jungle floor. It is relatively cool, with little undergrowth to hamper movement, but visibility is limited. It is easy to lose your sense of direction and difficult for rescuers to see you.

SECONDARY JUNGLE: Along riverbanks and the fringes of the jungle sunlight does penetrate to the floor, and growth is prolific. Undergrowth reaches heights of 10 feet (3 m) in a year. Moving is slow, hot work, hacking your way through with a parang or machete (see p. 249).

SUBTROPICAL RAIN FORESTS: Found within 10° of the equator, these forests have a season of reduced rainfall, even drought, with monsoons coming in cycles. More deciduous trees grow here, and undergrowth is dense.

Rescue signals must be set in clearings (often found near river bends), or—better—on rafts on the river.

MONTANE FORESTS: Found at altitudes above 3000 feet (1000 m). The Ruwenzori Range of central Africa is typical: a craterlike landscape covered in moss between ice-capped peaks. Plant growth is sparse, trees stunted and distorted. Low branches make the journey hard. Nights are cold, days hot and misty. Survival is difficult: make your way down the slopes to tropical rain forests.

SALTWATER SWAMPS: In coastal areas that are subject to tidal flooding, mangrove trees thrive, reaching heights of 40 feet (12 m). Their tangled roots are an obstacle above and below the waterline. Visibility is low, and passage is difficult. Sometimes channels are wide enough to raft, but generally progress is on foot. You won't starve—fish, mollusks, aquatic animals, and vegetation are plentiful—but it is a hostile environment with water leeches, caiman, and crocodiles. Where river channels intersect the swamp, you may be able to make a raft.

If you are forced to stay in a swamp, determine the high-tide level by the line of salt and debris on the trees and build a raised bed above it. Cover yourself for protection against ants and mosquitoes. Build your fire on a platform using standing deadwood for fuel. Decay is rapid in a swamp—choose wood that is not rotten.

FRESHWATER SWAMPS: Found in low-lying inland areas, their thorny undergrowth makes the journey difficult and reduces visibility—but survival is easy, and swamps are often dotted with islands, so you won't be chest deep in water all the time. There are often navigable channels and raw materials available from which to build a raft.

CLIMATE AND TERRAIN

SHELTER

There are ample materials for building shelter in most tropical regions. Where temperatures are high and shelters are exposed to the sun, make roofs in two layers with an air space 8–12 inches (20–30 cm) between to aid cooling. Double layers of cloth will help keep out rain if they are angled (see p. 161).

FIRE

Everything is likely to be damp. Take standing dead-wood, shave off the outside, and use that to start your fire. Dry bamboo and termite nests make good tinder.

FOOD

A wide variety of fruits, roots, and leaves are available. Bananas, papayas, mangoes, and figs are easily recognized, but you may find the wealth of tropical foods bewildering. See pp. 99–104 for a detailed guide. If you're not sure, use the tests described on p. 69 before you risk eating plants.

A wide range of mammals, reptiles, birds, and fish can be hunted, trapped, and fished (see pp. 107–156). Fish are easily digested, but in the tropics they spoil quickly. Clean them thoroughly, discard entrails, and eat them as soon as possible. Do not preserve them by smoking or drying.

> Fish in slow-moving water may be infested with tapeworms and other human parasites: boil them for 20 minutes. Water itself may be infected with amoebas, which cause dysentery: always boil.

DANGERS

INSECT ATTACK

Slashing your way through the jungle you may disturb bee, wasp, or hornet nests. Any bare skin is vulnerable to attack. Run! Don't drop anything—you won't want to go back for it. Goggles will protect the eyes. Insects, desperate for salt, will go for the sweaty parts of your body. Protect your armpits and groin against their painful stings.

MOSQUITO PROTECTION

Wear a net or T-shirt over your head, especially at dawn and dusk. Even better, take a strip of cloth 18 inches (45 cm) wide and long enough to tie around your head; cut it to make a fringe of vertical strips hanging from a band that will dangle around your face and over your neck.

Stay covered at night, including your hands. Oil, fat, or mud spread on hands and face may help repel insects.

Use bamboo or a sapling to support a tent of clothing and large leaves rigged over your upper half.

A smoky fire will help keep insects at bay.

COVER YOUR FEET

Good footwear and protection for the legs is essential. Wrap bark or cloth around your legs and tie it to make puttees as a defense against leeches and centipedes.

BEWARE OF HAIRY CATERPILLARS

Always brush theseoff in the direction they are traveling or small irritant hairs may stay in your skin and cause an itchy rash, which may fester in the heat.

CLIMATE AND TERRAIN

CLIMATE AND TERRAIN

BEWARE OF INVADERS

Keep spare clothing and footwear off the ground so that scorpions, snakes, and spiders don't creep in. Shake out clothes and check boots before putting them on; be wary when putting hands in pockets. Be careful when waking: centipedes nestle for warmth in the more private body regions. Protect armpits and groin against stinging insects attracted by sweat.

LEECHES

Their bite is messy but not painful. Left alone, they drop off when they have had their fill. Do not pull them off—the head may come off, leaving the jaws behind, which could turn septic. Remove with a dab of salt, alcohol, or a burning cigarette end, ember, or flame.

BEWARE OF THE CANDIRU

This minute, almost transparent Amazonian catfish, around 1 inch (2.5 cm) long, is reported to be able to swim up the urethra of a person urinating in the water —where it gets stuck by its dorsal spine. The chance of this happening is remote, but don't take the risk. Cover your genitals and don't urinate in the water.

RIVER DANGERS

Rivers can be home to dangerous creatures such as piranhas, stingrays, and electric eels. Look out for crocodiles or alligators and be careful when handling catfish, which have sharp dorsal fins and spines on their gill covers.

See pp. 340–356 for a guide to dangerous creatures and pp. 319–320 for first aid procedures if you are bitten or stung.

FOOD

The survivor must understand the body's nutritional needs and how to meet them. This chapter provides details of how to trap, snare, hunt, and fish, along with a miniature field guide to edible plants.

FOOD VALUES

A healthy body can survive on reserves stored in its tissues, but food is needed to supply heat and energy and to recover after hard work, injury, or sickness. Seventy calories per hour are required just for breathing and basic bodily functions. Work or major activity can burn up more than 5,500 calories daily. Save calories: do not squander energy.

A balanced diet is as important as having enough to eat. Vary your diet: it must include a range of elements that provide the right proportions of fat, protein, carbohydrates, minerals, and vitamins.

CARBOHYDRATES: Easily digested and a primary source of energy, they prevent ketosis (nausea due to the breakdown of body fats). They come in two forms: sugars, found in sugar, syrup, honey, treacle, and fruits; and starches, roots, tubers (always cook these), and cereals. One ounce (3 g) produces 12 calories.

FATS: A concentrated form of energy. They need a lengthy digestive process that requires plenty of water. Found in animals, fish, eggs, milk, nuts, and some vegetables and fungi. One ounce (3 g) produces 27 calories.

FOOD

PROTEINS: The main sources are meat, fish, eggs, dairy produce, nuts, grains, pulses, and fungi. One ounce (3 g) produces 12 calories

MINERALS: Phosphorus, calcium, sodium, potassium, chlorine, magnesium, and sulfur are among those that are required in quantity. Only small amounts are needed of fluorine, iron, and iodine. All are vital to good health.

TRACE ELEMENTS: These include strontium, aluminum, arsenic, gold, and tiny amounts of other chemicals.

VITAMINS: About a dozen of these are essential for humans. Vitamins D and K are synthesized by the body, but most come from external sources. Scurvy, beriberi, rickets, and pellagra all result from vitamin deficiency. Vitamin A aids vision and prevents eye diseases.

FOOD PLANTS

There are few places without some kind of vegetation that can be eaten. Plants contain vitamins, minerals, protein, and carbohydrates. Some contain fat and all provide roughage.

Do not assume that because birds or mammals have eaten a plant, it is edible for humans. Monkeys give some indication but no guarantee that plants are safe.

TESTING NEW PLANTS

Always adopt the following procedure when trying new plants as food. Never take shortcuts. Only one person should complete the whole test. If you are in any doubt at any stage of the test, do not eat it.

FOOD

EDIBILITY TEST

INSPECT: Try to identify it. Ensure that the plant is not slimy or worm-eaten. Don't risk old, withered plants.

SMELL: Crush a small portion. If it smells of bitter almonds or peaches—discard it.

SKIN IRRITATION: Squeeze some juice or rub slightly on tender skin (e.g. under your upper arm). If discomfort, rash, or swelling is experienced, discard it.

LIPS, MOUTH, TONGUE: If there is no irritation so far, proceed to the following stages, waiting 15 seconds between each to check that there is no reaction:

• Place a small portion on the lips
• Place a small portion in the corner of the mouth
• Place a small portion on the tip of the tongue
• Place a small portion under the tongue
• Chew a small portion

In all cases if discomfort is felt, e.g. soreness to throat, irritation, stinging, or burning, discard it.

SWALLOW: Ingest a small amount and wait five hours. During this time drink or eat nothing else.

EATING: If no reactions, e.g. soreness to mouth, repeated belching, nausea, stomach or abdominal pains are experienced, plant may be considered safe.

Should stomach trouble occur, drink plenty of hot water; do not eat again until the pain goes. If it is severe, induce vomiting by tickling the back of the throat. Swallowing some charcoal will also induce vomiting and may absorb the poison at the same time. White wood ash mixed into a paste with water will relieve stomach pains.

FOOD

GATHERING PLANTS

Gather plants systematically. Take a container out on foraging trips to stop the harvest from being crushed, which makes it go bad

LEAVES AND STEMS: Young growth will be tastier and more tender. Old plants are tough and bitter. Pull off leaves near stem—tearing them off may damage them.

ROOTS AND TUBERS: Choose large plants. If they are difficult to pull up, dig around the plant to loosen it, then prize it out with a sharpened stick.

FRUITS AND NUTS: Pick only ripe, fully-colored fruits from large plants. Hard green berries are indigestible. Peel fruits with tough, bitter skins. When nuts are ripe, they begin to fall from the tree. Shake the tree or throw a stick to knock other nuts down.

CAUTION! Some seeds and grains contain deadly poisons. Taste them, but do not swallow. Carry out the edibility test (see p. 69) and reject any seed that is unpalatable, bitter, or with a hot, burning taste, unless it is a positively identified pepper or spice.

The heads of some grain plants may have enlarged, black, beanlike structures in place of normal seeds. These carry a poisonous, hallucinogenic fungal disease that can be lethal. Reject the whole head.

FOOD

FUNGI: Medium-sized fungi are easy to identify and less likely to suffer insect damage. Pick the whole fungus to aid identification. Keep fungi separate until they are identified—poisonous ones will contaminate other food.

IDENTIFYING PLANTS

Only a small selection of plants can be described and illustrated here. Knowledge of even one or two plants that grow widely and at most times of year could make the difference between survival and starvation. Begin by thoroughly learning these few: Temperate zones: dandelion, nettle, dock, plantain; Subtropical and tropical zones: palm, fig, bamboo; Arid and desert zones: mescal, prickly pear, baobab, acacia (not in the Americas); Polar zones: spruce, willow (north), lichens (north and south), many temperate plant species that grow here in the summer; Coastal zones: kelp and laver.

IDENTIFICATION AIDS
(WITH A KEY FOR ILLUSTRATIONS ON pp. 73–106)

● *Location:* Plants only grow in suitable habitats. Learn these, and you can eliminate impossibilities.

▲ *Shape and size:* Is it tall and woody? Short and soft-stemmed? Bushy and branched?

◆ *Leaves:* Large or small? Spear-shaped or rounded? Toothed or lobed edges? Uniform in color?

❖ *Flowers:* Seasonal, but if they are present, note color, size, shape, single or clustered, where on plant.

Fruits and seeds: Fleshy? Hard? Note color, shape, size, single or clustered, pods or capsules, etc.

Roots: Unless unusual, no help for identification.

FOOD

PLANTS TO AVOID

Avoid any plant with milky sap, unless it is positively identified as safe (e.g. dandelion).

Avoid red plants, unless they are positively identified.

Avoid fruit that is divided into five segments, unless it is positively identified as a safe species.

Avoid plants with tiny barbs on their stems and leaves: these hooks will irritate the mouth and digestive tract.

Avoid old or wilted leaves—some develop deadly toxins when they wilt, e.g. blackberry, raspberry, plum, peach, and cherry. All may be eaten safely when they are young, fresh, and dry.

Avoid mature bracken—it destroys vitamin B in the body and can be lethal. Only eat tightly coiled "fiddle-heads." All northern temperate ferns are edible when they are young, but some are too bitter to be palatable, and others must have their hairy barbs removed before eating: break off young tips, close your hand over the stalk and draw frond through to remove the "wool."

 POISON!

There are two common poisons in the plant world, both easily detectable:

HYDROCYANIC ACID (prussic acid): tastes and smells like bitter almonds or peaches. The most notable example is the cherry laurel: crush a leaf and memorize the smell. Discard all plants with this smell.

OXALIC ACID: the salts (oxalates) occur in plants such as wild rhubarb and wood sorrel. Recognizable by the sharp, dry, stinging, or burning sensation when it is applied to the skin or tongue. Discard all plants that fit this description.

FOOD

EDIBLE PLANTS

In the spring and summer young shoots are tender. Some may be eaten raw; many are best cooked: wash them in clean water, rub off the hairs and boil in a little water so they cook in the steam. Leaves are rich in vitamins and minerals. Do not overcook.

1 **White mustard** ▲ 2 feet (60 cm). ● Grassy wasteland, Eurasia. Stem: hairy. ◆ Crinkly, deep lobed. ❖ Pale yellow. To eat: pick when young. Cook whole plant. Peppery leaves and flowers can also be eaten raw.

2 **Shepherd's purse** ▲ 2 feet (60 cm). ● Wasteland. ◆ Rosette; lobed, spear shaped. ❖ Small, white. To eat: boil leaves and mix with other plants.

3 **Primrose** ● Grassy and shady spots. ◆ Crinkly, tapering; basal rosette. ❖ Long stalked, 5-petaled, pale to bright yellow (pink, in some forms). All parts edible; young leaves are best. Primula genus, includes **cowslip** (3a) and **oxlip** (3b).

FOOD

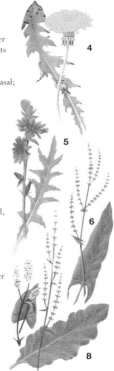

4 **Dandelion** ● Widespread.
◆ deep-lobed rosette. ❖ Large,
yellow to orange. Eat young leaves
raw; boil old ones, change the water
to remove the bitter taste. Boil roots
or roast for coffee.

5 **Chicory** ● Grassy wasteland.
▲ 4 feet (1.3 m). ◆ Thick, hairy basal;
leafy spikes. ❖ Blue, dandelion-
like. Prepare like a dandelion.

6 **Wild sorrel** ● Grassy
wasteland. ▲ 3 feet (1 m).
◆ Long, arrow-shaped.
❖ Spikes, tiny red and green
flowers. Cook young leaves to
reduce the sharp taste.

7 **Buckwheat** ● Open grassy
places, temperate climate.
▲ 2 feet (60 cm). Stem: red.
◆ Spear-shaped. ❖ Clusters; small,
pink or white. Seeds make grains.

8 **Curled dock** ● Grassy
wasteland. ▲ 3 feet (1 m).
◆ Long, narrow, with wavy
margin. ❖ Whorls, small, green.
Boil young leaves. Change the water
to remove bitterness. Rubbing
with dock leaves soothes nettle
stings. Many varieties exist:
prepare as above, use sparingly.

FOOD

*Some plants have edible stems.
If they are soft, peel off the outer,
stringy parts, slice, then boil.
The inner pith of some stems, e.g.
elder, can be extracted by splitting
stem and can be eaten. Use
fibrous stems to make twine.*

9 **Dead nettles** are smaller than
stinging nettles. ◆ Heart-shaped,
no stinging hairs. ❖ White (9), or
pinkish-purple (9a). Boil leaves.

10 **Stinging nettles** ● Widespread.
▲ Young plants 6–8 inches
(15–20 cm). ◆ Toothed, narrow ovals
covered in stinging hairs.
❖ Green spikes. Boil for at least
6 minutes to destroy the acid. Dry
and store leaves.

11 **Ribgrass** or **English
plantain** has spear-shaped leaves
and shorter flower spikes than the
greater plantain. ● Dry ground.
Prepare like greater plantain (below).

12 **Buck's-horn plantain** ● Dry
sandy and rocky areas. Small with
narrow, jagged leaves. ❖ Short spikes.
Prepare like greater plantain.

13 **Greater plantain** ● Grassy wasteland.
◆ Broad, oval leaves. ❖ Distinctive
spikes, tiny yellowish-green and
brown flowers. Prepare rather
bitter young leaves like spinach;
use expressed juice for wounds or
a decoction of the whole plant for
chest pains.

FOOD

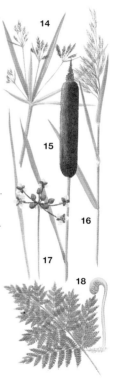

14 **Galingale** or **nut grass**
● Common in and by freshwater.
▲ 5 feet (1.5 m). Stems: 3-angled.
◆ Long, straplike. ❖ Forked,
clustered olive-brown flower head
turns yellow with fruit. Peel and
boil the tubers, or dry and grind them
for flour or coffee substitute.

15 **Cattail** ● In and by freshwater.
▲ 6–15 feet (2–5 m). ◆ Long,
narrow, grayish. ❖ Dark brown,
sausage-shaped. Rootstock/stems:
eat raw or boiled; cook leaves like
spinach, cook shoots like asparagus.
Mix pollen and water to make dough;
bake or cook on the end of a stick.

16 **Reeds** ● In and by freshwater.
▲ Up to 13 feet (4 m). ◆ Gray-green.
❖ Spreading, brown-purple flower
heads on tall canes. Cook the roots.
Punctured canes exude an edible gum.

17 **Flowering rush** ● Eurasia; in
and by freshwater. ▲ 5 feet (1.5 m).
◆ Rise from roots; very long,
straplike, 3-angled.
❖ Pink, 3-petaled. Peel and
boil the rootstock.

18 **Bracken** ● Widespread. Old
fronds are harmful: only eat young
shoots or fiddleheads, pulling off
woolly parts and boiling for 30
minutes. Eat sparingly. Roots can be
boiled or roasted.

FOOD

Many herbs grow wild.
Most can be dried, but not in
direct sunlight.

19 **Tansy** ● Grassy wasteland.
▲ 3 feet (90 cm). ❖ Toothed, dark
green, feathery leaflets.
❖ Buttonlike, bright yellow.
Poisonous in large quantity; leaves
and flowers make a vermifuge tea.
Strong smell keeps flies away.

20 **Marjoram** ● Eurasia; warm,
dry, grassy areas. ▲ 2 feet (60 cm).
◆ Small, oval, stalked. ❖ Clusters,
small, purplish-pink. Use the infusion
for coughs and digestive complaints;
chewed leaves relieve toothaches.

21 **Ramsons** ● Eurasia; wooded
areas. ◆ Bright green. ❖ White, starlike
at the top of stem. Wild garlic. Use any part.

22 **Borage** ● Eurasia; grassy wasteland.
▲ 1–2 feet (30–60 cm). ◆ Pointed, oval.
❖ Blue, star-shaped. Smells like
cucumber. All parts are edible raw or
cooked. Use the infusion for fevers.
Stems produce salt when they are cooked.

23 **Wild angelicas** ● Damp grassy and
wooded areas. ▲ 5 feet (1.5m). Stems: hollow,
sometimes purplish. Opposite pairs of broad,
toothed leaves. ❖ Heads of tiny greenish
white or pink flowers. Boil the aromatic leaves,
stems, and roots. Use an infusion for colds
or externally for stiffness. Do not confuse
this with water hemlock.

FOOD

ROOTS AND TUBERS

Roots are the starchiest between the fall and the spring. All roots should be thoroughly cooked. Scrub them in clean water, boil until soft, then roast on hot stones in embers. To cook more rapidly, cut them into cubes. Use a sharpened stick to test if they are done.

1 **Wild parsnips** ● Grassy wasteland. ▲ 3 feet (1 m). ◆ Hairy, pungent, with toothed leaflets. ❖ Tiny, yellow, dense flower heads. Eat the roots raw or cooked.

2 **Comfrey** ● Ditches, damp areas. ▲ 3 feet (1 m). ◆ Spear-shaped, taper to the stem. ❖ Clusters of cream or mauve bell-shaped flowers. Eat the roots raw or cooked. See p. 330 for other uses. Do not confuse this with foxglove.

3 **Salsify, oyster plant,** or **vegetable oyster** ● Dry wasteland. ▲ 2–3 feet (60–90 cm). ◆ Long, grasslike. ❖ Large, purple, dandelion like. Cook the roots and young leaves.

4 **Woolly lousewort** ● N. American tundra. Hairy, low-spreading. ❖ Pink. Root: yellow. Eat this raw or cooked. Beware: some other louseworts are poisonous.

FOOD

5 **Jerusalem artichoke**
● Wasteland. Sunflower-like: very tall, hairy. ◆ Large, rough, oval leaves. ❖ Large, yellow. Do not peel before cooking.

6 **Wild calla lily**
● Near water. ▲ Small. ◆ Long-stalked, heart-shaped. ❖ Green, fingerlike organ enclosed in a leaflike hood, pale on the inside, from which red berries arise. Roots must be cooked. Avoid other parts.

7 **Arrowheads**
● Aquatic. ▲ 1–3 feet (30–90 cm). ◆ Large; arrow- or spear-shaped, straplike below the water. ❖ Three rounded petals. Tubers are edible raw, but are best cooked.

8 **Water chestnut**
● Eurasia, aquatic. ◆ Diamond-shaped, floating. ❖ Small, white. Gray, hard 1 inch (2.5cm), two-horned seeds are edible raw or roasted.

The flowers of some plants are edible, e.g. limes, basswoods, roses, hops, elder, primrose, camomile. These are best used for teas and in medicinal infusions.

FOOD

FRUITS

Many fruits are familiar from their cultivated forms. From the summer on they are an important food source.

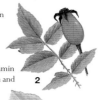

1 **Barberry** ● Scrub, dry moorland. ▲ 9 feet (3 m). ◆ Oval. ❖Yellow. Thorns in groups of three stems. Berries: bright red, very acidic, rich in vitamin C.

2 **Wild rose** ●Temperate areas. Resemble straggly, plain garden roses: thorned stems. ❖White or pink. Seed cases (rose hip) rich in vitamin C: chew to extract the juices or crush and boil to a syrup.

3 **Brambles (blackberry)** and **wild raspberry** ● Scrub, woods, open ground. ◆Toothed. ❖White, sometimes pinkish. Berries: juicy, segmented, ripen from green through red to purplish-black in the late summer. Raspberry bushes are less straggly, ripen to red earlier in the summer. Eat these raw.

4 **Dewberries** Like brambles, but the berries are smaller with fewer segments than blackberries.

5 **Wild strawberry** ● Dry, grassy areas, woodland. Small, scrambling plants. Fruits (hidden under leaves) resemble small, cultivated strawberries. Eat them fresh.

FOOD

6 **Hawthorn** ● Scrub, wasteland. Spiny shrubs or small trees. ◆ Deep-lobed leaves. ❖ Clusters, white or pink. Berries: red. Flesh is creamy. Eat them raw. Young spring shoots are edible too.

7 **Crab apple** ● Scrubland, woods. Short, spiny trees. ◆ Oval, toothed, downy; reddish-brown twigs. ❖ White, pink, or red flowers. Fruits look like cultivated apples. Very bitter. Eating too many causes diarrhea. Best when cooked with other fruitss.

8 **Wild cherry** ● Woodland. ▲ 80 feet (24 m). ◆ Small, pale green to red. Shiny reddish-brown bark. ❖ White or pinkish. Fruits are red or black: some kinds taste sour.

9 **Blackthorn** or **sloe** ● Eurasian scrub, woodland. ▲ 13 feet (4 m). Bush with dark brown twigs, long thorns. ◆ Oval. ❖ White. Small bluish-black fruits are very acidic and are best cooked down to a jam.

To make jam: boil the fruits, then simmer until mushy. Allow them to cool and store in an airtight container. Fruits lacking in pectin (the setting agent) may be supplemented by adding pectin-rich fruits, e.g. crab apples.

FOOD

10 **Juniper** ● Mountainous and northern areas. ▲ 15 feet (5 m). Tall or small prostrate bush. ◆ Gray-green, needlelike. Avoid young, green berries; cook ripe bluish-black ones with other food.

11 **Rowan** or **mountain ash** ● Woods, rocky areas. ▲ 50 feet (15 m). Smooth, grayish bark. ◆ Small, toothed leaflets. ❖ White. Clusters of small orange berries. Taste is sharp when raw. Best cooked down to a jam.

12 **Wild mulberry** ● Woods. ▲ 18–60 feet (6–20 m). ◆ Oval, sometimes deeply lobed. ❖ On catkins. Red or black fruits look like 2–3-inch (5–7-cm) long blackberries. Edible raw.

13 **Wild grapes** ● Widespread in warm climates. Straggly, high climbing. ◆ Large, heart-shaped, coarsely toothed. ❖ Greenish. Grapes amber to purple. Eat the fruit raw. Boil young leaves.

Some fruits can be dried for storage. Lay them in a single layer on a sheet, out of direct sunlight. Protect them from any moisture, e.g. rain and dew. The process takes 10 days.

NUTS

Nuts supply proteins and fat.

1 **Pine** ●Temperate and
northerly areas. Cone-bearing trees.
◆ Clusters of slim evergreen
needles. Heat the mature cones to
release seeds. Edible when raw, but
also tasty roasted (and store better).
Needles and bark are also edible.

2 **Walnut** ●Temperate areas
▲ Up to 90 feet (30 m). ◆ Many
toothed, narrow leaflets; furrowed
bark. Blackish-brown nuts are first
enclosed in a thick, green husk.

3 **Pistachio** ●Warm climates.
Mediterranean east to Afghanistan.
Trees. ▲ Up to 30 feet (10 m). ◆ Small
oval leaflets. Clusters of nuts with
green kernels and reddish skin.
Eat them raw or parch on embers.

4 **Oak** ● Occurs in great variety.
◆ Many have lobed leaves, all bear
acorns. Shell and boil them several times,
changing the water to ease bitterness
or steep in cold water for 3–4 days.
Can be buried with ash and charcoal,
watering occasionally, then roast.
Good as flour or coffee substitute.

5 **Hazel** ●Thickets, wasteland.
Tall shrubs. ◆ Toothed, oval to heart-
shaped. ❖ Brownish-yellow catkins.
Nuts come in ovoid, leafy, bristly, or
hairy husks.

FOOD

FOOD

EDIBLE PLANTS

The following are a further selection of the food plants available. If you cannot find any of the plants illustrated or described here, use standard edibility tests. Although one part may be edible, another may be poisonous. Test leaves, stems, roots, etc. separately.

Currants and gooseberries

Bushy shrubs in woods, scrub, and wasteland. Leaves are toothed, maplelike. Flowers are small, 5-petaled, greensih-white to purple. Red, purplish-black, or yellow berries. Eat currants raw. Cook gooseberries.

Wild onions

Long, grasslike leaves; cluster of 6-petaled purplish, pink, or white flowers tops stem. Easily detectable by the smell. Edible bulb may be 10 inches (25 cm) underground.

Thistles

Spiny, ridged stems; spear-shaped, prickly leaves, purple flowers. Remove prickles and boil young leaves. Peel tender shoots: eat raw or boiled. Cook roots of young, stemless plants. Eat nut at base of flower head.

Clovers

Abundant in grassy areas. Trefoil leaflets and dense, rounded heads of small flowers of white to greenish-cream or shades of red. Leaves are best boiled.

Wild rhubarb

In open, grassy places southern Europe to China. Resembles cultivated rhubarb, but leaves ragged and dissected. Eat stalk only, as other parts are harmful. Boil.

Violets

Damp woods. Veined, crinkly, heart-shaped leaves; violet, yellow, or white flowers. Cook young leaves.

FOOD

POISONOUS PLANTS
Poisons by contact

1 **Poison sumac**, or **poison dogwood** ● Swamplands in southeastern U.S. ▲ 6–18 feet (2–6 m).
◆ Hairless, oval leaflets in opposite pairs; dark-spotted, smooth bark; clusters of white berries.

2 **Poison oak** ● N. American woods. Resembles poison ivy, but is smaller and always upright.
◆ Oak leaf-shaped. Berries.

3 **Poison ivy** ● N. American woods. ▲ 2–7 feet (0.6–2.1 m), trailing or upright. ◆ 3-part, variable.
❖ Greenish. Berries: white.

4 **Touch-me-knot**, or **jewelweed** ● Often found near poison ivy. ❖ Pale yellow or orange spotted. Seedpods that pop. Juice eases irritation from contact poisons.

Poisons by ingestion

5 **Death camas** ● N. America; grassy, rocky, lightly wooded places. ▲ 1–2 feet (30–60 cm). ◆ Long, straplike, rising from the base. ❖ 6-part, in clusters, greenish-white. Deadly. Do not confuse with wild onions or calla lilies.

6 **Thorn apple**, or **iimsonweed** ● Widespread in temperate areas and in the tropics. ▲ 3 feet (90 cm). ◆ Jagged toothed, oval. ❖ Solitary, large white trumpet. Fruits: spiny. Sickly smelling. All parts are deadly.

FOOD

7 Foxglove ● Wasteland.
▲ 5 feet (1.5 m). ◆ Rosette of basal
leaves. ❖ Tall, leafy spike, tube-
shaped purple, pink, or yellow.
All parts are highly toxic.

8 Monkshood ● Damp woods,
shady areas. ◆ Palm-shaped,
segmented. ❖ Hairy, hoodlike,
purplsih-blue or yellow. Poisonous.

9 Hemlock ● Grassy wasteland.
▲ 6 feet (2 m). Hollow purple-
spotted stems. ◆ Coarsely toothed,
lighter below. ❖ Dense clusters,
tiny, white. White roots.
Bad smelling. Very poisonous.

10 Water hemlock / cowbane
● Near water. ▲ 2–4 feet (0.6–1.3 m).
Stems: purple-streaked, branching.
Hollow rootstock. ◆ Small, 2–3
lobed leaflet. ❖ Clusters, tiny, white.
Smells bad. One mouthful can kill.

11 Baneberry ● Woods.
▲ 1–2 feet (30–60 cm). ◆ Toothed
leaflets. ❖ Small, usually white,
at end of stem. Berries: white
or black. All parts cause
dizziness and vomiting.

**12 Belladonna, or deadly
nightshade** ● Eurasia; woods
and scrub. ▲ 3 feet (1 m).
◆ Oval. ❖ Solitary, bell-shaped,
purple or greenish. Berries: shiny black.
All parts are poisonous, especially the berries.

FOOD

Some poisonous plants are easy to mistake for edible species. Do not take risks: identify carefully. Learn to recognize the following in addition to those illustrated:

Buttercups
Occur in a great variety of sizes worldwide. All have glossy, yellow flowers. Avoid: all cause severe inflammation of the intestinal tract.

Lupines
Grassland, clearings. 1–3 feet (30–90 cm). Spikes of "peaflowers," blue, violet, pink, white, or yellow. All parts cause fatal intestinal inflammation.

Vetches, or locoweeds
Grassland, meadows. 6–18 inches (15–45 cm). Small spear-shaped leaflets in opposite pairs; spikes of 5-petaled peaflowers, yellow-white, pink, lilac, purple.

False hellebores
Wet, swampy areas, grassland. 2–8 feet (0.6–2.6 cm). Lily-of-the-valley-like leaves, drooping clusters of white or greenish-yellow flowers. Can be lethal.

Henbane
Bare ground by sea. Sticky hairs, toothed, oval leaves. Flowers: cream, streaked purple. Bad smell. Deadly.

Virginia creeper, or woodbine
Vinelike climber. Long-stalked, palm-shaped leaves, toothed leaflets. Clusters of small, blue berries, smaller than wild grapes. As a principle, no plant with edible blue berries is vinelike with tendrils.

Buckthorns
Shrubs, sometimes small trees. Woods, scrubland. Oval, fine-toothed leaves. Berries: black and bitter tasting. Violent purgative. Avoid.

FOOD

TREES

BARK

Outer bark is inedible, but the thin, inner bark of certain trees can be eaten in the spring, when sap has started to flow. Peel back the bark near bottom of tree or from exposed roots to reveal the inner layer. It can be eaten raw, but boiling will reduce it to a gelatinous mass that can be roasted and ground for use as flour.

Trees with the best inner bark: slippery elm; tamarack; basswood; birch; aaspen; poplar; maple; spruce; wwillow (including ground-hugging arctic ones); pine.

Other uses for inner bark: Birch bark may be removed in large sheets and used to make shelters, river craft, and containers. Tear it into strips for lashings.

Gums and resins: Some trees, when they are cut, bleed sap that hardens into a lump. If it is soluble in water this is gum; if not, it is resin. Both are nutritious. Some types are highly inflammable and ideal for lighting fires.

Birch and maple syrup: Cut a V-shape into the bark, collect the sugary sap that runs out. Below the V make a hole in the trunk, insert a leaf as a drip spout to run sap into a container. Collect the sap daily and boil to thicken it down into a syrup.

Spruce tea: Boil fresh, green spruce needles in water to make a tea that is rich in vitamin C. Alternatively, chew tender, young needles, whose starchy green tips are especially pleasant in the spring. Spruces occur in the far north and are an important source of nourishment.

FOOD

POISONOUS TREES

The following trees contain irritant or poisonous substances. Do not eat any part of them.

Yew: straggling evergreen tree or shrub with flaky bark, dark green needles, and red, berrylike fruit.

Cedar: large, spreading, scented evergreens with erect cones.

Horse chestnut and **buckeye:** tall, with hand-shaped leaves, sticky buds, and white, pink, or yellow flowers. Do not confuse their poisonous, spiky-cased nuts with those of sweet chestnut.

Laburnum: small, broad-leafed tree with three-part leaves and long sprays of yellow flowers.

Black locust: N. American tree with dark graay bark, oval leaflets in opposite pairs, clusters of white flowers, and beanlike seedpods.

California laurel or **Oregon myrtle:** short-trunked N. American evergreen, averaging 50 feet (16 m) high with oval, leathery leaves, clusters of yellowish flowers, and green to purple berries. The foliage is pungently aromatic.

Moosewood or **moosebark:**occurs in northeastern U.S.A. 40 feet (12 m); light, white-striped bark, oval to spear-shaped leaves, olive to brown above, broad-petaled yellow-green flowers, and winged fruits.

Hickory: divided, often palm-shaped leaves, catkins, and, usually, rounded nuts. Some varieties have edible nuts, sap, and roots, but do not eat them until the species is positively identified.

See also p. 104.

FOOD

FUNGI

PREPARING FUNGI: Discard suspicious, discolored, or maggoty parts. Clean, slice, and boil. Many bracket fungi are bitter and tough: cook these thoroughly. Tender ground fungi can be added to soups and other foods.

> Fungi must be positively identified before eating. No reliable edibility tests exist—deadly kinds do not taste unpleasant, and no symptoms may appear for many hours after eating. There is no truth in folktales that a fungus is not poisonous once it is peeled or cooked, or that toxic kinds change color when they are cooked.

STORING FUNGI: Collect all you can when available and separate the caps from the stems. Place on rocks in the sun, caps gill-side up. With the *Boletus* species, remove spongy tissue under cap. When it is dry, store in airtight containers. To use, soak it in water then eat raw or add to soups.

IDENTIFYING THE POISONOUS AMANITAS

To avoid mistaking *Amanitas* for edible varieties:

Avoid fungi with white gills, a volva (cuplike appendage at base of the stem), and stem rings.

Avoid fungi that are wormy or decomposing.

Unless positively identified—discard.

OTHER USES FOR FUNGI

Many bracket fungi make excellent tinder.

Razor-strop fungus can be used to sharpen knives.

Puffball fungus will staunch and soothe bleeding cuts.

Tree fungi can be used in treating burns.

FOOD

EDIBLE FUNGI

*Learn to recognize the small
selection illustrated here—and
stick to them.*

1 *Fistulina hepatica*
(beefsteak fungus or ox
tongue). Tree fungus.
Found in the fall on oaks.
Reddish above, pinkish
below. Rough texture.
Resembles a large tongue.
Exudes blood-colored juice.
Young specimens are the best. Soak to
soften it, stew thoroughly.

2 *Armillaria mellea* (honey fungus).
Grows on broad-leafed trees,
conifers, and stumps, from spring to fall.
Tawny yellow, brown-flecked caps
1.25–6 inches (3–15 cm) across, white
gills, white flesh, and bootlace roots.

3 *Lycoperdon giantea* (giant
puffball). Grows on the ground.
Resembles a 1 foot (30 cm) soccer ball.
In woods and grassy places, in the late
summer to the fall. Smooth, white,
leathery. Yellows with age. Weighs up to
20 lbs. (9 kg). Simmer or fry young ones.

4 *Cantharellus cibarius* (chanterelle).
Apricot-scented, egg-yellow, funnel-
shaped, 1.25–4 inches (3–10 cm) across.
Pronounced, forking gills. Grows in
groups under trees, especially beech, from
the summer on. Stew for 10 minutes.
Do not confuse this with *Cortinarius speciosissimus*.

FOOD

Agaricus *fungi. Avoid any that stain yellow when they are cut or bruised or that smell of phenol. Some young button mushrooms are hard to distinguish from the deadly* **Amanitas.**

1 **Agaricus campestris** (meadow mushroom). Grassy places in the fall, rarely by trees. White cap up to 4 inches (10 cm) across, browning slightly in older specimens. Pink gills later turn dark brown. Eat it raw or cooked.

2 **Agaricus augustus** In clusters in woodland clearings, in the summer and fall. Smells of anise. Scaly, light brown cap up to 10 inches (20 cm) across. Young gills are pink, and later turn dark. Ringed stem.

3 **Lepiota procera** (parasol) By broad-leafed woods and in grassy clearings from the summer to fall. Tastes of almonds or Brazil nuts. Brownish cap, later with dark scales, up to 1 foot (30 cm) across with creamy white gills and a slender stem with a double white ring and brown bands.

4 **Coprinus comatus** (shaggy ink cap). In groups in open grassland in the summer and fall. Cylindrical cap with white or pale brown scales. Gills begin white, turn pink, then dissolve into a black, inky mess. Gather young ones with pale gills. These are poisonous if eaten with alcohol.

5 **Boletus edulis** In woodland clearings in the fall. Swollen stem, white flesh. Spongelike pores instead of gills. Dry well. Avoid any with pink or red spores.

FOOD

POISONOUS FUNGI

Do not use any fungi that you can't positively identify.

1 *Amanita virosa* (destroying angel).
White. Large volva, scaly stem,
cap up to 5 inches (12 cm) across.
Woodland in the summer and fall. Sweet,
sickly smelling. Deadly.

2 *Amanita phalloides* (death cap).
In woodland, especially oak or beech.
Olive green cap, up to 5 inches (12 cm)
across. Pale stem, large volva, white gills and
flesh. Lethal.
Symptoms for destroying angel and death cap
appear 8–24 hrs. after eating: vomiting,
diarrhea, thirst, sweating, convulsions.
Apparent recovery after one day, then
followed by a relapse and in 90% of
cases by death from liver failure.
No known antidote.

3 *Amanita pantherina*
(panther cap). In woodland,
especially beech. Brownish, white-
flecked cap up to 3 inches (8 cm), white gills,
2–3 hoops at the base of the stem.
Can be fatal.

4 *Amanita muscaria* (fly agaric). In pine
and birch woods in the fall. Bright red cap,
flecked with white, up to 9 inches (22 cm).
Causes severe gastro-intestinal
upset, delirium, hallucinations,
convulsions, then a comalike sleep.
Victim usually recovers.

FOOD

5 *Entoloma sinnuatum* (leaden entoloma). In groups in grassy areas and woods, especially beech and oak, in the summer and fall. Dull gray-white, deeply convex cap up to 6 inches (15 cm) across. Yellowish gills turn pink. Firm white flesh smells like cornmeal, bitter almonds, and radishes. No ring on the stem. Deadly.

6 *Inocybe patouillardii* In broad-leafed woods, especially beech, in the summer and fall. Begins whitish, turns yellow-brown. Cap up to 2.75 inches (7 cm), often split at the edges. Whitish gills turn olive-brown. Stains red when it is bruised. Can be confused with *agaricus* when it is young, but it lacks a ring on the stem. Causes vertigo, blindness, sweating, dilated pupils, delirium. Can kill.

7 *Paxilus involutus* In woods, especially birch. Solid yellow-brown cap with a rolled rim up to 5 inches (12 cm) across. Yellow-brown gills, straight, stout stem. Deadly. Do not confuse with the chanterelle.

8 *Cortinarius speciosissimus* In coniferous woods in the fall. Reddish to tawny brown. Flattish cap 0.75–3.25 inches (2–8 cm) - across. Rusty brown gills. The lighter-colored *C. orelanus* is also poisonous and found in broad-leafed woodland. Both have a radishlike smell. Deadly.

FOOD

ARCTIC AND NORTHERN PLANTS

In addition to these hardy arctic plants, many temperate species occur in summer in the far north.

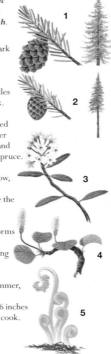

1 **Red spruce** ● Dry areas, N. America. ▲ 70 feet (23 m). Dark or yellow-green needles around hairy twigs. Rough, dark bark. Pendant cones. Eat young shoots either raw or cooked. Infuse needles for teas. Boil the edible inner bark.

2 **Black spruce** ● Moist areas, N. America. ▲ Smaller than the red spruce with shorter needles. Other similar species occur in America and northern Eurasia. Use as for red spruce.

3 **Labrador tea** ● N. America. ▲ 1–3 feet (30–90 cm). ◆ Narrow, rolled edges, whitish or hairy below. ❖ 5-petaled, white. Infuse the leaves for tea.

4 **Arctic willow** ● Tundra. ▲ 1–2 feet (30–60 cm). Shrub forms a mat with rounded leaves, shiny above. Yellow catkins. Eat the spring shoots, leaves, inner bark, young peeled roots. High in vitamin C.

5 **Ferns** ● Moist areas in the summer, far northern woods, near tundra. Eat only young fiddleheads up to 6 inches (15 cm). Remove hairs. Steam to cook.

FOOD

6 **Cloudberry** ▲ 1 foot (30 cm).
Bramblelike. ◆ Palm-shaped. ❖ White.
Berries: found at the top of the plant, pink,
ripening to orange/amber. Eat them raw.

7 **Salmonberry** ● N. America, Europe.
Like a small wild raspberry. Thornless,
with 3-part leaves. ❖ Purple-red.
Berries: red or yellow. Eat them raw.

8 **Bearberry** ● Arctic regions. Small, mat-
forming, woody evergreen. ◆ Club-
shaped. ❖ Pink or white. Berries: red,
in clusters. Cook them.

9 **Iceland moss** ● Lichen. ▲ Forms tufted,
gray-green or brownish mats up to
4 inches (10 cm), composed of strap-shaped
branches. ❖ Soak for several hours, then
boil it well.

10 **Reindeer moss**, or **reindeer lichen**
Lichen. ▲ 2–4 inches (5–10 cm). Often grows in
large clumps. Hollow, roundish, gray stems,
antlerlike branches. Soak for several
hours, then boil well.

11 **Rock tripe** Lichen. ❖ Roundish,
blisterlike gray or brown growths
attached to rocks by a central stalk.
Some kinds are warty, pebblelike;
others are smooth. Can cause irritation
if eaten raw. Soak in water overnight,
then boil it well. Then roast to make
them crunchy.

*If you kill a caribou, eat the
fermented lichens in its stomach.*

FOOD

DESERT PLANTS

Water is vital to desert survival.
Learn water-bearing plants.
Eat only if you have water.

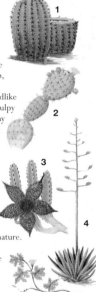

1 **Barrel cacti** ● Southwest U.S.
▲ 4 feet (1.2 m). Yields up to 2 pints
(1 L) of milky sap—an exception to the
rule to avoid milky sap. Slice off the top,
smash the inner pulp, then drink.

2 **Prickly pears** ◆ Thick, jointed, padlike
leaves. ❖ Red or yellow. Egg-shaped, pulpy
fruits. Eat the peeled fruit raw. Cut away
the spines, peel and cook tender young
pads. Roast the seeds for flour. Tap
stems for water. Beware: they are very
prickly. In Africa do not confuse them
with spurges (which have milky sap).

3 **Carrion flowers**, or **stapelia**
● Southern and tropical Africa.
Large plants; short, succulent stems
branch off into leaves like fat spines.
❖ Star-shaped, some hairy, give off a
stench of rotting meat when they are mature.
Tap the stems for water.

4 **Mescals** ● Africa, Asia, Europe, the
Americas—moist tropical areas and
deserts. ◆ Rosette of thick, sharp-
tipped leaves from which rises a long
flower stalk. Stalks that are not yet in
flower are edible when cooked.

5 **Wild gourds** ● Kalahari Desert, Sahara
east to India. Mat-forming, vinelike. Orange-sized fruits.
Roast the seeds, cook the young leaves, eat the flower raw, chew
the stems and shoots for water.

FOOD

6 **Date palm** ● Near water,
India to N. Africa. ▲ Tall, slender palms that
are crowned with tuft of leaves up to 16 feet
(4 m) long. Eat the fruits and growing tips
raw. Cook the young leaves. Sap from the
trunk can be boiled down.

7 **Baobab** ● Africa to Australia.
▲ Large tree with swollen, ridged
trunk, 30 feet (9 m) in diameter.
Tap the roots for water. Fruits,
4–8 inches (10–20 cm) long, and
seeds are edible raw. Boil the tender,
young leaves.

8 **Acacia** ● Africa to northern
Australia. ▲ Many types, all are
thorny, scrubby, medium-sized
trees with small leaflets.
Globular, 0.5-inch (1-cm)
flower heads, white, pink, or
yellow. Tap the roots for water.
Roast the seeds. Boil the young leaves
and shoots.

9 **Carob** ● Mediterranean, Sahara,
Arabia to India. ▲ Up to 50 feet
(15 m). ◆ Shiny, evergreen,
paired, with 2 or 3 to a stem.
❖ Small, red. Flat, leathery seedpods
contain a sweet pulp—eat this
raw. Hard, brown seeds can be
ground and cooked as porridge.

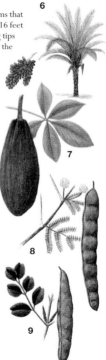

FOOD

TROPICAL PLANTS

1 **Sago palm** ● Damp lowlands.
▲ 30 feet (10 m). Spiny trunk.
◆ Long, arching. Spongy inner pith
provides sago.

2 **Nipa palm** ● Brackish estuaries
in S.E. Asia. ▲ 20 feet (6 m). ◆ Long,
fernlike, clustering at the base to form the
"trunk." Yields sugary sap, delicious
fruits, and an edible growing tip.

3 **Banana** or **plantain**
● All over tropics. ▲ 9–30 feet
(3–10 m). Large, straplike, usually
split light green leaves. Eat the buds,
growing tips, young stems, and inner
parts of the roots. Always cook the hard fruits.

4 **Fishtail palm** ▲ Average 30 feet (10 m).
Smooth, ringed trunk, long, arching leaves,
oval or wedge-shaped leaflets. Use as the sago
palm is used. Do not eat the fruits.

5 **Coconut palm** ● Moist tropics.
▲ Up to 90 feet (30 m). Large clusters
of nuts hang at the base of the leaves.
Coconut is inside the large, smooth husk.
Growing tip, milk, and the flesh of
the nut are edible. Boil the sap down.

**The growing tip, enclosed by a
crown of leaves or the bases of
leaf stems, is edible in most
palms—eat if it is not too bitter.
Avoid the fruits unless they are
positively identified.**

FOOD

6 **Bignay** ● S.E. Asian forests. ▲ 30–40 feet (10–13 m). Evergreen shrubs. ◆ Shiny, 6 inches (15 cm). Fruits: currantlike, with many seeds, 0.5 inches (1 cm) across. Ripen from green to white to red then black. Edible when raw, but they are best in jam.

7 **Mango** ● Moist places. Medium to large evergreen tree. ◆ Narrow, dark green clusters. Fruits: oval, 3–5 inches (7.5–13 cm); ripens from green to orange. Eat the fruits raw. Leaves may cause an allergic reaction.

8 **Sugar apple**, or **sweetsop** ● Widespread. ▲ 15–18 feet (5–6 m). Tree. ◆ Oval to spear-. shaped ❖ Magnolia-like flowers. Fruits: aromatic, pulpy, green-gray, segmented.

9 **Soursop** ▲ Up to 28 feet (12 m). Fruits: avocado-like, green, leathery, spiny. Weigh up to 4.4 lbs. (2 kg).

10 **Wild fig** ● Tropical and subtropical areas, some species in deserts. Straggly trees, aerial roots, leathery evergreen leaves, rounded at the base. Fruits: pear-shaped, grow directly from the branch. Edible raw. Avoid any that are hard and woody or hairy.

FOOD

11 **Ceylon spinach** ● Most tropical areas. Vinelike. ◆ Thick, circular to oval or heart-shape, green to purple-red. ❖ Fleshy, purplish. Cook the young leaves and stems.

12 **Tamarind** ● Widespread. Densely branched tree. ▲ Up to 80 feet (25 m). ◆ Evergreen leaflets. ❖ Pale yellow, red-streaked. Eat the pulp of brown seedpods raw. Use the seeds and young leaves as a potherb. Peel and chew the bark.

13 **Peanut** ● Widespread. Small bushy plant. ◆ Oval, in pairs. ❖ Yellow flowers and stalks leading to wrinkled seedpods. Nuts ripen underground and store well.

14 **Yam beans** ● In large patches in most of the tropics. Climbing plants with knotty, turniplike roots. ◆ Irregular, 3-part. Tubers are crisp, sweet, and taste of nuts. Seeds are harmful raw: boil them well.

Food deteriorates rapidly in the tropics. Do not pick more than you need.

FOOD

15 **Water spinach** ● Near freshwater, S.E. Asia. Usually floating plant. ◆ Green leaves. ❖ White. Old stems arestringy. Boil the young leaves and shoots.

16 **Lotus** ● Aquatic. Asia, Africa, N. America. ◆ Long-stalked, bell-shaped, blue-green leaves stand clear out of water. ❖ Pink, white, or yellow. Boil the young leaves, peeled stems, and rootstalk. Remove the bitter embryo and boil or roast the ripe seeds.

17 **Water lily** ● Lakes, rivers, streams in tropical Africa, India, the Americas. ◆ Heart-shaped, float on water. Large edible tubers; cook the stems; seeds are bitter but nourishing.

18 **Wild yam** ● Occurs in a wide variety in light forests and clearings in tropical and subtropical areas. Twining, vinelike stems. Some types bear edible, aerial tubers leading to underground tubers. They store well if kept dry. Some are poisonous raw; so always cook them: peel tubers and boil and mash them.

15

16

17

18

FOOD

19 **Wild rice** ● Widespread in tropics. ▲ 3–4 feet (90–120 cm). Coarse grass. Thresh and winnow the grains to remove husks; boil or roast them and pound to store as flour.

20 **Sugarcane** ● Cultivated all over the tropics, grows wild. Coarse, tall, aromatic, thick-stemmed grass. Chew the canes raw to extract a sweet juice.

21 **Millets** Grasses are several feet tall, with sausagelike heads of grain. Pound to a meal and use in stews or as porridge.

22 **Bamboo** ● Moist areas. Rapidly growing, edible young shoots (22a) are at the base of the plant. Split the tough outer sheath and cook it like asparagus. The seeds of the flowering plant are also edible. Be careful: plants under tension may shatter or lash.

In addition to the plants illustrated here, you will recognize relations of cultivated varieties such as avocado and citrus fruits. Always apply the edibility test to unknown plants, using very small amounts.

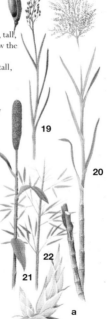

FOOD

POISONOUS TROPICAL PLANTS

1 **Physic nut**, **Barbados nut**, or **purging nut**
● Wooded areas in the tropics. Small tree.
◆ Large, lobed, ivylike. ✤ Small, green-
yellow. Fruits: yellow, apple-sized, with 3 large
seeds. Seeds taste sweet but are a violent purgative.

2 **Strychnine** ● Mostly in India, but other
species occur throughout the tropics. Small
tree. ◆ Oval, opposite pairs. Fruits:
orangelike, white to yellow-red. Seeds
are deadly.

3 **Castor-oil plant** ● Scrub and wasteland
all over the tropics. Shrublike. ◆ Arranged
like fingers on a hand. ✤ Yellow, spikes.
Prickly, 3-seeded seedpods. Seeds are a violent
purgative, sometimes even fatal.

4 **Duchesnia** ● Waste ground in warm
parts of Asia, N. America. ◆ 3-part, trailing.
✤ Yellow, not white. Fruits: red,
strawberry-like, and highly poisonous.
Can be lethal.

Other plants to avoid

White mangrove ● Mangrove swamps.
Pale bark, pencil-like roots. ◆ Spear-
shaped or oblong. ✤ Yellow. Round, white
berries. Sap blisters the skin; can even blind.
Nettle trees ● Widespread, often near
water. ◆ Spear-shaped, sharp-toothed.
✤ Drooping spikes, like common nettle.
Sting like a nettle's, only worse. Poisonous seeds.
Pangi ● S.E. Asia (mostly Malaysia). Tree. ◆ Heart-shaped,
in spirals. ✤ Green spikes. Clusters of large, brownish,
pear-shaped fruits. All parts are poisonous, especially the fruits
(contains prussic acid).

FOOD

SEASHORE PLANTS

The following plants thrive in salty conditions, but many other edible plants grow near the coast.

1 **Orachs** ● Salty ground. Some grow inland. Pale-stalked.
◆ Pale green, spear-shaped.
❖ Small, green-white spikes. Cook the young leaves.

2 **Sea beet** ● European coasts. Sprawling, red-tinged. ◆ Long-stalked, dark green. ❖ Small, green clusters. Boil the leaves or eat it raw.

3 **Sea rocket** ▲ 1 foot (30 cm).
◆ Fleshy, blue-green, lobed.
❖ Lilac/purple. Egg-shaped seedpods Peppery leaves and young seedpods can be eaten raw or as a potherb.

4 **Glasswort** or **Pickleweed**
● Widespread in saline areas, mud flats. Plump, greenish-yellow jointed stems up to 1 foot (30 cm) high. ❖ Minute, scarcely visible at the junctions of stems.
(**Rock samphire** is no relation—it grows on shingle and cliffs; cook and suck its fleshy, hairless stems and gray-green leaves.)

5 **Scurvy grass** ▲ 10 inches (25 cm). ◆ Dark green, heart- or kidney-shaped. ❖ Small, white or pink. Very bitter, leach in the water. Rich in vitamin C.

FOOD

SEAWEEDS

Seaweeds anchor to the bottom in shallow waters or float on the open sea. Coastal weeds are often stratified: green forms grow in surface waters, red in shallow water, and brown a little deeper. Wash seaweeds in freshwater before eating them, to remove salt.

1 **Sea lettuce** ● Found on rocks and stones in the Atlantic and Pacific oceans, especially where water runs into the sea. Light green leaves. Wash and boil them.

2 **Enteromorpha intestinalis** ● Rock pools and salt marshes in cool waters. Pale green; podlike, unbranched fronds up to 2 feet (50 cm). Whole plant is edible in early spring, fresh or dried and pulverized.

3 **Kelps** ● Rocky shores of the Atlantic and Pacific oceans. Short, cylindrical stem; thin, long, wavy olive-green to brown fronds. Edible raw but they are best boiled.

4 **Lavers** ● Atlantic and Pacific oceans. Thin, satiny red, purple, or brown fronds. Boil until tender, then mash them. Use as a relish or mix it with grains to make cakes.

Some seaweeds are purgatives. Use the edibility test on p.69.

ANIMALS FOR FOOD

Your humane instincts must be balanced against the
expediencies of survival. Study each species' habits:
where it sleeps, what it eats, and where it drinks. Learn
how to best make a kill and what traps to set. The
younger the animal, the more lean the meat will be. Most
species put on extra fat to get them through the winter.

FINDING GAME

TRACKS AND SIGNS: If you can read the subtle signs that
animals leave, you will know what hunting/trapping
methods to use.

Only large, powerful mammals venture out during
the day. Most small mammals eat at night, as do those that
hunt them. Trails between watering/feeding places and
homes are clearest on wet ground, snow, and damp sand.
Determine the age of the tracks by their sharpness and
moisture content: the clearer they are, the more recent.

In the early morning check tracks from ground level.
If dew and spiderwebs have been disturbed, the tracks
are fresh. Tunnels through undergrowth and broken
twigs along a track will indicate the size of the animal
that is responsible. If trampled leaves have not wilted and
broken twigs are green and supple, the trail is fresh.

FEEDINGS SIGNS: Gnawed bark, discarded food, and the
remains of prey, reveal an animal's presence and suggest
bait for traps. For details see pp. 108–119.

DROPPINGS: Size and quantity indicate the type of
animal; old droppings will be hard and odorless, fresh
ones wet and still smelling. Flies draw attention to them.

FOOD

Break open a dropping to check for clues as to what the animal has been eating, then bait your trap accordingly. Copious bird droppings indicate the presence of nesting sites. Seed-eating birds' droppings are small and mostly liquid (indicating water within reasonable range); meateaters' pellets contain indigestible parts of their prey.

ROOTINGS: Some animals turn ground over in search of insects and tubers. Crumbly, fresh earth means that it has recently been dug. A muddy wallow is a sign of pigs.

SCENT AND SMELL: Listen to noises and register smells. In cold climates a large animal's breath forms a cloud of condensation that can be seen from faraway.

BURROWS AND DENS: Some are easy to find. Hidden ones may be given away by tracks or droppings nearby.

MAMMALS

The following illustrated tracks are not drawn to scale. Most tracks are typical of a family of animals, varying according to species. Where 2 are shown, track 1 is right front, track 2 is right hind.

WEASEL GROUP

Stoats, mink, marten, and polecats are all secretive and have sharp, dangerous teeth.

Traps: Spring snares with bait bars and deadfalls. Bait with offal or birds' eggs.

Tracks: Indistinct except in soft ground. Five well-spaced claws and toes; the hair on the main pad often smudges. Fore and rear prints overlap.

FOOD

WILD DOGS

Foxes and other species are found from deserts to the Arctic. Wolves are confined to the northern wilderness. Canines can be very dangerous. Their superb senses make it pointless  to stalk them. Remove the anal glands before cooking. Boil thoroughly.

Traps: Snare foxes: try stepped-bait or toggle, bait-release, baited-hole-noose. Minimize human scent.

Tracks and signs: Walk on their toes. Print shows four pads and claw tips—outer pad is shorter than inner, with a large main pad to the rear. Elongated, tapered droppings show remains of fur, bones, and insects. Fox scent pungent. In soft ground fox dens can be dug out.

WILD CATS

Wild cats occur on all continents except Australia and Antarctica, but are not common. They are secretive and generally nocturnal. Kills of big cats may be scavenged if they are unattended, but beware of big cats. Small cat meat is like rabbit. Stew it thoroughly.

Traps: Bait powerful spring snares with offal, blood, or meat. Cats have fast reactions and may leap clear of deadfall traps.

Tracks and signs: Walk on their toes, with claws retracted when walking (except cheetah). Droppings elongated, often hidden. Strong-smelling urine.

FOOD

MONKEYS AND APES

Confined to the tropics, they usually live in extended family groups, often in trees. Even small monkeys can inflict a bad bite. Intelligent and difficult to stalk. Very edible.

Traps: Perch or baited spring-spear trap, spring snare, or hole noose. Bait with fruits or colorful objects.

Signs: Few take the trouble to conceal themselves, and most are noisy.

SEALS

Track shows the belly dragging in the center. Arrow indicates the direction of travel. See p. 44 for details.

BATS

Found everywhere except very cold climates. Active at night. Hibernating meat-eaters. Plump fruit bats are especially good for eating. Remove wings and legs, gut and skin like a rabbit. Vampire bat can transmit rabies: stay well covered if sleeping rough within its range.

Traps: Knock down from roosts when sleeping by day.

Signs: Roosting colonies easy to spot. Often in caves.

CATTLE

Cattle live in herds near water. Bison and other wild cattle are found in N. America (protected species), Africa, and S. Asia. Old bulls are especially dangerous.

FOOD

Traps: Powerful snares, spring traps, and deadfalls.

Tracks and signs: Heavy, two distinct hoofprints, narrow at the top, bulbous at the rear. Droppings are like cow pies. They make excellent fuel.

WILD SHEEP AND GOATS

Sheep tend to live in small flocks in inaccessible places. Goats are even more sure-footed than sheep and almost impossible to approach.

Traps: Snares or spring snares on trails. In rocky areas natural obstructions are ideal for deadfalls.

Tracks and signs: Cloven hooves, two slender pointed marks not joined, tip splayed out in sheep, sometimes in goats. Illustration: domestic sheep (left), chamois (right). Globular droppings are like that of domestic sheep.

DEER AND ANTELOPE

Deer, found in densely-wooded countrysides on every continent except Australia, vary from the moose to tiny forest deer of the tropics. Antelope and gazelles are equally varied and widespread. All are shy and elusive, with superb hearing and smell. Most are active atdawn and dusk, and—

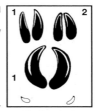

except those in arid areas—are never far from water Their meat smokes well. Use hides and antlers.

FOOD

Their horns are weapons and can gouge and stab.

Traps: Snare or deadfall small types. Use leg spring snares spear traps and deadfalls for larger ones. Bait with offal.

Tracks and signs: Cloven hooves form two oblongs. Reindeer marks are rounded. The illustration shows, in relative scale, doe deer front and hind track (top); and reindeer (bottom).
Notice the dew-claw impression on the reindeer track. When walking, the front and rear prints overlap; and when running, they are spaced apart. Droppings are oblong to round pellets, usually in clumps. Look for scrapes on saplings and nibbled and frayed bark, also for long scratches where antlers have been rubbed.

WILD PIGS

Some have thick hair, and all are pig-shaped with snouts and tusks. They are hard to stalk—listen for snores and creep up on sleeping ones.

Their meat must be boiled well. Their tusks inflict severe injuries, often dangerously close to the femoral artery on the upper leg. Beware!

Traps: Strong spring snares, deadfall, pig spear traps.

Tracks and signs: Cloven hooves leave deerlike marks. Droppings are often shapeless, never long, firm, or tapered. Look for ground that has been disturbed by mud wallows or rooting.

FOOD

RABBITS AND HARES

Rabbits are widespread and easy to catch. Most live in burrows, often in large numbers and use well-worn runs—the places to set snares. Hares do not live in burrows and usually do not have regular runs.

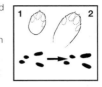

Traps: Simple snares. A spring snare will lessen the chance of your meal being stolen by other prey.

Tracks and signs: Hairy soles leave little detail on soft ground. Distinctive combination of long hind and short front feet. Hares have 5 toes on front feet, but inner is short and rarely leaves a print. Hind foot is narrower, 4-toed. Rabbits are similar but smaller. Droppings are small, hard, round pellets. Bark nibbled at bottom shows two incisor marks. Rabbits thump a warning.

RABBIT STARVATION

It is not possible to survive on rabbits alone, no matter how many you eat. The body needs minerals and vitamins that rabbits do not provide: make sure to balance your diet with vegetation.

SMALL RODENTS

Rats, mice, guinea pigs, cavies, capybara, coypus, and other members of the rodent family may be tempted into cage traps—most species are too small to snare. Tracks of different types are not easy to distinguish. Rats carry diseases. When gutting, be careful not to rupture the innards. Cook them thoroughly.

FOOD

SQUIRRELS AND PRAIRIE DOGS

They are found everywhere except Australasia and the poles, hibernating in cold areas. Alert and nimble, most are active during the day and night. Beware of their sharp teeth—they are savage in defense. Ground-living varieties make burrows. Most are excellent for eating.

Traps: Small spring snares attached to bait bars are the best. Use split fruit or an egg to attract. For tree squirrels set 2 inch (5 cm) loop snares on a pole leaned against a trunk.

Tracks and signs: Chewed bark, gnawed nuts, and cones beneath a tree, or an untidy nest of twigs.

KANGAROOS

With wallabies and other relatives, limited to Australia. Large types can strike a blow with hind feet. Most are active at night. Edibility is fair, but difficult to catch.

Traps: Deadfalls, spring snares.

Tracks and signs: Two prints resembling giant rabbit tracks (front legs are not used for locomotion).

OPOSSUMS

Small, nocturnal scavengers of S. America and the U.S. Similar, unrelated animals are found in Australasia.

Traps: Bait with fruits, eggs, etc. Very inquisitive.

FOOD

RACCOONS

Cat-sized, nocturnal animals with bushy, banded tails and black masks. Found widely in N. America.

Traps: Baited spring snares.

CAMELS

Roam wild in desert countries. They can spit and inflict powerful bites. They require a very powerful spear or projectile weapon.

REPTILES

CROCODILES AND ALLIGATORS

Found in most subtropical and tropical areas. Avoid large ones. In areas where they live always assume they are around for they can lie underwater unseen. Their tails can inflict a scything blow almost as damaging as their teeth. Tail meat is very tasty.

Traps: Set them by water for small crocodiles only or catch on a line with stick wedged in bait to lodge in throad. Kill with a sharp blow between the eyes.

LIZARDS

Some lizards are venomous (see p. 348). Most are timid, but big iguanas and monitors can inflict a bad bite and have powerful claws. Small ones move fast, but try to catch them by the tail. Sometimes they can be trapped in a pit or may fall into a solar still.

FOOD

TURTLES AND TORTOISES

Most live in the water, only emerging to lay eggs. A few are terrestrial. Net or drag them from the water. On land use a stick to turn them onto their backs. Stay out of the way of jaws and flippers. Kill with blow to the head. Cut through belly and discard the guts, head, and neck. Best when boiled. Very rich, only eat in small amounts. Tortoises can retract their heads—stab, then roast ungutted in embers. When shell splits, they are ready.

AMPHIBIANS

Frogs are all edible, but their skins may be poisonous—so remove before cooking. Active at night near water. Dazzle them with a light and club them.

Toads have warty skins and may be found far from water. Most have highly toxic skin—do not eat it.

SNAKES

Do not tackle poisonous or large ones. Use a forked stick to pin it down just behind the head. Strike back of head with another stick. Tree snakes can be clubbed and knocked to the ground. Club again to make sure!

Never pick up or get close to a snake until you are sure that it is dead. Some can feign death convincingly.

BIRDS

All birds are edible, but some taste better than others. Game birds are good to eat but are well camouflaged and wary. Birds of prey must be boiled thoroughly.

Traps: Cage traps, deadfalls, and spring snares can be used for birds that take bait. Nooses on branches may catch roosting birds. In wooded areas set traps in

FOOD

clearings or by riverbanks. Small birds are easy to catch or lime and can be attracted by bait. A crude dummy owl will lure small birds.

Tracks and signs: In the desert and on snow tracks may help locate birds that are hiding in close cover. Droppings may indicate a night roost. Alarm calls may help locate other animals.

Fall molt: Birds molt completely in the fall and are unable to fly more than short distances. Ducks, geese, and game birds are easy to catch at this time.

Nests: Eggs are easily available from ground nesters. Approach colonies carefully—crawling not walking—to get within stone-throwing or clubbing distance. Some guard their nests tenaciously. Be prepared for attack.

Flightless birds: Large birds, such as ostriches, should be treated with caution: they can deliver powerful kicks.

INSECTS

Rich in fat, protein, and carbohydrates. Overcome your squeamishness. Look in nooks and crannies of trees and in moist, shady spots. Look for beetle grubs—pale in color, with three short legs—on trees with peeling bark and in decaying stumps. Collect living specimens. Avoid any that look sick or dead, have a bad smell, or produce a rash when handled. Be careful: scorpions, spiders, and snakes also shelter in nooks and crannies.

Most are edible raw, but they are more palatable cooked. Boiling is the safest. Alternatively, roast by placing them on hot stones or in the embers of a fire. Remove the legs and wings from larger insects—fine hairs can irritate the digestive tract. To eat a hairy caterpillar, squeeze to extract the innards and do not eat the skin. Take the armor casing off beetles.

FOOD

Small insects can be mashed into a paste and cooked or dried to a powder, then used to thicken other foods such as soups or stews.

 Do not gather insects that are feeding on carrion, refuse, or dung—they may carry infections. Avoid grubs found on the underside of leaves, they often secrete toxins. Use as fish bait.Brightly colored insects and caterpillars are usually poisonous. Large beetles often have powerful jaws.

TERMITES

Found in warm climates. Most only eat vegetation, but big ones have sharp jaws and will bite anything. Termites build mounds up to several feet high. Break off pieces and dunk them in water to force termites out. A piece of the nest placed on embers will produce a fragrant smoke that will keep mosquitoes away. When fishing, suspend a piece of nest above a pool; termites falling from it will be good bait. Alternatively, insert a twig into the nest and gently withdraw it. Termites will bite it and hang on—but you won't catch very many.

Remove the wings from large termites before boiling, frying, or roasting. The eggs are nutritious too.

BEES , WASPS, AND HORNETS

Bees are edible throughout their life cycle. Honey is easily digestible and highly nutritious, but it is difficult to collect. Nests are found in hollow trees or caves or under an overhanging rock. Strike at night: make a torch from a bundle of grass and hold it close to the entrance so that the nest fills with smoke. Seal the hole. This kills bees, providing an instant meal and a supply of honey.

FOOD

Remove wings, legs, and stingers, before eating. Boiling or roasting improves flavor. Honey may be eaten, and wax used to waterproof clothing or make candles. In some places there is a slight risk that honey may contain concentrations of plant poisons. Smell will be one guide, but use the edibility test given for plants.

Wasps and hornets are dangerous. Hornets sting on sight, and the pain is extreme. Search for a safer meal.

ANTS

Most ants have a stinging bite. Some shoot formic acid. They must be cooked for at least 6 minutes to destroy the poison. They are then safe to eat.

LOCUSTS, CRICKETS, AND GRASSHOPPERS

All have plump bodies and muscled legs. Swat with a leafy branch or clothing. Remove the wings, antennae, and legs. Eat raw or roast them to kill parasites.

SNAILS, SLUGS, AND WORMS

They must be eaten fresh after special preparation.

Snails are found in freshwater, saltwater, and on land. They are rich in proteins and minerals. Ones with brightly colored shells may be poisonous. Sea snails should be left alone unless they are positively identified. Starve snails or slugs for a few days or feed them only on herbs and safe greens so that they can excrete poisons. Place in a saltwater solution to clear out the guts. Boil for 10 minutes, adding herbs for flavor.

Worms are high in protein. Starve them for a day, or squeeze them between your fingers to clear muck out. Can be sun or force-dried—leave them on a hot stone —then ground them into powder to thicken other food.

FOOD

DANGERS

The numerous diseases carried by mosquitoes, ticks, and other insects, and the unseen dangers of parasites you may pick up from food or water, as well as various waterborne diseases, are much more serious than attacks by animals.

DANGEROUS CONFRONTATIONS

Attacks by animals are rare, but large animals can be dangerous. Stay out of their way. Use self-control, do not unintentionally provoke the animal to attack.

If you come face-to-face with a large animal, freeze. Slowly back away and talk in a calm manner. Avoid sudden movements and remember that animals can smell fear—many huntesr have soiled themselves and given themselves away. Do your best to stay calm.

If an animal appears to charge, it may be that you are blocking its escape route. Move out of the way.

If an animal gives chase (or you don't have the nerve to freeze or sidestep), zigzag when you run. Some animals—e.g. rhinos—have bad eyesight or charge in a straight line.

Nocturnal predators have excellent night vision, but their color vision is bad. They cannot see stationery objects well. Freeze if it hasn't already seen you.

Shouting and making a commotion *may* put off a predator.

Climbing a tree is the last resort, you may be treed for a long time. Don't choose a thorn tree if you can help it, you may get badly scratched and become trapped on an extremely painful perch.

FOOD

TRAPS AND TRAPPING

It is easier to trap than to hunt small prey. Your choice of baits and site is important. Food may be scarce, but a little used as bait may bring rewards. Be patient and give the traps time. Animals will be wary until they get used to them—that is when they will run into them.

> Regular checking is essential. Leaving a trapline unchecked will prolong an animal's pain and increase the risk of your catch struggling free—animals will bite off a limb to escape—or being poached by predators.

Establish as large a trapline as you can. Collect game and reset traps, repairing when necessary and removing any that are repeatedly unfruitful. Accept a proportion of failures, but if the bait is gone without the trap being fired, it is an indication that the trigger mechanism is too tight or the bait was insecurely fixed. Check both when you reset the trap.

Set traps on game trails or runs. Look for natural bottlenecks, e.g. where the track passes under an obstruction. Do not place a trap close to an animal's lair—it will be alert to anything unusual close to home.

When alarmed, animals panic and take the shortest route to cover. That is when the crudest and most obvious traps will be successful.

MANGLE, STRANGLE, DANGLE, TANGLE
Deadfalls mangle. Snares strangle. Saplings can take the prey in the air—it dangles. The higher the sapling, the more effectively it lifts the animal. A net tangles. Some traps combine two or more of these principles.

FOOD

RULES FOR TRAPS

1 **Avoid disturbing the environment:** Don't tread on a game trail—leave no sign that you have been there.

2 **Hide your scent:** Handle traps as little as possible and wear gloves if you can. Do not set a trap of pinewood in a wood of hazel. Mask human scents by exposing the snare to campfire smoke.

3 **Camouflage:** Hide freshly-cut ends of wood with mud. Cover ground snares to blend in naturally.

4 **Make them strong:** An ensnared animal will fight for its life. Any weakness in the traps will soon be exposed.

Snares

Snares can be improvized from string, rope, twine, or, ideally, nonferrous wire with a running eye at one end through which the other end passes before being anchored to a stake, rock, or tree. A snare is a free-running noose that catches small game by the throat and large game around the legs.

A wire snare can be supported off the ground on twigs, which can also be used to keep a suspended string noose open. Set the snare a hand's length from an obstruction to trap rabbits.

FOOD

> USING A SIMPLE SNARE FOR SMALL ANIMALS
> Make the loop a fist-width wide.
> Set it four fingers above the ground and a hand's
> width from an obstruction.
> Anchor securely. Support loop with twigs if necessary.

When constructing a snare under tension, use a sapling to lift the game off the ground. The trap is then more effective: the animal is less able to struggle, and predators can't get at it. Hazel is ideal for this.

SPRING SNARE: This is good for rabbits and foxes. Set on a trail by a natural bottleneck caused by a deadfall or rock.

Cut a notch in trigger bar (a) to fit a notch in upright (b). Drive an upright stake into ground. Attach snare to trigger bar and tie cord to sapling to keep tension. Bar disengages, lifting game into air.

BAITED SPRING SNARE: Ideal for medium-sized prey.

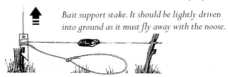

Bait support stake. It should be lightly driven into ground as it must fly away with the noose.

FOOD

BAITED SPRING LEG SNARE: Push the prongs of a natural fork of wood (or 2 sticks tied together) into the ground. The line from a bent sapling is tied to a toggle and to the snare; toggle is then passed under the fork. Bait is attached to a separate bar. Ideal for large game: deer, big cats, and bears. For deer bait with blood or scent glands to arouse its curiosity.

Upper end of toggle presses against fork; lower end is prevented from pulling back through by the bait bar between it and the fork.

SPRING TENSION SNARE: Used for small animals. Set on a trail. *The switch line secures one end of snare arm (b) while the other rests on keeper stick (a). Keep switch line near the end of snare arm (c).When game gets ensnared, snare arm is dislodged from keeper stick and switch line slips off the other end.*

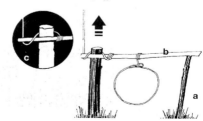

TRAPEZE SPRING SNARE: Use this to cover two game trails in open countryside.

Once ensnared, the prey's struggle disengages snare arm, regardless of the direction from which it approached.

ROLLER SPRING SNARE: This is good for rabbits and foxes.

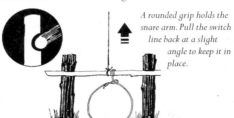

A rounded grip holds the snare arm. Pull the switch line back at a slight angle to keep it in place.

A wide area can be covered using several snares on a long, horizontal bar. Use this where the game trail widens.

FOOD

Platform trap: Set this in a small depression on a game trail. Place the snares on platforms on either side. When the platform is depressed, the trigger bar is released and game is held by the leg. Ideal for deer, big cats, and bears.

A platform of sticks or stiff bark rests on the bottom bar. The upper bar fits in the notches.

Stepped bait release snare: Set this in clearings. It will catch small carnivores and pigs.

Two forked sticks hold down a crossbar engaging with a baited, notched upright stake (attached to a line in tension), holding it in place and carrying snares.

The retaining bar should be squared off to fit the square-cut notch on the bait stick.

FOOD

Deadfall traps

These traps work on the principle that when the bait is taken, a weight falls on the prey.

 Large versions of traps can be dangerous for humans. Toggle release and deadfall traps are easily set off accidentally. In a survival situation ensure that everyone knows where the traps are. In survival practice keep people away from them and never leave a trap set up at the end of an exercise.

Setting a deadfall trap is risky. You cannot do it on your own. Keep the mechanism to the side of the trail, away from the dropping weight. Balance is critical—you are unlikely to get it right the first time.

TOGGLE TRIP-RELEASE DEADFALL: A mechanism similar to the toggle-release snare, but here the release bar keeping the toggle in position presses one end of the toggle upward. A line from the toggle passes over a tree limb to support a weight (e.g. logs) above the trail. A tripline runs aboveground beneath the suspended weight to a securing point.

Run a tripline under a forked stick so that it will pull the trigger bar sideways when it is operated.

FOOD

BALANCE LOG: A forked stick, its ends sharpened to dislodge easily, one fork baited, supports one end of a crossbar. The other end rests on a fixed support, held there by the heavy logs or rock with rests on the bar. The trap collapses when the bait is taken.

Angle the bait beneath the trap.

DEADFALL TRAP: A weight suspended over the trail pulls the line carrying it against a retaining bar that is held by short pegs secured in a tree trunk at a slightly downward angle. Make sure the line is long enough and the anchor is weak enough to allow the weight to reach the ground.

FIGURE 4 DEADFALL TRAP: Balance a horizontal bait bar at rightangles to an upright stake with a locking bar that supports a weight, positioned over bait, pivoted on a sharpened tip of an upright stake.

The bait bar is notched on top to engage the locking arm and square cut on the side to fit the upright stake. The locking arm is sharpened at the end for quick release and notched at the center to pivot on the upright stake.

Spear traps

These traps can be lethal to humans. Always stand behind the spear when you are setting it and mark it with signs to warn humans that the trap is there. Except in a survival situation, never leave spear traps set and unsupervised.

DEADFALL SPEAR TRAP:
The same mechanism as the deadfall trap (see p.128), but rocks add weight and sharpened sticks deliver a stabbing blow.

FOOD

SPRING SPEAR TRAP: A springy shaft with a spear attached is held taut over the trail. A slip ring made of smooth material is attached to a trip wire and acts as a release.

The toggle (a) and a short line are fixed to an upright stake and hold spear shaft in tension. A further rod through the ring is tensed between the near side of spear shaft and far face of the upright stake, securing the trap.

Bird traps

NETS: Stretch a fine net between trees where birds roost. Alternatively, a fine twine crisscrossed between trees across their flight path will damage birds that fly into it.

BIRD LIME: Boil holly leaves and any starchy grains in water; simmer until you have a gooey mess. Spread this onto branches and perching places. Birds will get stuck in it when they alight.

SUSPENDED SNARES: Hang a line of snares across a stream a little above water level. This works best among reeds and rushes.

FOOD

BAITED HOOKS: Bury fishhooks in fruits or other food. The hook gets caught in the bird's throat.

NOOSE STICKS: Tie fine nooses 0.5–1 inch (1.25–2.5 cm) in diameter in horsehair. Place a stick in a roosting or nesting spot with nooses on top. Do not remove it as soon as the first bird gets entangled—it will attract others into the trap.

FIGURE 4 TRAP: This mechanism (see *figure 4 deadfall on p. 129*) can be used with a cage made from a pyramid of sticks tied together and balanced over the bait. For small birds lay all the sticks in place, then lay another two sticks, the same length as the bottom ones, on top and tie them tightly to the bottom layer—tight enough to keep all the others in place. Larger animals are stronger; for them each stick must be individually tied.

FOOD

RUNNING NOOSE: Use a noose attached to a long pole to pull down roosting birds. Go to a roosting site on a bright night. Slip the noose over bird, tighten as you pull.

STALKING WATERFOWL: Get up close by getting into the water and camouflaging your head with reeds or vegetation. Cautiously approach the nesting area, bearing in mind that birds can be ferocious in self-defense.

Where large gourds are available, make holes on one side to see and breathe through, then place over the head. Throw several other gourds into the water to prepare the birds. The hunter then floats with the current among the birds, grabs them from below, and strangles them underwater.

PIT TRAP: Find or dig a hole 3 feet (90 cm) deep in an area where ground-feeding birds are common. The pit's width depends on the type of birds. Spread grain or bait around the hole and more inside it. First taking the bait around the hole, birds will enter it to get more. Rush them: in their panic they are unable to spread their wings sufficiently to take off from inside the hole.

SEAGULLS
Seagulls can be caught by wrapping food around a stone and throwing it into the air. The gull swallows the bait while still in flight, gulps down the stone with it, and the weight change causes it to crash. Obviously this is a technique for use over land rather than at sea. Be ready to dispatch the bird as soon as it hits the ground.

HUNTING

FOOD

Close observation and a knowledge of animals make it easier to find prey and take advantage of terrain.

Proceed quietly. Move slowly and stop regularly. To avoid stumbles and reduce noise, carry your weight on the rear of your foot, testing the next step with the toes before transferring your weight. Hunt against the wind.

> If an animal catches a glimpse of you, freeze. It may be more curious than frightened. Remain still until the animal looks away or continues feeding.

Hunt at first light, moving uphill, and return to camp in the afternoon. Tracks are easier to read when moving uphill; thermal currents build up with the heat of day and carry scents upward, so by returning downhill the scent of game reaches you before yours reaches them. If you must hunt in the evening, go out at least an hour before dusk so that your eyes can develop night vision, but your prey will probably see better than you do.

Get as close as you can to your prey and take steady aim at a point just to the back of the front shoulder. A hit here will drop most animals instantly.

If an animal drops, wait 5 minutes before moving in. Stand back and observe. If it is hurt, loss of blood will weaken it, and when you do approach, it will be unable to bolt. If a wounded animal moves away, wait 15 minutes before following, otherwise it will run all day.

> Avoid large animals unless you are really confident of a first-shot kill—or you could end up becoming the hunted and not the hunter.

FOOD

WEAPONS

Bow and arrow

This is the most effective of improvised weapons: easy to make, it takes only a short time to become proficient.

A well-seasoned wood is best for the bow. Long-term survivors should put wood aside to season it. Tension in unseasoned wood is short-lived, so make several bows and change them as soon as one loses its spring.

Yew is ideal, but hickory, juniper, oak, white elm, cedar, ironwood, birch, willow, and hemlock (the tree) are good alternatives.

MAKING THE STAVE: Select a supple wand. To determine the correct length, hold one end of the stave at the hip with the right hand, reach sideways with the left hand, and mark the extent of your reach as the length of your bow.

SHAPING THE BOW: Stave must be 2 inches (5 cm) wide at the center, tapering to 0.6 inches (1.5 cm) at ends. Make notch about 0.5 inches (1.25 cm) from ends (a) to take bowstring. Remove bark if you wish. Once whittled into shape, rub bow with oil or animal fat.

FOOD

FITTING THE STRING: Cut rawhide to 0.1 inches (3 mm) wide or use string or twisted fibers from nettle stems to make a bowstring. If the bow has lots of give, use shorter string. The string should only be under slight tension—the main tension is added when you pull it back to shoot.

Secure the string to the bow with a round turn and two half hitches at each end. If the wood is unseasoned, release one end when the bow is not in use to relax its tension.

MAKING ARROWS: Use straight wood—birch is the best. Make arrows 2 feet (60 cm) long, 0.25 inches (6 mm) wide. They must be as straight and as smooth as possible.

At one end make a notch that is wide enough to fit the bowstring and 0.25 inches (6 mm) deep.

FLIGHT ARROWS:
(a) Split the feathers, from the top, down the center of quill.
(b) Leave 0.75 inches (20 mm) of quill at each end to tie to the arrow.
(c) Tie 3 flights, equally spaced, around the shaft.
Flights increase accuracy. Paper, cloth, or leaves can also be used.

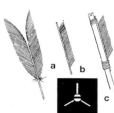

FOOD

ARROWHEADS: The arrow itself can be sharpened and hardened in fire, but a tip of tin or flint is better. Split the end of the shaft, insert arrowhead, and bind tightly with wet sinews—they dry hard, securing the head firmly.

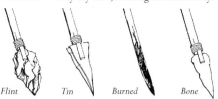

Flint   *Tin*   *Burned*   *Bone*

For details of how to make flint arrowheads see p.198.

ARCHERY TECHNIQUE: Fit the arrow into the bowstring. Raise the center of the bow to eye level. Hold the bow just below the arrow, extending the arm forward. Keep the bow arm locked and draw the string smoothly back across the front of your body, with the arrow at eye level and lined up with the target. Sight along arrow. Release string.

ARROW BURNS: Arrow flights rubbing against the hand and cheek can cause friction burns. Protect the cheek with a piece of cloth pulled tight to the face. Wear a leather mitten or fit a leather guard between the fingers and wrist to protect the hand.

FOOD

Slingshot

A sling is a simple leather pouch in the middle of a length of thong or rope (any strong fabric will do if you don't have leather). Attach the pouch as one piece threaded through, or two tied or sewn on.

SLINGSHOT TECHNIQUE: *Use round, smooth pebbles that are 0.75 inches (2 cm) across. Swing the sling above head in a circle lined up to your target. Release one end of rope, and ammunition should fly at the target. Experiment with sling length to achieve accuracy and distance.*

Catapult

Take a strong, pliable forked twig (hazel is ideal) and a piece of elastic material (rubber from a tire or elastic from clothing). Thread or sew a pouch into the center of the elastic, tie the ends to each side of the fork. Use stones as missiles.

Load several pebbles at a time when using slingshots or catapult against birds.

FOOD

Spears

A straight staff that is 6 feet (1.8 m) is ideal for a jabbing spear; 3 feet (90 cm) is best for throwing. Make a spear thrower from a piece of wood half that length to improve accuracy.

Add a sharp point of flint or a flattened cone of tin to the spear tip. Or securely bind a knife on—but do not risk this if you only have one knife.

SPEAR THROWER: *Take a tree limb twice the width of spear, with a branch stump to serve as a handle. Split down the center, using the knife as a wedge. Gouge out a cleanly cut groove along most of upper face of the thrower. Leave a solid portion as a buffer to add thrust.*

Hold the spear at shoulder level and aim at your target, bringing the holder sharply forward then downward.

FOOD

THE DANGERS OF HUNTING

Few animals will attack except in self-defense, but don't camp on a trail or near an animal watering spot.

DON'T PROVOKE A BEAR ENCOUNTER

Bears are scavengers and will come to camps in search of food. Don't get close or try to catch them. A bear can easily kill a human. Use noise to drive them away—the same goes for other scavengers, e.g. hyenas.

INJURED AND CORNERED ANIMALS

Most animals try to escape when hurt. By preventing them from doing so you are forcing them to fight.

STAY CLEAR

Crocodiles and alligators should be given a wide berth. Large, horned animals may wound you before you can reach your weapon. Many animals, not just those with hooves, have deadly kicks—including ostriches.

BITES

Many small animals have sharp teeth and will attack ferociously. Chimpanzees and other monkeys can be very bad-tempered. Thoroughly clean any bites: they may cause tetanus. Some animals carry rabies.

SNAKES AND STINGING INSECTS

Get used to checking clothing, beddingm and equipment for reptiles and insects. If you awake to find one in your sleeping bag, move gently and calmly to get rid of them or to free yourself.

FOOD

HANDLING THE KILL

Before approaching, check that your prey is dead. Use a
spear or tie your knife to a long stick and stab a large
animal in its major muscles and neck. Loss of blood will
weaken it, allowing you to move in and club the head.

*Two people can carry a large
animal tied to a bough. Place the
pole along the belly and use the
clove hitch round each pair of legs.
Lash animal to pole and finish
with clove hitch around pole. If it
has horns, tie these up out of the
way or cut off head.*

    Butcher game on the trapline. Other meat-eaters will
be attracted and may become trapped. Use entrails to bait
traps. Only carry to camp what you can manage without
exertion: at camp it will only attract flies and scavengers.
Cache the remainder for collection later.

HIDING THE KILL
Suspend a carcass from a bough, out of reach from
the branch. A cache in the crook of a tree will keep
meat away from ground predators but will still be
accessible to climbing predators. Where vultures are
present the cache will be impossible to protect.

FOOD

 HEALTH HAZARDS—DISEASED ANIMALS
All animals have lymph nodes in their
cheeks. If large and discolored, the animal is
sick. Any animal that is distorted or discolored around
the head should be boiled and care should be taken
in preparation: cover cuts or sores in your skin when
handling meat.

PREPARING THE KILL

Waste nothing: make use of the parts you cannot eat.
Prepare the kill in four stages:

Bleeding: Essential if meat is to keep.
Blood is valuable food—rich in vitamins and minerals,
including salt—that are essential to survival.
Keep cool in a covered vessel.

Skinning: Hide or fur can be used.

Gutting: Remove gut and recover offal.

Jointing: Produces suitable cuts for cooking.

BLEEDING: Hang the animal's head down. Tie ropes
around hock (not ankle) and hoist it up to a branch or
build a frame, placing a receptacle below to catch blood.

For a frame: drive strong posts into the ground and
tie firmly to make A-frames. Rest a horizontal bar on top.

Bleed the animal by cutting the jugular vein or carotid
artery in its neck. When the animal is hanging, these will
bulge clearly. Make a cut either behind the ears—stab in
line with ears to pierce the vein on both sides of head at
the same time—or lower down in the V of the neck,

FOOD

before artery branches. Unless you have a stiletto knife, the latter is the best. Cutting the throat from ear to ear risks contamination of blood with the contents of the stomach. Bleed pigs thoroughly if the meat is to be saved.

SKINNING: While the flesh is still warm, remove any scent glands (deer have them behind the knees of the rear legs; felines on either side of the anus). Remove the testicles of males. To remove the hide, cut through the skin as shown by broken lines on the illustration above.

1   Make a ring around the rear legs just above the knee.
2   Cut around the forelegs in the same place.
3   Cut down the inside of the rear legs to the crotch; cut a circle around the genitals.
4   Extend the cut down center of the body to the neck. Do not cut into the stomach and digestive organs. Lift the skin as you go, slip in the knife, sharp edge outward, and cut. Draw the knife slowly down, cutting away from your body.
5   Cut down the inside of the forelegs.

FOOD

Now ease the skin of the rear legs from the flesh. Use the knife as little as possible. Roll the skin outward, fur inside itself, and pull down. When the back legs are clear, cut around the tail. Insert your hand down the back of the carcass and use your fingers to separate flesh from skin. Next, peel the skin from the forelegs. Separate the single piece of hide from the neck with a strong twist of the head. Cut through the remaining tissues.

If alone, lay the carcass down a slope and scoop an impression in the ground to hold the collecting vessel.

Skin small animals by making an incision over the stomach (do not pierce). Insert thumbs and pull out. Free legs and twist head off. If you have no knife, snap off lower part of the leg and use sharp edge to cut skin.

GUTTING: Remove guts and offal from the suspended carcass by pinching the abdomen as high as possible and making a slit big enough to take two fingers in the pinched flesh. Insert your fingers and use them as a guide for the knife to cut upward then downward, using your hand to prevent guts from spilling. Cut down as far as the sternum. Then let guts spill out, hanging down. Remove kidneys and liver. Cut through the membrane to chest cavity and remove heart, lungs, and trachea. You should be able to see daylight through anus—check it is clear.

JOINTING MEAT: Large animals can be quartered by first splitting them down the backbone, then cutting each side between the tenth and eleventh ribs. Hindquarters contain steaks (rump and fillet) and choicer cuts. Forequarter meat is stringier and needs slow cooking to tenderize. Cuts vary according to the type of animal.

FOOD

OFFAL

Liver: Eat this as soon as possible. Little cooking is required. Remove the bile bladder in the center with care, don't allow it to taint the meat. Avoid mottled or white-spotted liver.

Stomach: Tripe is easy to digest. Remove the stomach contents (good invalid food, as it is already broken down, so boil it lightly), wash the tripe and simmer it slowly with herbs.

Kidneys: Boil these with herbs. The white fat surrounding them (suet) can be rendered down to use in pemmican; see p. 192.

Lungs: Do not eat if mottled with black and white spots. If pink and blemish free, boil them or use them for bait.

Heart: Roast or use to liven up a stew.

Intestines: Ideal sausage skins: turn them inside out and wash. Then boil well. Mix equal proportions of fat and meat, then stir in the blood. Stuff the skins with this mixture and boil it well. If smoked, sausages keep for a long time.

Sweetbreads (pancreas): Boil or roast this.

Tail: Skin and boil it to make soup.

Feet: Clean them well, then boil to make stew.

Head: Large animal heads are meaty. Boil tongue to make it tender and skin it before eating. Brain will make headcheese and provide a solution to cure hides. Boil whatever is left, or the whole head with small animals.

Bones: Boil these for soup—marrow is rich in vitamins. They can also be made into tools.

FOOD

HANGING: Eat offal as soon as possible, but rest of meat is better hung to make it tender and to kill parasites. In moderate temperatures leave carcass hanging for 2–3 days. In hot climates preserve it or cook at once.

PREPARING SHEEPLIKE ANIMALS: Follow the instructions for large animals, then split into two down center of the spine. Remove the rear leg (cut through the joint) and the front leg. Cut off the neck and loose flesh below the ribs. Cut inbetween the ribs and vertebrae. Preserve the fillet, which is found in the small of the back.

PREPARING PIGS: Do not skin. Gut, then place over hot embers and scrape the hair off (loosen it with water just hotter than your hand can bear). Boil to kill parasites.

PREPARING REPTILES: Discard the internal organs. Cook it in skin. Cut off the head far down, behind the poison sacs; open vent to neck, keeping the blade turned outward—don't pierce the innards. Skewer to suspend it. Ease the skin down toward the tail.

PREPARING BIRDS: To kill them, stretch the neck and cut the throat or cut just under the tongue to sever the main artery. Hang it head-down to bleed. Meateaters harbor parasites, so handle them as little as possible. Pluck while the body is still warm. Hot water will loosen the feathers (except those of waterfowl). Make an incision from the vent to the tail, insert your hand and draw out guts. Retain heart and kidneys. Cut off head and feet. Boil meateaters and old birds; young ones can be roasted on a spit or in an oven. Leave skins on and eat them.

FOOD

FISH AND FISHING

Fish contain protein, vitamins, and fats. They differ widely in size, eating habits, and diet, but all can be attracted and caught with the appropriate bait. Angling is not the most effective method of catching fish—the night line and gill net will get better results—but if you have plenty of time, it is a pleasurable pastime.

WHERE TO FISH: If it is hot and the water is low, fish retreat to deep, shaded waters. In cold weather they seek shallow spots where the sun warms the water. At any time fish like to shelter under banks and rocks.

When a river is in flood, fish in slack water, e.g. on the outside of a bend or in a small tributary.

WHEN TO FISH: Leave lines out overnight and check them just before first light. If a storm is imminent, fish before it breaks. Fishing is bad after heavy rain.

IMAGE REFRACTION: *Fish can see more on the bank than you think. Sit or kneel when you are fishing, so you are less likely to be in sight. Stay back from the edge and try to keep your shadow off the water.*

INDICATIONS OF FISH FEEDING: Fish are likely to take the bait when you see them jumping out of the water. Clear ring ripples breaking on the surface are another sign. Where lots of little fish are darting around, they may be being pursued by a larger predatory fish.

FOOD

ANGLING

You can improvize hooks from all types of materials. Here (from left to right) are a pin, a thorn, a bunch of thorns, nails, bone, and wood.

Large hooks will catch large fish, but small ones catch both large and small. A rod is not essential (you can fish with a hand line), but it makes it easier to catch fish and cast away from the bank.

ANGLING WITHOUT HOOKS: *Eels and catfish swallow without biting. To catch them, tie a blob of worms on a line (a) and pull them out as soon as the bait is taken.*

A small, sharp piece of wood attached to the end of the line and held flat along it by the bait (b) will, when the bait is swallowed, open out across the throat of the fish (c).

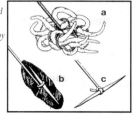

BAIT: Fish are more likely to take bait native to their water: berries that overhang it or insects that breed in it. Examine stomach contents of your first catch for clues.

FOOD

USING FLOATS AND WEIGHTS

A small, floating object attached to the line, visible from the bank, will show you when you have a bite. Its position will help control where the line descends.

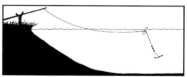

Small weights between the float and the hook stop the line from trailing along the water or too close to the surface, while leaving the hook itself in movement. Your survival kit includes a small split lead shot. Slip the groove along the line and squeeze it to fit tightly.

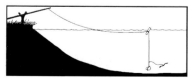

To get a deeper hook position, extend the line to a weight below the hook.

Any suitable bait, when scattered on water, will attract fish. Put the same bait on your hook to catch them. Suspend a termite or ant nest over the water, and the falling insects will prove to be an irresistible draw to fish.

SPINNING: Fish will attack a shiny object drawn through the water: try coins, buttons, tin, or buckles. Thread a propeller shape to a piece of wire, and it will spin with the current. Attach your hook to the end of the spindle.

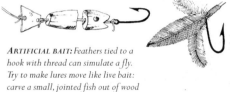

ARTIFICIAL BAIT: Feathers tied to a hook with thread can simulate a fly. Try to make lures move like live bait: carve a small, jointed fish out of wood (hazel is the best for cutting through), thread the segments, and decorate it with color or glitter.

LIVE BAIT: Cover the hook completely with worms, insects, maggots, or small fish. A hook can be placed through a small fish or grasshopper without killing it. The distressed movement of the bait will attract fish.

FOOD

NIGHT LINES: Weight one end of a line and attach worm-baited hooks along it at intervals. Anchor the free end securely on the bank. Put this out overnight—use in daytime too, but change the worms regularly because fresh wriggling ones attract more attention.

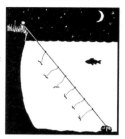

OTTER BOARD: To fish farther than you can cast a line, make a board with a movable, pivoted rudder. Set a bar at the front end of the rudder and attach two control lines. Suspend baited hooks below. Float the board out into the lake. If the winds are favorable, mount a sail, but first add a keel: gouge holes to fix the dowel supports and tie on a flat stone (not so big as to conflict with the rudder). Extra movement of the board indicates a bite.

FOOD

JIGGING OR SNAGGING: *When you can see fish but they are not taking the bait, tie several hooks to a pole and lower it into the water. Suspend a bright object 8 inches (20 cm) above the pole, and when the fish go to inspect it, sharply pull the hooks up to catch them.*

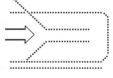

FISH TRAPS

In shallow streams build a channel of sticks or rocks that fish can swim into but not turn around in (arrows here indicate the current).

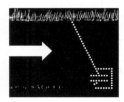

BOTTLE TRAP: *Cut a plastic bottle off just below the neck. Invert the neck inside the bottle. Use bait to entice them in. Once in, the fish can't get out.*

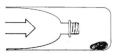

FOOD

A similar trap can be made for larger fish using a hollow log. Make a lattice cone out of twigs for the entrance and block the other end of the log.

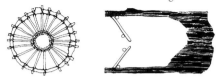

WICKERWORK TRAPS: Hazel or other pliant twigs can be used to make a trap that allows the current to flow through it and to a fish looks like streambed debris.

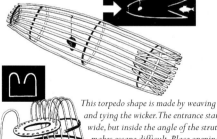

This torpedo shape is made by weaving and tying the wicker. The entrance starts wide, but inside the angle of the struts makes escape difficult. Place opening downstream, against the current.

The lobsterpot trap utilizes holes in a circle of board to make it easier to shape. This trap sits on the bottom. Bait will attract eels and crayfish.

FOOD

OTHER TECHNIQUES

Fish snares: Large fish can be caught in a noose line attached to the end of a pole or passed down inside a length of bamboo. Pass the loop over fish from tail end and sharply pull up so that the noose traps the fish.

Eel bag: Tie fresh offal and straw or bracken in a cloth (not plastic) bag. Attach a line and weight to the end of the bag and allow it to sink. Leave it overnight and pull it out in the morning. Eels will chew their way into the bag and will still be wriggling in the straw when you catch it.

Gill net: If you have a net, set floats at the top and weight the bottom, then stretch it across a river. It will soon empty a stretch of water, so do not use for long.

Attracting and driving: A flashlight held above water at night will attract fish. Pull nets to trap the fish, then spear or club them. A mirror placed on the riverbed will reflect either sun or moonlight and attract fish.

Spearing: Sharpen a long stick to make a spear. Try to get above the fish and strike down swiftly. Make sure that you are not casting a shadow over the fish. Aim slightly below it, to allow for the refraction of its image.

Muddying: Receding floodwater leaves isolated pools. Stir up the mud at the bottom of the pool with a stick or by stamping in the water. Fish will try to escape to clearer water. Scoop them out.

Explosives: Explosives kill nearby fish and force to the surface those that are farther away.

Guns: Fish can be shot in the water, but do not submerge the gun barrel—it will explode, and the detonation will blow back at you.

FOOD

Fish narcotics

Some plants stupefy fish to make them come to the surface. This works the best in slack, warm waters. Do not use in closed pools—the fish supply can't be restocked.

> The following plants are only toxic to cold-blooded animals, but they should not be eaten by humans.

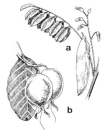

Derris (a) Found in S.E. Asia to Australia. Woody, vinelike plants with oval leaflets in opposite pairs and purple flowers in seedpods. **Powder the roots and throw them into the water.**

Barringtonia (b) A tree with the same distribution as derris, often near coasts. **Crush seeds inside their pods and throw into the water.**

Desert rose (Adenium) *(c)* Found in tropical and southern Africa and Arabia. Shrubs or small trees with thick, fleshy leaves. The E. African species illustrated here has spirals of blunt, oval leaves and clusters of tubular pink flowers. **Crush the stems and roots.**

Soap plant (d) Found in N. America, in dry open or scrubland. Narrow, grasslike leaves, white starlike flowers. **Crush the bulbous root and throw it into the water.**

Dead fish floating on the surface of the water—unless you have caused them to be there—may be diseased and unfit to eat.

ARCTIC FISHING

The technique of fishing through ice is effective on any frozen lake or river where the ice is thick enough to bear your weight but not too solid that it can't be penetrated.

Bait the hook in the usual way. If the line is carried back up against the underside of the ice, weight it below the hook. Set up multiple angling points. To signal when you have a bite, make a pennant from bright-colored cloth or cardboard and attach it to a light stick. Tie this firmly at rightangles to another stick that extends the diameter of your hole by at least 30%. Now attach the line to the lower end of "flagpole" and rest flag on the side of hole with line at its center. When fish takes bait, the crosspiece will be pulled over the hole and flag jerked upright. Be ready to pull your catch up quickly before a seal gets to it.

ICE NETTING: Make several holes in ice 16 inches (40 cm) wide and twice that distance apart. Attach retaining loops to a weighted net at intervals to match holes. Put loop at one end around a stick that is wider than the hole. With hooked pole, haul net through to next hole and anchor the next retaining loop. Continue until fully extended.

FOOD

PREPARING FISH

All freshwater fish are edible. Those that are under 2 inches (5 cm) long need no preparations: eat them whole. Larger fish must be gutted.

As soon as the fish is caught, cut its throat to bleed it and remove the gills. To gut it, slit from the anal orifice to the throat. Remove offal (use for hook bait). Keep the roe, which runs down the side of fish. Scaling is not necessary, but to scrape scales off, pull a knife from tail to head (a). Fish skin can be eaten. To skin eels and catfish, pass a stake through fish, place it across two upright stakes, cut skin away, and pull it down toward tail (b).

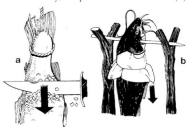

PREPARING CRUSTACEANS: Eat these as soon as possible. Boil for 20 minutes. Crabs have poisonous parts, so twist off claws and legs; with crab on its back, place your thumbs under flap at tail, push up. Pull flap up and away from body and lift off—this prevents stomach contents from tainting flesh. Push down and out on mouth with your thumbs, to make the mouth and stomach come off in one piece. Lungs are harmful: discard them.

CAMP CRAFT

In a survival situation it is vital to know where to set up camp, how to build a shelter from the materials available, how to make fire, cook, and preserve food, and how to improvise tools, clothing, and equipment.

SHELTER AND MAKING CAMP

An accident, exhaustion, or sudden fog may leave you stranded. Local conditions and materials will determine the type of shelter you can build. While there is still daylight to see by, scour the vicinity for the best natural shelter from wind, rain, and cold before night sets in.

A wrecked plane or vehicle may provide shelter or materials from which one can be built, but if there is a risk of fire or fuel tanks exploding, wait until it has burned out before attempting to salvage anything.

BAD PLACES TO CAMP

Exposed hilltops (go down, seek shelter on lee side).

Valley bottoms and deep hollows—damp and more liable for frost at night.

Hillside terraces where the ground holds moisture.

Spurs that lead down to water, which are often routes to animals' watering places.

Too close to water: you will be troubled by insects, and heavy rainfall may cause rivers to swell and flash floods to occur. Even old, dry watercourses are at risk.

Near solitary trees, which attract lightning.

Near bees' or hornets' nests.

CAMP CRAFT

WHERE TO CAMP

You should be sheltered from the wind, near water—but clear of any risk of flooding—with a plentiful supply of wood closeby (in forest areas, stay to the edges where you can see and be seen). Check above your head for deadwood in trees that could crash down in high winds. Don't camp across a game trail. Bear in mind that the sound of running water can drown out other noises that might indicate danger, or the sound of search parties.

TYPES OF SHELTERS

For immediate protection rig up a makeshift shelter while you construct something more permanent. If you are walking to safety, build temporary shelters at each stop; if it is light enough, they can be carried with you.

HASTY SHELTERS: Where no materials are available for constructing a shelter, make use of natural cover. In completely open plains sit with your back to the wind and pile any equipment behind you as a windbreak.

BOUGH SHELTERS: Branches that sweep down to the ground or partially broken boughs can provide shelter, but make sure they are not likely to fall off the tree.

Make a similar shelter by tying a broken-off bough to the base of another branch where it forks from the trunk (a).

CAMP CRAFT

ROOT SHELTERS: The spreading roots and trapped earth at the base of a fallen tree make a good windbreak. Fill in the sides between extended roots for added shelter.

NATURAL HOLLOWS: Even a shallow depression will provide protection from the wind, but you must deflect any downhill flow of water if it is a hollow on a slope.

Make a roof to keep the rain off and warmth in. A few sturdy branches laid across the hollow can support a light log laid over them, against which shorter sticks can be stacked to give pitch to the roof—and so allow water to run off. Consolidate with turf, twigs, and leaves.

FALLEN TRUNKS: A log makes a useful windbreak if it is at the right angle to the wind. With a small trunk, scoop out a hollow in the ground on the leeward side.

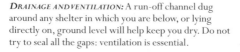

A log also makes an excellent support for a lean-to of boughs.

DRAINAGE AND VENTILATION: A run-off channel dug around any shelter in which you are below, or lying directly on, ground level will help keep you dry. Do not try to seal all the gaps: ventilation is essential.

STONE BARRIERS: A shelter is more comfortable if it is high enough to sit in, so increase its height by building a low wall of stones around your hollow. Calk inbetween the stones with turf and foliage mixed with mud.

SAPLING SHELTERS: If suitable growth is available, select two lines of saplings, clear the ground between them of obstructions, and tie the tops together to form a frame for sheeting. Weight down the edges of the sheeting with rocks or timber. A similar shelter can be made from pliable branches driven into the ground.

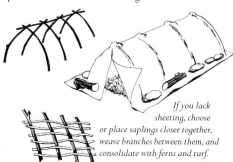

If you lack sheeting, choose or place saplings closer together, weave branches between them, and consolidate with ferns and turf.

CAMP CRAFT

Shelter sheet: With a waterproof poncho, groundcloth, plastic sheeting, or canvas, a number of shelters can be made.

Make use of natural shelter (a) or make a triangular shelter with the apex pointing into the wind (b). Stake or weight down the edges. If it is long enough, curl the sheeting below you, running downhill (c). Use dry grass or bracken as bedding.
Do not lie on cold or damp ground.

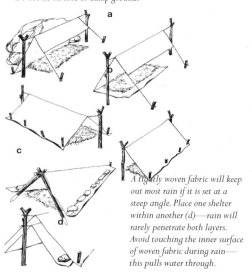

A tightly woven fabric will keep out most rain if it is set at a steep angle. Place one shelter within another (d)—rain will rarely penetrate both layers. Avoid touching the inner surface of woven fabric during rain—this pulls water through.

CAMP CRAFT

TEPEES: The quickest type to erect has three or more angled support poles, tied where they cross to make a cone. They can be tied on the ground and then lifted into place before covering it with hides, birch bark, or sheeting. Leave an opening at the top for ventilation.

Wider angles will give greater area but will shed rain less easily.

A parachute, suspended from its center, makes an instant tepee. Peg down the bottom edge.

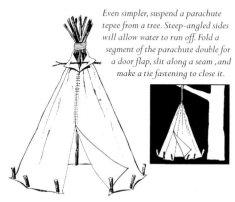

Even simpler, suspend a parachute tepee from a tree. Steep-angled sides will allow water to run off. Fold a segment of the parachute double for a door flap, slit along a seam ,and make a tie fastening to close it.

Stick walls and screens

Build walls by piling up sticks between upright stakes driven into the ground and (if possible) tied at the top. Use this to make one side of a shelter, to block an opening, or for a heat reflector behind a fire. This can be used instead of large rocks to dam a stream.

To make a very sturdy stick wall, increase the space between the upright stakes, use two stacks of sticks, and fill up the gap with earth.

COVERINGS: Use springy saplings, plant stems, grasses, and long leaves to make wattle and woven coverings for roofs and walls. First make the framework from less pliable materials, either in situ or as a separate panel to attach later. Tie the main struts into position. Weave in the more pliant materials.

If no ties are available, drive vertical stakes into the ground and weave saplings between them. Calk with earth and grasses.

If suitable, firm crosspieces are scarce, weave creepers between the upright stakes. Very large leaves, tied or weighted down, can be overlapped like tiles or shingles to keep the rain out.

CAMP CRAFT

Long grass can be bunched up and woven, or use birch bark to make tiles. Ring a birch tree with even 2 foot (60 cm) cuts and remove the bark (a). Attach pairs of canes or creepers across a frame (b). The upper ends of tiles are gripped between the canes; the lower ends rest on those below (c).

OPEN LEAN-TO SHELTERS:
If there is nothing to lean a roof against (and no need to keep out heavy rain or blizzards) use panels of wattle or grass-covered frames.

Erect a horizontal crosspiece between trees or on simple supports. On the windward side lean a panel of wattle, or saplings at 45 ° to make a roof. Add side walls (a). Build your fire on the leeward side and build a reflector (b) on the other side to preve fromnt heat escaping.

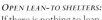

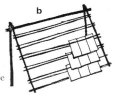

Tropical shelters

In rain forests and jungles, where the ground is damp and crawling with insects, a raised bed is preferable. Unless the nights are cold, the number one priority will be to stay reasonably dry. The following are useful materials.

BAMBOO: A very versatile building material found in damp places from India through to China, parts of Africa, Australia, and the southern U.S. and which can be used for supports, flooring, roofing, and walls.

Split the bamboo vertically to make roofing and guttering to collect rainwater. Split stems, laid alternately to interlock with each other, form waterproof pantiles.

Flatten the split bamboo for walls, floors, or shelving by cutting vertically through the joints every 0.5 inches (1.25 cm) around the circumference. It can then be smoothed out.

The paperlike sheaths formed at the nodes can be used for roofing material.

 Be very careful when collecting bamboo. Some stems are under tension, and when they are cut they explode into sharp slivers. Split bamboo can be razor-sharp and cause serious injuries. The husks at the base of bamboo stems carry small stinging hairs that cause severe skin irritations.

CAMP CRAFT

THATCH OF LEAVES: When thatched, atap and other large leaves make the best roofs and walls for jungle shelters. Look for any plant with a similar structure—the bigger and broader, the better.

a

Atap (a) is the best when used horizontally, splitting each leaf in two from the tip (b) and tearing it into two halves along its length. Do not try to split i from the thick end as it will break. There are barbs at each leaf tip, so handle it carefully.

b

Closely layer then halves of the atap on a roof frame (c). Walls can be less dense.

c

Another method involves not splitting the leaf, but instead folding the leaflets on one side across to the other side and interweaving them (d). This is easiest if you work from one side and then the other, but it requires practice.

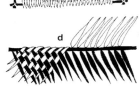

d

CAMP CRAFT

Three-lobed leaves or leaves cut in this way (e) can be locked over a frame thatching without any other fixing being necessary to keep them in place (f).

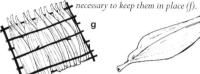

Elephant grass and other large leaves can be woven between the crosspieces (g). Only a small number are needed to produce a shelter very quickly.

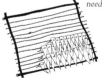

Long, broad leaves can be sewn along the battens with vines (h).

Palm and other long-stemmed leaves can be secured by twisting the stem around the batten and over the front of the leaf, where it is held by the next leaf (i). Leaves must overlap those below on the outside of the shelter.

CAMP CRAFT

Arctic shelters

In polar areas caves and hollows form simple shelters. If you carry a bivouac, increase its protection by piling up loose snow around and over it, as long as it can support the weight. At very low temperatures snow is solid, and you need spades and ice saws to cut into it or make blocks out of it.

Snow or rock caves are easily recognizable, but also look for spaces left beneath conifers where snow has built up around them. A medium-sized tree may have a space right around the trunk (a), or a large one may have pockets in the snow beneath a branch (b). Try digging under any tree that has spreading branches on the leeside.

Even soft snow can be built into a windbreak. Cut and stack the blocks (c). Use another set of blocks to anchor a ground cloth or poncho along the top, use others to secure the bottom edge, and more to close up the sides.

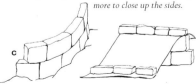

CAMP CRAFT

> BUILDING IN SNOW
> Cut compacted snow—using a saw, knife, shovel, or
> machine—into blocks 18 x 20 inches (45 x 50 cm)
> wide by 4–8 inches (10–20 cm) thick. These provide
> insulation, while allowing the sun's rays to penetrate.

Snow trench: This is a one-person shelter for short-
term use only. Mark out an area the size of a sleeping bag;
cut out blocks the entire width of the trench. Dig down
at least 2 feet (60 cm). Along the top of the sides cut a
ledge around 6 inches (15 cm) wide and the same depth.

*Place the snow bricks on each side of the ledge and lean them in
against each other to form a roof (a).*

Put your equipment under a sleeping bag as insulation.
Block the windward end with a block or piled snow. At
the downwind end dig an entrance or have a removable
block. Fill in the gaps with snow. This shelter is best when
built on a slight slope with an entrance at the lower end.

Snow cave: Dig into a drift of firm snow. Create three
levels inside: build a fire on the highest, sleep on the
center one, and stay off the lower level, which will trap
the cold. Drive two holes through the roof: one for a
chimney, and one to ensure adequate ventilation.

CAMP CRAFT

Use a block of snow as a door, keeping it loose fitting and on the inside so that it won't jam. Smooth off inside surfaces to discourage drips. Make a channel around the internal perimeter for melting snow.

IGLOO: An efficient snow house. Make sure the entrance does not face into wind (erect a windbreak if necessary). *Mark out a circle 13.5 feet (4 m) in diameter and tramp it down to consolidate the floor. Cut and lay a circle of blocks on the perimeter. Dig a tunnel (a),*

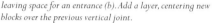

leaving space for an entrance (b). Add a layer, centering new blocks over the previous vertical joint.

　　Each new layer should be placed halfway over the lower tier, so the igloo forms a dome shape. Shape the entrance arch as you go. Seal the top with a flat block. Make ventilation holes near the top and bottom (not on the side of prevailing winds, or so low that snow blocks the hole). Fill in other gaps with snow. Smooth off the inside to remove drippoints.

　　Inside the igloo build a sleeping level higher than the floor and create a lower cold level for storage.

Sweating should be avoided, so take your time when building a complex structure and rest frequently.

Adequate ventilation is essential to prevent carbon monoxide poisoning and to allow moisture to escape.

The smaller the shelter, the warmer it will be, but it will not be possible to heat it much above freezing.

CAMP CRAFT

LIVING IN A SNOW HOUSE

Make sure you have a supply of fuel in the shelter.

Knock snow off boots and clothing before entering.

Mark the entrance so that it can be found easily .

Keep shovels and tools inside to dig yourself out.

Stop drips by placing a piece of snow on the source.

Relieve yourself indoors in containers.

No matter how low the external temperature gets, inside a snow house it will not drop below 0°F (-10°C). An oil burner or fat on bones are alternative heating fuels when there is no wood or casiope.

Long-term shelters

If you decide that there is no hope of rescue and it is impracticable to make your own way to safety due to distance, time of year, lack of equipment, or your physical condition, make a permanent shelter.

CAVES: Those situated above a valley will be dry, even if water seeps through in some places from above. They are weatherproof and require little aside from a barrier of rocks or wattle to close off the entrance. Caves may be inhabited by wild animals, so approach them with caution. Dry plant matter on the ground will provide insulation. A good fire will make animals leave (allow them an escape route). Build the fire at the back of the cave so that smoke goes up to the roof—smoke from a fire near the open mouth of a cave will be blown in. If you seal the entrance, make sure you leave a gap for smoke to escape.

CAMP CRAFT

 Check for the possibility of a rockfall inside or outside the cave. You could be trapped or injured by falling rocks.

LIGHT STRUCTURES: Follow the methods outlined for the lean-to structure (see p. 164). Extend it with a less angled roof and a front wall or build vertical walls and roof them over with deep eaves to allow extra shade and ensure that rain runs off. In hot climates the walls can be fairly open lattice to allow air to pass through. Grasses and mud will seal cracks. In climates with heavy rainfall use leaves or bark like tiles on the top.

If you have bamboo or other strong materials to build a firm frame in tropical climates, raise the floor of your shelter off the ground to keep other creatures out.

SOD HOUSE: Cut sections of turf 18 x 6 inches (45 x 15 cm) and build with them like bricks, overlapping them to form a bond. Keep the structure low—big enough to sit in but not to stand in. One side could be open, facing your fire. Slope the sides to give pitch to the roof, which will be supported by spars of wood. Lay turfs on the roof as well or cover it with grass.

FIRE

Fire is essential to survival. It provides warmth, protection, and a means of signaling; it boils water, cooks, and preserves food; it heats metal to make tools and to bake pots. You must learn to light a fire anywhere an in any conditions. It is not enough to know all the methods—you have to be an expert at them.

Remember the fire triangle.
Its three sides represent air, heat, and fuel.
If any one of these is removed, the triangle collapses and the fire goes out.

PREPARATION

Ensure that there is adequate ventilation for your fire. The more oxygen is introduced, the brighter the fire; by reducing ventilation the fire burns less fiercely, needing less fuel. Collect sufficient supplies of tinder, kindling, and fuel. Prepare a fireplace so you can control the fire.

The fireplace

Choose a sheltered site. Except for signaling purposes (see pp. 273–275), do not light a fire at the base of a tree. Clear away leaves, twigs, moss, and dry grass from a circle 6 feet (2 m) across until you have a bare earth surface.

If the ground is wet or covered in snow, build a platform from a layer of green logs covered with a layer of earth or a layer of stones.

CAMP CRAFT

TEMPLE FIRE: This is a raised platform of green timber. Four upright stakes support crosspieces in their forks. Place a layer of green logs across them and cover this with several inches of earth. Light the fire on top of this. A pole across the upper forks on diagonally opposite upright stakes can support cooking pots.

In windy conditions dig a trench and light your fire in it.

Alternatively, encircle your fire with rocks to retain heat and save fuel. They serve as heated pot stands and can be used as bed warmers.

 Avoid placing wet or porous rocks near fires, especially rocks that have been submerged in water—they may explode when they are heated, producing dangerous flying fragments that could take an eye out if you are close to the fire. Avoid slates and softer rocks. Test them by banging them together and do not use any that crack or sound hollow.

CAMP CRAFT

Tinder

Tinder is any material that only takes a spark to ignite it.
Birch bark, dried grasses, wood shavings, bird down,
waxed paper, cotton fluff, fir cones, pine needles,
powdered, dried fungi, or scorched or charred cotton are
excellent tinder, as is the fine dust produced by wood-
burrowing insects and the inside of birds' nests.

Kindling

Kindling is the wood used to raise flames from tinder.
Small, dry twigs, resinous and softer woods are the best.

> Tinder and kindling must be dry. Don't collect it from
> the earth. If the outside of kindling is damp, shave it
> until you reach dry wood.

Make fire sticks
*Shave sticks with shallow cuts to
"feather"them.This will
make the wood catch
light quicker.*

Fuel

Use dry wood to get a fire going. Once it is established,
mix green and dried-out damp wood.

Hardwoods, such as hickory, beech, and oak, burn
well, are long lasting, and give off great heat.

Softwoods burn fast and give off sparks: the worst
culprits are alder, spruce, pine, chestnut, and willow.

CAMP CRAFT

Dry wood across two supports that are high enough above a fire that they won't be set alight. Lay green logs beside the fire,

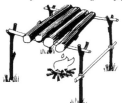

tapering away from the wind, so they shelter the fire while they dry.

A basic woodshed is vital in wet weather. Position it where fire will warm it but away from stray sparks.

Save energy: don't chop logs, break them over a rock (a)

or feed them over the fire, letting them burn through in the middle (b).

Split logs without an ax by placing a knife on the end of a log and hitting it with a rock (c). Once it is started, the split can be widened with a wooden wedge plugged in the gap and driven downward. Don't do this if you only have one knife —it could get damaged.

CAMP CRAFT

OTHER FUELS

Animal droppings: dry well, mix with grass and leaves.

Peat: found on moors. Soft and springy underfoot, it looks black and fibrous. Dry it before burning. It will need ventilation when it is burning.

Coal: sometimes found on surface in northern tundra.

Shales: rich in oil, burn readily. Some sands also contain oil and burn with a thick smoke—good signals.

Combustibles: petroleum, hydraulic fluid, engine oils, and insect repellent. If soaked in oil, tires, upholstery, and rubber seals are flammable.

Animal fats: use a tin for a stove and burn it with a wick.

BURNING OIL AND WATER: *Pierce a small hole in the base of a tin can for each liquid and attach tapered sticks to govern the flow (a). The oil and water run down a trough to a metal plate. To increase the flow, pull stick out; push it in to reduce*

Try 2–3 drops water: 1 drop oil. First light a small fire under the plate to get it hot. Light the mixture itself on top of the plate. It is highly volatile and will burn almost anything.

CAMP CRAFT

BURNING OILS: Mix gasoline with sand and burn it in a ventilated tin can, or dig a fire pit. Burn oil by mixing in gasoline or antifreeze. Do not set a light directly to any liquid fuels: make a wick for the flame.

LIGHTING FIRES

Form a tepee of kindling around bed of tinder. If windy, lean kindling against a log on the leeside. Ignite the tinder. Add larger sticks once kindling has caught fire— or light a bundle of dry match-thin twigs and place them in the tepee.

Matches are the easiest way to start a fire. Carry the nonsafety type in waterproof containers, packed so that they can't rub, rattle, or ignite. Split them in half to make them last longer. To strike split matches, press the flammable end against the striking surface with your finger.

Strike a damp match by stabbing obliquely instead of pulling it along the striker strip.

If your hair is dry and not too greasy, roll a damp match in it. Static electricity will dry out the match.

CAMP CRAFT

Whenever you strike a match, light a candle. Many things can then be lit from it, saving matches. Even a small candle will last a long time if it is used carefully.

SUNLIGHT THROUGH A LENS: *This can ignite tinder. Use your survival kit magnifying glass, telescope, or camera lens. Focus sun's rays to form a tiny, bright spot of light. Keep it steady and shield it from the wind. Blow it gently as it glows.*

POWDER FROM AMMUNITION: *Break open a round and pour gunpowder on the tinder (a) and use a flint—or leave half the powder in the cartridge case and stuff a piece of cloth in (b). Chamber the round and fire it into the ground. The smoldering cloth will be ejected. Place it on the tinder to ignite.*

FLINT: A stone found in many parts of the world. Strike it with steel, and hot sparks fly off (a)—or use a saw edged blade from your survival kit (b) for more sparks.

LIGHTING FIRES WITH BATTERIES: Attach two pieces of wire to a battery. If you have no wire, use metal tools. If using a car battery, remove it from the vehicle first.

Slowly bring the bare ends of two pieces of wire together. A spark will jump across just before they touch. Aim it at the tinder. A small piece of cloth with a little gasoline on it is the best tinder.

FIRE BOW: The friction of a hardwood spindle rotated on a softwood base produces wood-dust tinder, and then heat. Both the spindle and the base must be dry.

Gouge a small depression at the near end of the baseboard. Cut a cavity below this for the tinder. Shape the spindle evenly. Make a bow from a pliable shoot and a hide, twine , or a shoelace. Use a hollow piece of stone or wood to steady the top of the spindle and exert downward pressure. Wind bowstring once around spindle. Place spindle in the depression, hold the steadying piece over its end, and lightly push down while moving the bow backward and forward so that the spindle spins. Increase speed as spindle starts drilling. When it enters cavity, apply more pressure and bow vigorously.

CAMP CRAFT

Keep the spindle upright and steady and bow strokes even. It helps if you kneel with one foot on baseboard. Continue bowing until a glowing tip drops onto the tinder. Blow on it gently to ignite it.

HAND DRILL: A variation on the fire bow.

Cut a V-shaped notch in a hardwood baseboard. Make a small depression. Use a stem of hollow softwood with a soft pith core for the spindle. Roll the spindle between the palms of your hands, running your hands down it as you go to press it into the depression. When friction makes the spindle tip glow red, blow gently to ignite the tinder. Put a pinch of sand in the spindle hole to increase friction.

FIRE PLOW: Cut a straight groove in a softwood baseboard and then plow the tip of a hardwood shaft up and down it. This produces tinder, and then ignites it.

CAMP CRAFT

LIGHTING FIRES WITH CHEMICALS

The following mixtures can be ignited by grinding with rocks or by putting under a friction point in a fire drill. Mix carefully and avoid contact with metal. Keep dry.

Potassium chlorate and sugar mixed 3:1.

Potassium permanganate and sugar mixed 9:1.

Sodium chlorate and sugar mixed 3:1.

Potassium chlorate is found in some cough drops.

Potassium permanganate is part of your survival kit.

Sodium chlorate is a weedkiller.

 Handle chemicals with care. Sodium chlorate ignites from percussion—DO NOT shake or spill it (spillage can ignite when it is stepped on)!

TYPES OF FIRES

Fires for warmth

Only surfaces that are facing an outdoor fire are warmed by it.

A reflector not only reflects heat but also makes smoke go upward. Use one to reflect heat into a sleeping shelter.

Build a fire near a rock. Sit between the two so that the rock reflects the heat and warms your back. Add a reflector.

If there is no rock to reflect heat, build a second reflector to go behind you.

CAMP CRAFT

SNAKE HOLE FIRE: In the side of a firm earth bank dig a chamber around 18 inches (45 cm) deep. From above drive a stick down into the chamber, maneuver it a little to make a chimney, removing the dirt that falls below.

This fire is ideal for smoke preserving meat and fish. Build the fire in the chamber. The entrance is best placed downwind in windy conditions.

Cooking fires

TRENCH FIRE: *Dig a trench 12 x 36 inches (30 x 90cm) and 12 inches (30 cm) deep, plus the depth of a layer of rocks with*

which you should line the bottom. Build a fire on the rocks. Even when it dies down, the rocks will stay hot enough to make a grill. A spit placed across the embers is ideal for roasts.

HOBO STOVE OR VAGABOND STOVE: *Punch holes in the bottom and around the bottom sides of a 5-gallon oil drum. Cut out a panel on one side, 2 inches (5 cm) from the bottom, through which to stoke the fire. Set the drum on a ring of stones to allow ventilation beneath.*

CAMP CRAFT

COOKING

Cooking makes food more appetizing and easier to digest. It destroys bacteria and parasites that may be present, and neutralizes poisons. But when heated, food loses some nutritional value. Never cook it longer than is necessary.

Use the fire to boil water, then let the flames die down and use the embers and hot ash for cooking.

Never leave your fire unattended when cooking.

Having lit a fire, always have water boiling—unless it is in short supply—for drinks, sterilizing wounds, etc.

Do not just balance a can on the fire. Support vessels on rocks or suspend them over the fire for stability.

COOKING METHODS

BOILING: Cans and metal boxes are ideal for boiling water. Make a handle, hang them from a pot support, or use tongs to move them. Punctures can be repaired by hammering in small plugs of wood—when they are wet, they will expand and stop leaks. Improvize pots from a thick piece of bamboo or sections of birch bark—but do not let them boil dry.

To cook in a bamboo stem, angle it across the heat of the fire, supporting it on a forked stick driven into the ground.

Boiling conserves natural juices—always drink the liquid unless you are boiling out toxic substances.

CAMP CRAFT

Any dead animal that is not actually decomposing can be eaten if you only use the large muscle areas. Cut into 1 inch (2.5 cm) cubes and boil for 30 minutes. Only eat a little and wait a half hour—most toxins act in that time or less. If there are no bad effects, then eat.

ROASTING: Skewer the meat on a spit and rotate it over hot embers or beside a blazing fire. Continually turn the meat to keep the fat moving over the surface.

A spit should be set up on one side of a fire to allow for a drip tray to catch the fat for basting. Fierce heat cooks the outside, leaving the inside undercooked, so a slow roast is best. Cut off the outer meat, then continue roasting to cook the inner flesh.

GRILLING: This wastes fat—only use when food is plentiful.

Rest wire netting or a grid of green sticks on rocks over the embers—or use a long stick on a forked support to hold food over the fire. Wrap the food around the stick.

BAKING: This requires an oven. Cook the meat on a dish and baste it with its own fat. Slow cooking on a steady heat tenderizes the meat. Baking is also ideal for root vegetables.

CAMP CRAFT

A large metal box with a hinged lid—and a catch that you can use as a handle—can be set up to open sideways. If it has no catch, let it open downward. Place a support in front, to rest the lid on. Prop it closed and avoid a tight fit that could build up dangerous pressure inside. If no box is available, make a clay dome, set a fire inside, and scrape this out before cooking. Leave a small aperture that can be sealed easily while baking.

Sit the box on rocks so that a fire can be lit under it. Build up rocks and earth or clay around the back, sides, and top, but leave a space behind and make a chimney hole from above, leading to this space.

STEAMING: This is a good way to cook vegetables and fish. Punch holes in a can and suspend it inside a larger can or put something in the bottom of the large can to keep the inner one above the water. Cover the outer can, but do not seal it or the pressure could cause it to explode.

Improvise a steamer out of bamboo: between the inner compartments make a hole that is just big enough to let water through to fill the bottom section. Make a lid (not too tight) for the top. Water boiled in the lowest section will produce steam to cook food in the top one.

CAMP CRAFT

FRYING: This is a good way to vary your diet, if fat is available. Any sheet of metal that can be made into a curve will work to fry in. Some large leaves (e.g. banana) contain enough oil not to dry out before the cooking is done. Try the leaves out first before cooking food on them and only fry over embers.

COOKING IN CLAY: This requires no utensils. Wrap food in a ball of clay and place it in the embers. Heat radiates through the clay, which protects against food scorching. Animals must be cleaned and gutted first but do not need to be prepared otherwise: when the clay is removed, spines, scales, or feathers from small birds come away with it, but big birds should be plucked. Not advisable for root vegetables—skins are too nutritious to lose.

HANGI: This is another way of cooking without utensils. It requires kindling, logs, and round rocks the size of a fist. Do not use stones that may explode (see p. 174).

Dig an oval hole with rounded sides 18–24 inches (45–60 cm) deep; place the kindling at the bottom. Lay logs across the hole, place another layer at right angles, interspersed with stones. Build up 5 or 6 more alternating layers, and top these off with stones. When the kindling is set alight, the logs will burn, heating the stones above them, until eventually it all falls into the pit.

CAMP CRAFT

Remove the embers and ash, place the food on top of the hot rocks, with the meat in the center and vegetables to the edge. There must be a gap between the food and the earth. Lay saplings across the pit and cover with sacking, leaves, and earth. Uncover after 1.5 hours; your meal is ready.

The hangi can be used to boil water collected in a waterproof sack, as long as the fabric won't melt. Place tied-up sack in the hangi. This takes around 1.5 hours.

Useful utensils

TONGS: *Tie 2 branches so that they spring apart—use a tapering piece of wood between them under the lashings. Grip is improved if one branch has a forked end. Use for holding hot pots.*

POT ROD: *Drive a sturdy, forked stick into the ground near the fire. Rest a longer stick across it with one end over fire. Drive the bottom of the long stick into ground and weight it with rocks. Cut a groove near the tip to prevent pots from slipping off, or tie on a strong hook.*

SWINGING POT HOLDER: *Bind 2 forked sticks together so that forks fit in opposite directions on a firm upright stake. The cantilever action will maintain the height you set it at, and a push sideways will swing the pot away from the flames.*

VARIABLE POTHOOK: *Cut a strong piece with several branches from a small tree or bush and trim branches to 4–5 inches (10–12 cm). Strip off the bark, which may hide rotten wood.*

CUP: *Cut a section of bamboo just below a joint, then cut just below the next joint up. Smooth off the edges to prevent splinters.*

SPOON: *Scribe a spoon shape on a flattish piece of wood with a knife point. Whittle to the required shape. Never cut toward yourself.*

BIRCH BARK CONTAINERS: *Use the inner layer of bark to make cooking vessels. Sew or tie them near the top to prevent them from unfolding. Make a second vessel with a larger base for a lid.*

A circle, folded into quarters, will make a cone-shaped cup or a boiling vessel if it is suspended.

CAMP CRAFT

COOKING TIPS

MEAT: Cut into cubes and boil. Pork is prone to worms and liver fluke; venison is prone to worms. Marinade tough meat in citric juices for 24 hours before cooking.

OFFAL: Check the liver: only if it is firm, odorless, and free from spots and hard lumps, can it be eaten. Boil, then fry it if you want. Hearts: parboil then bake. Brains: skin the head and boil, simmering for 90 minutes. Strip all the flesh from the skull, including the eyes, tongue, and ears. Blood: collect in a container and leave covered until a clear liquid comes to the top. When separation seems complete, drain it off. Dry the residue by the fire to form a firm cake. Use it to enrich soups and stews.

FISH: Stew or wrap fish in leaves and place it in hot embers (avoid toxic leaves).

BIRDS: Boil all carrion. Old birds are tough and are best when boiled. Stuff young ones with herbs or fruits and then roast them.

REPTILES: Gut, then cook in their skins. Place in hot embers, turning continually. When skin splits, the meat can be removed and boiled. Some snakes have poisonous secretions on their skins and others have venom glands in their heads, so cut off before cooking. If you are not sure if they are safe, be careful when handling. Skin frogs (many have poisonous skins), then roast them on a stick.

SHARKS: Cut shark into small cubes and soak overnight in fresh water. Boil it in several changes of water to get rid of the ammonia flavor.

CAMP CRAFT

SHELLFISH: Safest boiled. All seafood goes bad quickly. Drop into boiling salted water and boil for 10 minutes.

INSECTS & WORMS: Best boiled. Cook and mince them by crushing in a can—or dry on hot rocks, then grind into a powder with which to enrich soups and stews.

EGGS: Boil, or roast after first using a sharp stick or knifepoint to pierce a small hole in one end. Place on warm embers to cook slowly. If a boiled egg contains an embryo chick, remove the embryo and roast it.

GREEN VEGETABLES: Wash and boil until tender. Can be steamed if you are sure that they are safe. Add to stew after the meat is cooked. Eat fresh greens raw as a salad.

ROOTS: Any toxins are destroyed by heat. Try boiling for 5 minutes then place in a hole dug beneath the fire, cover with ash and embers and leave until tender.

LICHENS & MOSSES: Soak overnight. Add to stews.

SAGO: Fell a sago palm at base of the trunk and trim the tip just below last line of flowers. Divide the trunk into sections cut lengthwise. Using each section as a trough, pound the pith into a mash, then knead it in a container of water and strain through a cloth. A starchy paste will form in the water. Roll this into sticky balls and cook.

PALM SAP: Choose a fat stalk with a flowering head (at the base of the crown on trunk). Bruise it with a club then cut off head. Sweet juice will flow from the end of the stalk. Bruise and cut daily to stimulate flow. Drink raw or boil then cool it to produce lumps of pure sugar.

CAMP CRAFT

PRESERVING FOOD

If food is not plentiful or it is limited by season, ensure that supplies keep safely.

Do not store food in direct sunlight, near excessive warmth or moisture, or where scavengers may ruin it.

Wrap it in airtight and waterproof materials—or store it in containers with good seals. Label supplies and separate different foods to avoid cross-flavoring.

Check supplies occasionally to ensure they are fine.

DRYING

Wind and sun can dry food out, but it is easier to force-dry it over a fire. Dried foods are less vulnerable to molds and maggots. Meat with a high fat content is difficult to preserve. Cut off most of the fat and rub salt into the flesh. Hang the salted meat in a cool, airy place.

SMOKING: This dehydrates meat and coats it with a protective layer. Smoking can be done in a smoke tepee. Get a fire started to produce hot embers. Have a pile of green leaves ready.

To build a smoke tepee, drive three sticks into the ground to form a triangle and tie the tops together. Build a platform between them and set a fire beneath them.

Hardwood leaves are ideal, but avoid holly and other toxic leaves, as well as conifers, which may burst into flames. Do not use grass. Make sure that there are no flames left and pile leaves over the embers.

Cut meat into fat-free strips, 1 inch (2.5 cm) by 0.5 inches (6 mm), gut and fillet fish. Cover the tepee with a cloth to keep the smoke in. If you don't have a cloth, pile boughs and turfs on the frame and seal it. Leave it for 18 hours and ensure that little or no smoke escapes.

To avoid risk of embers setting tepee alight, build a snake hole fire (see p. 183); erect tepee over a chimney.

BILTONG: Cut strips, as for smoking; hang them in sun, out of the reach of animals, 6–10 feet (2–3 m) above-ground. They can take 2 weeks to dry. Protect them from rain and dew. Turn the strips to ensure all surfaces are dried and keep flies off so they don't lay eggs.

To dry fish, cut off the head, tail, and gut. Split it open, remove the backbone, and score inner flesh. Lay it on hot, sun-baked rocks. Fish less than 3 inches (7.5 cm) long do not need to be gutted.

Fish can also be smoked. They will be easier to hang if they are cleaned and gutted without removing the backbone, head, or tail. Suspend them by one side of the head.

CAMP CRAFT

PEMMICAN: This is concentrated food made from biltong and ideal for provisions to carry on treks. Before setting out take equal quantities, by weight, of biltong and rendered fat. Shred and pound the meat. Melt the animal fat over the shredded meat and mix it together well. When it is cold, pack it in a waterproof bag. It will keep for a long time, especially in cold climates.

Nuts and cereals

Place on hot rocks from the fire, turning frequently until dried. Store them in damp-proof containers.

Fruits, fungi, and lichens

Fruits and berries can be dried whole or cut into slices and dried by the sun, smoke, or heat. Fungi also dry easily. Fruits can be eaten dry. Add fungi to soups or soak in water for several hours to regain their texture.

To store lichens, soak overnight, boil well, and allow to dry. Grind them into a powder then boil again to form a thick syrup, which adds body to other foods.

PICKLING AND SALTING

Citric acid from limes and lemons can be used to pickle fish and meat. Dilute the juice and water 2:1, mix well, and soak the flesh for at least 12 hours. Transfer it to an airtight container with enough solution to cover meat.

Vegetables can be preserved by boiling and then storing them in saltwater. To make sure a brine solution is strong enough, add salt until a potato or root vegetable will float in it. Another method of using salt is to tightly pack layers of salt and vegetables. Wash off the salt when you need to use them.

CAMP CRAFT

ORGANIZING THE CAMP

If no command structure exists between a group of survivors, establish an organizing committee with particular responsibilities. A roster is essential for daily chores. Everyone who is able should take their turn to do unpleasant tasks, unless their skills are in such high demand that it would be a waste of their abilities.

> Staying busy eliminates boredom and keeps morale up. People who are injured should get lighter jobs. At all times there must be someone in camp who is able to operate the signals if a search aircraft appears. If numbers allow, avoid venturing from the camp alone.

A nightly gathering will provide discipline and an opportunity to debrief and discuss new strategies.

Boredom is dangerous for a lone survivor, and objectives should be set each day whether they are practical or for entertainment. A regular routine helps morale.

CAMP HYGIENE

Strict hygiene should be maintained in the camp.

CAMP LAYOUT

Latrines must be downhill of camp and away from the water supply to avoid the risk of seepage.

Establish a collection point for drinking water. Ensure that noone washes upstream of it. Downstream choose a point for ablutions and laundry and downstream of that a place for cleaning cooking utensils.

Latrines and garbage disposal should be far away from camp—preferably downwind—but not so far as to be inconvenient. Cut a track to make access easier.

CAMP CRAFT

Never urinate or defecate near your water supply. Latrines must be established, even for a lone survivor. Do not use disinfectant—after defecating cover the feces with earth. Make a latrine cover to keep flies out and always replace it. If a latrine starts to smell, dig a new one. Fill in the old latrine and burn the old timbers.

DEEP TRENCH LATRINE:
Dig a trench 4 feet (1.25 m) deep and 18 inches (45 cm) wide. Build up the sides with logs, rocks, or earth to sitting height. Seal the gaps. Lay logs across it to leave just a hole for use. Pour wood ash onto logs to make a seal and deter flies.

Cover the opening with a wooden lid, flat rock, or a large leaf weighted with stones.

URINAL: *Dig a pit 2 feet (60 cm) deep. Fill it three-quarters full with large stones and top it up with earth, with a bark cone set into it as a funnel.*

CAMP CRAFT

INCINERATOR: Garbage should be burned. Make a fire in the latrine area using a large can as an incinerator. Bury unburned garbage in a pit.

CAMP DISCIPLINE

Do not prepare game in camp: bleed, gut, and skin it on the trapline to attract game to traps, not to camp.

Keep food covered and off the ground.

Replace lids on containers immediately after use.

Stow clothing and equipment where it cannot get wet or burned. Keep things tidy: hook mess kits and cooking utensils on twigs and branches.

Never leave the fire unattended.

SOAP: Washing with soap leaves the skin less waterproof and more prone to attacks by germs. However, soap is an antiseptic, better than many others, such as iodine, which destroy body tissue as well as germs. It is ideal for scrubbing your hands before administering first aid. Save supplies for this.

MAKING SOAP: Two ingredients—an oil and alkali—are needed. The oil can be animal or vegetable fat, but not mineral. The alkali can be produced by burning wood or seaweed to produce ash.

To make soap, wash the ash with water and then strain and boil it with the oil. Simmer it until the excess liquid has evaporated and allow it to cool. This soap is not antiseptic. Add horseradish roots or pine resin to make it antiseptic. Too much alkali in the mix will dry out the skin, leaving it sore

CAMP CRAFT

TOOLS

STONE TOOLS: Split a cobble with a blow from a hard, smooth pebble to form a flat face. The blow should be at an angle of less than 90°. Shape by hitting it using the edge of another stone (a), then create a platform on one side (b), from which a series of flakes can be struck vertically downward (c). Then strike it with softer stones and hit and press small flakes away with a piece of antler or hardwood. Flakes may be used as scrapers, to cut edges, and as arrowheads.

BONE TOOLS: Bones, antlers, and horns make useful digging implements, gougers, and hammers. Cut them with stone tools or grind them with coarse stones. A shoulder blade is a good shape for a saw (a). First split it in half, then teeth can be cut along it with a knife. A small bone scraper (b) could also be made, with the edge ground to be sharp. Ribs are ideal for shaping into points (c). To make a bone needle, choose a suitably sized bone and sharpen it to a point. Burn an eye with a piece of hot wire or scrape it with a knifepoint or a piece of flint. Don't heat the knife in the fire.

AXES

CAMP CRAFT

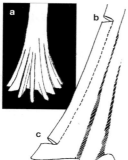

To improvize a handle for an ax head, use any straight, knot-free hardwood. The flukes of a buttress tree (a) are ideal; curved slightly, straight-grained, and easy to work. Cut two notches into the fluke of a buttress, spaced to the desired length (b to c).

Hit along the side of the fluke close to the cuts. It will split away at their depth.

ATTACHING THE AX HEAD: Whittle the handle into shape, with one end cut to fit the hole in the axhead, cutting a notch in that end. Make a wedge to fit the notch. With the head in place, drive in the notch, then soak the ax in water overnight to tighten the ax head on the shaft. Always check ax heads for tightness before use.

CAMP CRAFT

TO ATTACH A STONE AX HEAD: Select a hardwood handle. Tie a band of cord around it 9 inches (23 cm) from one end. Split the end as far as this band (use a knife and a wedge or the ax head flint). Insert flint and tie end.

SHARPENING AN AX: Use a file to get rid of burrs, and use a whetstone to make the sharp edge. A file is a one-way tool—it works when it is pushed, not pulled.

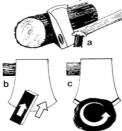

Prop the ax head between a log and a peg (a). Always sharpen inward from the cutting edge to avoid producing burrs. Use a file or a rougher stone first to remove the burrs (b). Finish with a smooth stone, using a circular motion. Don't drag stone off cutting edge. Push onto blade. (See pp. 23–25.) Turn ax over. Repeat process, circling in opposite direction (c).

USING AN AX: Swing an ax in an arc that feels natural with a firm grip and always away from your body, hands, and legs. Make sure that, if you miss your target and follow through, the ax will not strike you or anyone else. Never throw an ax on the ground. Sheath it or bury the blade in a log.

CAMP CRAFT

Tree felling

Check overhead for dead branches and hornets' nests.
Clear creepers and branches that could deflect your
blows. Cut the branches off from the outside of the join.

*Cut from both sides of the tree, first
chopping out a notch at an angle of
45°, and another on the opposite
side at a lower level, on the side to
which you want the tree to fall (a).
Do not cut more than
halfway before starting
the other notch.*

A tree with most of its branches on one side will fall
in that direction, regardless of the placement of the cuts.

Use a steady rhythm of blows. Use too much effort
with the ax, and your aim will suffer. Alternating the
angle of the stroke will prevent the ax from jamming. Too
steep of an angle will cause the ax to glance off, straight

on will make it jam or be
inefficient. Aim for 45°.

*SPLITTING LOGS: Stand
behind the log with your feet
apart. Swing down to cut the
side away from you (a). Do not
chop downward (b). To split a
small log, angle it against
another log (c). Do not put your
foot on it.*

CAMP CRAFT

BROKEN HANDLES: Ax handles break when the axhead misses the target and the handle takes the impact (a). To remove a broken handle, put it in a fire, burying the metal in the earth to prevent it from losing temper—single-headed (b) or double-headed (c).

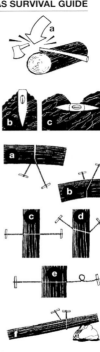

USING A FLEXIBLE SAW:
Always use a flexible saw so that the cut opens (a) rather than closes (b), causing it to jam. Don't pull too hard, or the saw will break. Keep the wire taut (c), pulling straight and never at angles (d). Maintain the rhythm when 2 people saw. A kink (e) may break the saw.

It is usually easier for a single person to cut a log by pulling it upwards(f). Keep the log off the ground and at an angle to keep the cut open. Alternatively, to remove a branch, pull it down from above (g). This could be dangerous. High branches can be removed by attaching strings to the saw toggles for extra reach. Be ready to jump clear of the branch.

FURNISHING THE CAMP

CAMP CRAFT

BEDS

Avoid lying on cold, damp ground. In the tropics raise the bed up to provide a current of air. In cold climates keep a fire going throughout the night and build a screen to reflect heat back on the sleeping area. On dry ground stones heated in the fire and then buried under a thin layer of soil beneath the bedding will keep you warm.

A-FRAME BEDS: Drive two pairs of posts into the ground at an angle, leaving a little more than your height between the pairs. Tie the tops together. On hard ground cross members will be needed between the feet of each A-frame and between the two A-frames.

TUBE BED: Make a tube of strong material, sewn or thonged together. A large, heavy-duty plastic bag is suitable. Do not use any fabric that might give out under your weight or seams that might come apart.

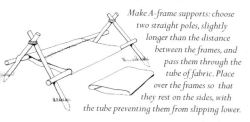

Make A-frame supports: choose two straight poles, slightly longer than the distance between the frames, and pass them through the tube of fabric. Place over the frames so that they rest on the sides, with the tube preventing them from slipping lower.

BOUGH BED: Fir tree branches arranged in alternate layers make a comfortable and fragrant bed.

LADDER BED: Make A-frame supports and select poles, as for the tube bed, and add a number of crosspieces. Strong, springy saplings are the best. Tie end rungs to the A-frame, jutting out on either side. Make these of strong timber and tie them securely. Attach a ladder over frames and tie in place. Lay a bedding of ferns or leaves.

SEATS: Never sit on damp ground. Use a log or tie together a couple of low A-frame supports and rest a bough across them.

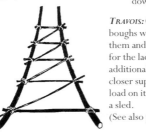

LADDER: Tie crosspieces to two long poles set at an angle, not parallel, so that the rungs won't slip down.

TRAVOIS: Choose two boughs with some spring to them and tie crosspieces, as for the ladder. Add additional struts to provide closer support. Pull the load on its runners like a sled.
(See also p. 245.)

ANIMAL PRODUCTS

SKINS AND FURS

Properly prepared skins are supple, strong, and resist tearing. They have good thermal insulation and are permeable to air and water vapor. For moccasins, shelters, shoelaces, thongs, water bags, or canoes, the fur is removed, but for warm clothing, bedding, or a good insulating groundcloth, it is should be left on.

Remove the fat and flesh by scraping the skin, using an edge of bone, flint, or wood. Be careful not to cut it. Remove every trace of flesh. Ants and other insects may help if you lay the skin on the ground. Watch to make sure that they do not start to eat the skin itself.

To cure it, stretch the skin as tight as possible and leave it in the sun to dry. Rubbing in salt or wood ash will aid the process. Do not let it get damp until the process is complete. If little or no sun is available, force-dry it over a fire, but only use the heat and smoke and keep it away from the steam of any cooking pots.

SHOELACES AND LASHINGS: Cut short shoelaces straight from skin, along its length. For greater length, cut in a spiral, keeping width consistent to avoid weak points.

SINEW AS THREAD: The hamstring and the main sinews of the legs can be dried and used as thread, bowstrings, short ropes, and arrowhead bindings. They look like strong, white cords. Sticky when wet, they dry hard.

BLADDER: The bladder of a large animal can be used as a water carrier, so can the stomach. Tie off the openings to seal them.

CAMP CRAFT

CAMP CRAFT

CLOTHING

Salvage towels, blankets, seat covers, curtains, sacking from the wreckage—any fabric can be used for garments, bedding, or shelter.

Improve insulation by adding layers. Wear one sock over another and stuff dry grass or moss between them. Grass, paper, feathers, animal hair, etc. can be stuffed between other layers of clothing.

Use plastic bags and sheets to improvize waterproofs or cut off large sections of birch bark. Discard the outer bark and insert the inner layer under outer clothing.

Improve water-repellent qualities by rubbing animal fat or the tallow from suet into your clothing. Do not do this in situations of intense cold, where the reduction in insulation would be too great a loss.

Cut shoe soles from rubber tires, make holes around the edges for thongs to tie them over wrapped feet or to sew onto fabric uppers.

Tie on several layers of foot wrappings with thongs or use a triangular shape. Fold one point back over the toes and make slits in the front. Bring other points from behind heel, through slits and tie around ankle.

Tie long leaf strips and fibers around a belt or neck band to hang down as a grass skirt or cape.

Cut a head hole in a blanket or carpet and use this as a poncho. Tie at the waist or thong sides.

Sew together small skins. Fur on the inside will give greater insulation, but on outer garments the suede side sheds snow better.

CAMP CRAFT

ROPES AND LINES

Match the type, thickness, and length of rope you carry
to the demands that you expect to make on it. Nylon has
advantages in very damp climates and when weight is
critical, but it can melt and is slippery when it is wet.

Rope around 0.5 inches (9–10 mm) is recommended
for lashings, throwing, and mountaineering. It can be used
for safety lines and for climbing, provided belay and
rappelling techniques are used—it is not thick enough for
a hand over hand and foot grip.

Climbing rope must be elastic, to absorb shock
without putting strain on anyone who falls.

TAKING CARE OF ROPE

Rope should be protected from exposure to damp or
strong sunlight and, if it is made from natural fibers,
from attacks by rodents and insects.

If it does get wet, do not force-dry it in front of a fire.
Do not drag it or leave it on the ground. Dirt can
penetrate and work away at the fibers.

Try to keep rope for the job for which it was intended—
do not use clothesline for climbing or climbing rope for
lashing,although in a survival situation you may have to
use the same piece of rope for many purposes.

THROWING A ROPE

A coil of rope is easier to throw than a loose end. Have a
large knot or weight on the throwing end. Make sure that
you keep ahold of the other end! Always overthrow a
lifeline so that the recipient has a chance of catching part
of the rope, even if they miss the end.

CAMP CRAFT

TO THROW A ROPE: Coil half the rope on the fingers and palm of your right hand, raise the index finger and coil remainder on the other fingers only. Pass the second coil back to the left hand. As you throw, release the right-hand coil a split second before the left.

FOR A LONG THROW: Tie a suitable missile to the end of the rope. Coil the rope carefully on the ground or loop it loosely over the other hand so it will pull out freely.

Don't risk losing your end. Tie it to an anchor such as a heavy stone. Use a killick hitch (see p. 219).

If you are throwing a weighted rope over a branch, stay out of its way as it swings back toward the throwing point. If you are throwing a lifeline, make sure that you don't knock out the person you're trying to help.

MAKING ROPE

Vines, grasses, rushes, barks, palms, and animal hairs can all be used to make ropes or lines.

The stems of nettles make excellent ropes and those of honeysuckles can be twisted together to make tight lashings. The stronger the fiber, the stronger the rope. Some stiff fibers can be made flexible by steaming or warming them. While pliable vines and other long plant stems can be used for short-term purposes, they may become brittle as they dry out. A rope made from plant fibers that are twisted ("spun") or braided together will be more durable.

The tendons from animals' legs also make good strings, but they tend to dry hard. (They are also very useful as binding on arrowheads and spear heads; see pp. 135–137).

KNOTS

It is important to select the right knot for the task at hand. You never know when you may need to tie a knot, so learn their uses and how to tie—and untie—each one.

> In the instructions for individual knots that follow, the end of the rope or cord being used to tie the knot is referred to as the "live end" to distinguish it from the other end of the rope, or the "standing part."

CAMP CRAFT

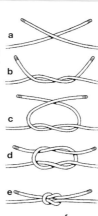

REEF KNOT: Used to tie ropes of the same thickness. It holds firmly under strain, yet can be easily untied. It is not reliable for ropes of different diameters, nor for nylon. It can be tied in other materials—use for first aid. It will lie flat against the patient.

Pass right end over left (a) and then under it (b). Take left over right (c) and under it (d).

Check it—the 2 loops should slide on each other. Tighten them by pulling both strands on each side (e). To be extra sure, finish it by making a half hitch with the live ends on either side of the knot (f).

CAMP CRAFT

Simple knots

These knots are made quickly and will help you
understand the more complicated knots that follow.

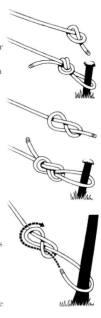

OVERHAND KNOT: Make a loop
and pass the live end back
through it.

OVERHAND LOOP: A fixed loop for
throwing over a projection.
Double the end of rope and tie an
overhand knot with the loop.

FIGURE EIGHT: An end-stop.
Make a loop. Carry the live end
first behind, then around, the
standing part. Bring it forward
through the loop.

FIGURE EIGHT LOOP: Made in
the same way as the figure eight,
but with the line doubled, using
the loop as the live end. It can be
used over a spike anchor for
a belaying rope.

REWOVEN FIGURE EIGHT: Use this
when the top end of a projection
is out of reach. Make a loose
figure eight along the rope. Pass
the live end around the anchor
and feed it back around the figure
eight, following exactly. Ease it
tighter.

Connecting ropes

CAMP CRAFT

SHEET BEND: If it is made correctly and the strain is not erratic, this won't slip. **1** Make a loop in one rope. Take live end of the other (a) all the way around behind the loop to the front, carry it over itself, and then tuck it down through the loop. **2** Pull it tight and ease it into shape as the strain is increased.

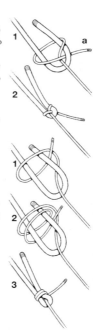

DOUBLE SHEET BEND: A more secure variation of a sheet bend— use this on wet ropes and where strain is not constant.
1 Make a loop in the thicker rope. Take live end of thinner rope (a) through the loop, beneath thicker live end, and then forward on the outside of the loop and all the way around it. Bring thin live end back between itself and outside of the thick loop. **2** Take thin live end completely around the loop again and back through the same place on outside of thick loop.
3 Pull it tight and ease into shape.

If not tightened, these knots tend to come loose. Do not use on smooth lines, e.g. nylon fishing line.

CAMP CRAFT

FISHERMAN'S KNOT: This is ideal for connecting springy vines, wires, slippery lines, and gut fishing line (soak gut first to make it pliable). It is very secure but hard to untie. Not recommended for bulky ropes or nylon lines.
1 Lay lines beside each other, with the ends in opposite directions. Carry live end of one line around the other and make a simple overhand knot. **2** Repeat with the live end of other line.
3 Partially tighten knots and slide them toward each other. Ease them to rest against each other, completing tightening process.

DOUBLE FISHERMAN'S KNOT: A stronger version of the above. Do not use on nylon fishing lines, nylon ropes, or bulky ropes.
1 Carry live end of one line around the other, then around both. **2** Carry the live end back through the two loops.
3 Repeat with the end of the other line. **4** Slide the 2 knots together and tighten, easing them to rest tightly against each other. Apply strain gradually.

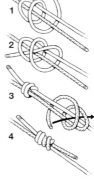

CAMP CRAFT

TAPE KNOT: Used to connect flat materials, e.g. leather, webbing, tape, and sheets or other fabrics. **1** Make an overhand knot in the end of one tape. Do not pull it tight. **2** Feed the other tape through it so that it exactly follows the shape of the first knot. **3** Live ends should be clear of the knot so that they will not slip back when you tighten it.

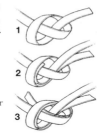

Loop making

BOWLINE: A fixed loop that will neither tighten nor slip under strain. Used at end of a lifeline. **1** Make a small loop a short distance along the rope. **2** Bring the live end up through it, around the standing part and back down through the loop.
3 Pull on the live end to tighten it, easing the knot into shape. Finish with a half hitch.

RUNNING BOWLINE: A loop that tightens easily. Make a small bowline and pass the long end of rope through the loop. Never tie a running bowline around the waist, it acts like a hangman's noose and could kill.

CAMP CRAFT

TRIPLE BOWLINE: A bowline made with a double line. Form a loop, pass the doubled live end through the loop, behind the standing part, and back through the loop. This produces 3 loops that can be used for hauling equipment, or as a sit-sling or lifting harness with one loop around each thigh and the other around the chest. It takes practice—learn it before you need to use it.

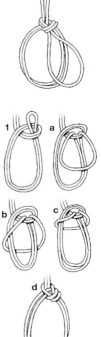

BOWLINE-ON-THE-BIGHT: Used to support or lift someone from a crevasse. The loops will not tighten or jam, forming a bosun's chair, one loop fitting around buttocks, the other around the upper body. Practice before you use it.
1 Using a doubled line, form a loop and pass the live end through it. **2** Bring this end down (a) and over the end (b) of the larger double loop that is now formed. Ease it back up to behind the standing part (c). Pull on the large double loop to tighten it (d).

CAMP CRAFT

MANHARNESS KNOT: A nonslip loop. It can be made along the length of the rope, but it does not require access to an end. Several loops can be put on a rope for harnessing people together. It is also a good way of preparing a rope for climbing. Toes and wrists can be put into the loops to carry weight, allowing you to rest.
1 Make a loop in the rope—look closely at the drawing.
2 Allow the left side of rope to cross over loop. **3** Twist the loop. **4** Pass it over the left part of the rope and through upper part of the original loop. **5** Pull the knot gently into shape. Ease it tight and test carefully.

Note: If it is not eased tight correctly, the loop may slip.

Different ways of making this knot may be found where the loop is not twisted at **3**. The final strength of the loop does not appear to be affected, either by making this twist or not, nor if the twist straightens out during use.

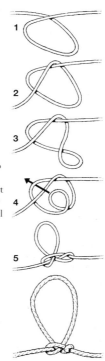

CAMP CRAFT

Ladders

Tie as many manharness knots in a rope as you need for handholds and footholds. Add rungs using strong sticks or pieces of wreckage.

Use 2 ropes or a long rope, doubled, with manharness knots placed evenly along both sides to make a rope ladder. As you make loops, pass sticks through the corresponding loops and ease it tight to hold sticks firmly. Allow sticks to project a few inches on either side of the ropes and test it for strength.

LADDER OF KNOTS: A series of overhand knots tied at intervals along a smooth rope will make climbing it much easier.
1 Leaving a reasonably long free end, make a half hitch near the end of a short piece of log. **2** Continue making loose half hitches along the log—the diameter of which will hold the spacing of the knots. **3** Pass the starting end back through all the loops and then slide them all off the end of the log. **4** As each turn of rope comes through, the center of the half hitch loops to the other end. Shape it and tighten each knot.

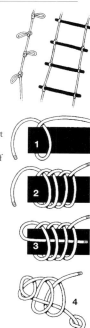

CAMP CRAFT

HONDA KNOT: A free-running noose with a circular loop that is ideal for lassoing. If you only have one rope, don't use it as a lasso—this causes wear and damage to the rope.

a Start with an overhand knot.
b Form a loop farther down the rope.
c Double the rope into a bight between the loop and the knot.
d Pass the bight through loop.
e Tighten the loop around bight.
f Pass long end of rope through new eye formed by the bight.

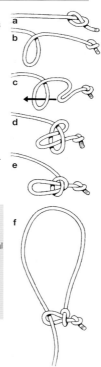

Before lassoing an animal, consider its strength. A big animal may wrench the rope away, depriving you of a meal and a rope. If the rope is anchored to you, you may be dragged along and injured. Instead, use a firm anchor—a tree or rock—to take the strain.

CAMP CRAFT

Hitches

Used to attach ropes to posts, bars, and poles.

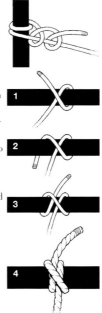

ROUND TURN AND TWO HALF HITCHES: The best way to secure a rope to a post. These can take the strain from any direction. Carry the rope behind the post, then around again. Bring live end over and back under the standing end and through loop that has been formed. Tighten it and repeat half hitch to make knot secure.

CLOVE HITCH: This is effective when strain is perpendicular to the horizontal. Not as good when the strain comes at an angle or is erratic.

1 Pass live end over and around the bar. 2 Bring it across itself and around the bar again. 3 Bring the live end up and under itself, moving in the opposite direction to the standing end.

4 Close it up and pull it tight.

CAMP CRAFT

TIMBER HITCH: Used as a starting knot for lashings and for hoisting and dragging or towing heavy logs. **1** Bring live end around bar and loosely around the standing end. **2** Bring it forward and tuck it beneath rope encircling the bar. Twist around as many times as will comfortably fit. Tighten the knot by gently pulling on the standing end until a firm grip is achieved.

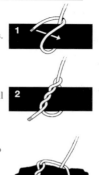

KILLICK HITCH: To secure a line to an anchoring weight, make a timber hitch around one end of weight and tighten it. Bring line along weight and make a half hitch.

MARLINSPIKE HITCH: A temporary knot for securing a mooring line to a post or for dragging over the top of an upright peg. By attaching a short, stout stick to the line, it is possible to gain extra grip for a firmer pull.

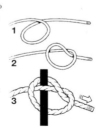

1 Form a loop in the rope—study drawing carefully. **2** Bring one side of loop back up over the standing end. **3** Drop this over the pole—the pole coming between the extended loop and the standing part. Pull live end to tighten it.

CAMP CRAFT

QUICK-RELEASE KNOT: A secure knot, but it will come untied with a single, sharp tug on the live end. Recommended for temporarily anchoring lines.

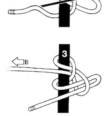

1 Carry a bight, around a post or rail. **2** Bring a bight from the standing end through the first bight. **3** Form the live end into a further bight and push doubled end through loop of second bight. Pull on standing end to tighten knot. **4** To release, pull sharply on live end.

Shortening rope

SHEEPSHANK:
Triple the line.
Form half hitches

in outer lengths and slip them over adjoining bends. Or, instead of half hitches, when a loop is formed in the standing part, pull a bight through it and slip this over bend in rope. Tighten as you gradually increase tension.

Make a
sheepshank more
secure by passing
a stick through

the bend and behind the standing part (a). Or, if you have
access to the rope's end, pass that through the bight (b). A
stick would make this more secure.

> Never cut a rope unnecessarily: a connected rope only
> has half the strength of a continuous one. Use sheep-
> shank to shorten it or to leave out a damaged section.

CAMP CRAFT

Securing loads

WAKOS TRANSPORT KNOT: Used
to secure a high load or to tie
down a roof. For maximum
grip, pull down with all your
weight, then secure with 2 half
hitches. If it comes loose, undo
the hitches, retighten, and
secure. **1** Make a loop in the
rope. Further down, toward the
end, make a bight. **2** Pass bight
through loop. **3** Make a twist in
new lower loop. Pass end of
rope around securing point and
up through this twist. **4** Pull end
to tighten. **5** With the end make
two half hitches around lower
ropes to secure. Undo these to
adjust and retighten.

PRUSIK KNOT: A sliding loop. This will not slip under tension, but it will slide along when tension is released. A pair of prusiks provide handholds and footholds for climbing or for swinging along a horizontal line. Slide them along the main rope as you proceed. Also good for tent guys.
1 Pass a bight around main rope, pull ends through. Keep it loose.
2 Take ends over again and back down through loop. Ease it tight. Do not allow circuits to overlap.
3 This gives the appearance of four turns on the main rope (a). Mountaineers take ends around and back through to give the appearance of six turns on main rope (b). **4** A prusik knot can be made using a fixed spliced loop: pass bight over main rope and back through itself, then repeat.
5 For use as a tensioning line attach along the guy, etc., and secure ends (a) to an anchor.

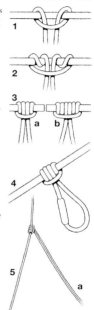

When this is used for climbing, or for traveling along a rope, a spliced loop (4) is the safest. If you have no spliced loop, connect the ends after a knot is made. Test the joins rigorously before use.

Lashings

Methods of lashing differ according to the position of the components. These techniques are invaluable when making rafts, shelters, etc.

SQUARE LASHING: For lashing spars that cross at right angles. **1** Make a timber hitch carrying line alternately above and below both spars in a complete circuit before securing it. Then bring the rope counterclockwise over and under both spars. **2** After three or four circuits make a full turn around a spar and circuit in the opposite direction. **3** Complete circuits with a half hitch around one spar and secure it with a clove hitch on a spar at right angles.

ROUND LASHING: Used to lash spars alongside each other or to extend length of a spar. Begin with a clove hitch around both spars (a), then bind the rope around them. Finish knot with a clove hitch at the other end (b). Force a wedge under the lashings to make them very tight. If spars are vertical, hit the wedge in downward.

CAMP CRAFT

CAMP CRAFT

DIAGONAL LASHING: Used when spars do not cross at right angles or when spars need to be pulled toward one another for tying.

1 Begin with a timber hitch around both spars, placed diagonally.

2 Frap (lash) both spars with a few turns of rope over a timber hitch, then make a full turn under the bottom spar. **3** Frap across other diagonal, then bring rope back over one spar and make two or three circuits above upper spar and below lower. **4** Finish with a clove hitch on a convenient spar.

SHEAR LASHING: Used to tie ends of two spars at an angle, e.g. for an A-frame. Begin with a clove hitch (a) around one spar. Bind, not very tightly, around both. Bring rope between spars and frap a few times around binding. Finish with a clove hitch around other spar (b). Tighten by opening up shears (c). A similar method can be used around three poles to make a tripod. Make turns around all three legs and frappings in the two gaps. The feet of A-frames and tripods should be anchored to stop them spreading.

Fishing knots

CAMP CRAFT

HOOK ON TO GUT: Turl knot. Soak gut. Thread through eye of a hook. Make an overhand loop and pass a bight through it (a) to form a simple slip-knot (b). Pass hook through slip-knot (c); pull tightly around shank.

HOOK ON TO NYLON I: Half blood knot. Thread end through eye. Make 4 turns around standing part. Pass live end through loop formed next to hook (i). Pull it taut and cut it off close to the end (ii).

HOOK ON TO NYLON II: Two turn turl knot. Thread hook. Pass live end around standing part to form a loop and through it. Twist live end twice around side of loop. Hold loop and pull twists tight. Pass hook through loop (1). Pull on the standing part to tighten the loop on the hook (2).

JAM KNOTS: To secure improvized hooks to a gut or cord. With an eye: thread gut. Make two turns around hook and bring live end up through turns (a). Ease tight and test for strength. Without an eye: make loop around lower part of shaft. Make two half-hitches from upper end downward and pass live end through lower loop (b). Pull on standing part to tighten.

LOOP IN NYLON I: Double overhand loop. Double the line to make a bight. Tie an overhand in it (a). Twist end through again (b). Pull it tight (c) and cut off the end.

LOOP IN NYLON II: Blood bight. Form a bight. Twist the end of it back around the standing part (i). Bring the end back through the new loop (ii). Pull tight and cut off the loose end.

JOINING LOOPS: With free ends: pass each line through the other loop (1) and pull it tight (2). With only one end free: make a loop on one line. Take live end of the other line through loop, around it, and back through, and then tie off with either of the knots for hooks onto nylon.

JOINING NYLON: Double three-fold blood knots. Place ends alongside each other and twist one three times around the other. Bring live end back and pass it through the space where the two lines cross over the other line and under its own standing end (a). Repeat in the opposite direction with the other line. Live ends then point in opposite directions (b). Ease it tight.

READING THE SIGNS

In addition to being able to read and make a map, your survival depends on interpreting natural signs to help you find your way and anticipating the weather.

MAPS

Choose your maps carefully. Make sure that the scale is appropriate to your needs. Most importantly, make sure that you can interpret the information that is given.

INTERPRETING MAPS

ALTITUDE: Since height cannot be reproduced on paper, altitudes are recorded as contour lines, representing a series of points at the same distance above sea level. However, they do not record what happens in between.

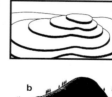

Closely grouped contour lines indicate a steep slope (a). Larger spaces between contour lines show gentler inclines (b). The rise in the ground is not comparable to the scale of the distance shown between them (on a 1:50,000 map, contours at 0.2 inches (5 mm) would indicate a gradient of 1 in 25).

READING THE SIGNS

SCALE: The scale of a typical walker's map is 1:50,000, i.e. each measure represents a distance that is 50,000 times greater on the ground. Not all features can be shown to scale: roads, paths, streams, and rivers are usually given standardized widths. Study the key and master the way the information is presented—which symbols represent which features (swamps, woodlands, buildings).

COORDINATES: Map grids are either based on degrees of latitude and longitude or on ground measurements. For example, on British Ordnance Survey maps, grid lines represent areas that are 1 km (0.62 miles) apart with the diagonal across them as 1.5 km (0.9 miles). A position can be described by a coordinate made up from the line references from two adjoining sides. This is an easy way of telling rescuers your location or fixing a rendezvous.

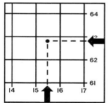

The point marked with a dot can be described as 15.5 x 62.8 using the coordinates from the sides of this grid. The map reference is usually expressed as 6 digits: 155628. Any letter area codes on the map should be included.

NORTH ON MAPS: Unless they are lines of longitude, grid lines do not indicate north and south. Remember that a compass does not point to true north but to magnetic north—the difference varies according to where you are in the world. If your map doesn't indicate magnetic north, you can find it from the North Star (see p. 235).

In the northern hemisphere point the compass at the North Star. Notice the difference between the pointer and indicated north. Line the compass up with the grid lines on the map to discover their variation. If you follow magnetic bearings, you must compensate for the variation. If unable to make appropriate corrections, continually check your position against visible features.

MEASURING DISTANCES: As-the-crow-flies distances can be measured using a ruler, which is then matched against the scale. Gradients make a difference. For example, a gradient of 45 ° will add another 269 feet (82 m) to a horizontal map distance of 656 feet (200 m).

YOUR OWN MAPS: If you do not have a map, make one. Find the best vantage point and study the terrain. Notice the number and direction of ridges—you won't be able to see what lies between them, so leave gaps to be filled in as you gain information from other vantage points.

Mark anything of interest on your map: watercourses, rocky outcrops, landmarks, and areas of vegetation. Plot positions of your traps, animal lairs, and places for foraging for food, fuel, and stones for implements. It will be much easier than relying on your memory.

WORKING OUT DIRECTIONS

The sun rises in the east and sets in the west, roughly speaking. At noon in the northern hemisphere the sun will be due south; in the southern hemisphere it will be due north. The hemisphere is indicated by the way that shadows move: clockwise in the north, counterclockwise in the south.

READING THE SIGNS

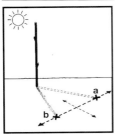

SHADOW STICK METHOD 1:
Place a 3 foot (1 m) stick upright on a patch of flat ground. Mark where tip of shadow falls (a). Wait 15 minutes and mark the new shadow tip (b). Connect the two for the directions of east and west—the first mark is west. North and south are at right angles to the line.

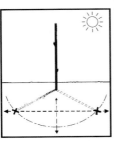

SHADOW STICK METHOD 2:
Mark the first shadow tip in the morning. Draw an arc at exactly this distance from the tip, using the stick as the center point. The shadow shrinks at midday. In the afternoon, as the shadow lengthens, mark the exact spot where it touches the arc. Connect them to give east and west—west is the morning mark.

DIRECTION BY WATCH: A traditional analog watch with two hands can tell direction, as long as it is set to true local time (ignoring daylight savings and conventional time zones). The closer to the equator you are, the less accurate this method is.

READING THE SIGNS

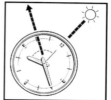

In the northern hemisphere, hold watch horizontally. Point hour hand at the sun. Bisect the angle between hour hand and the 12 mark to give a north–south line.

In the southern hemisphere, hold watch horizontally. Point the 12 toward the sun. The midpoint between 12 and the hour hand will give a north–south line.

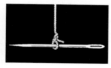

IMPROVISED COMPASSES:
A piece of ferrous metal wire (a sewing needle is ideal) repeatedly stroked in one direction against silk will become magnetized and can be suspended so it points north.

Stroking it with a magnet will be even better than using silk—stroke the metal smoothly from one end to the other in one direction only.

Suspend the needle in a loop of thread so that balance is not affected. Kinks or twists in the thread must be avoided.

READING THE SIGNS

A floating needle can be used in the same way as the suspended one on p. 231. Lay the needle on a piece of paper, bark, or grass and float it on the surface of water.

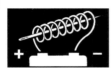

A power source of 2 volts or more, e.g. a battery, can be used with a short piece of insulated wire to magnetize the metal. Coil wire around the needle. If the wire is uninsulated, wrap needle with paper or cardboard. Attach ends of wire to battery terminals for 5 minutes.

A razor blade can also be used as a compass. Magnetize the blade by stropping carefully against the palm of your hand, then suspend.

Use other methods to establish the general direction of north, then mark the relevant end of your new "compass" to indicate north. Work up your needle's magnetism occasionally and always check your readings against the sun.

READING THE SIGNS

PLANT POINTERS

Plants can give an indication of north and south. They tend to grow toward the sun, so flowers and most abundant growth will be to the south in the northern hemisphere, and to the north in the southern. Moss on tree trunks will be greener and more profuse on that side.

If trees have been felled, the pattern of the rings is more widely spaced apart on the side toward the Equator.

A South African plant, the north pole plant, leans toward the north.

The compass plant is North American and directs its leaves in a north–south alignment so that its profile from east or west is very different from that of north or south.

WIND DIRECTION: If the direction of the prevailing wind is known, it can be used to maintain direction.

Where a strong wind always comes from the same direction, plants and trees may be bent that way. Birds and insects will usually build nests on the leeside.

DIRECTION BY THE SKIES

Using the moon

As the moon orbits the earth over 28 days, the shape varies according to its position. When it is on the same side of the earth as the sun, no light is reflected from the sun (a): this is the new moon. It then reflects light on its apparent right-hand side in a gradually increasing area as it waxes. At the full moon it is on the opposite side of the earth from the sun (b), and then it wanes, the reflecting area reducing to a narrow sliver on the apparent left-hand side.

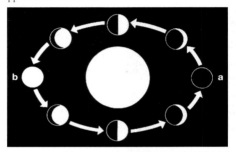

If the moon rises before the sun has set, the illuminated side will be on the west. If it rises after midnight, the illuminated side will be the east. Thus the moon gives a rough east–west reference in the night.

Using the stars

The stars stay in the same relation to each other. Their passage over the horizon starts 4 minutes earlier each night—a 2-hour difference over a month.

In the northern hemisphere groups of stars remain visible throughout the night, moving around the only star that does not seem to move: the North Star (a useful navigational aid, located almost above polar north).

THE NORTHERN SKY: The Big Dipper or Plow (a), Cassiopeia (b), and Orion (c) all circle the North Star (d), but (a) and (b) are recognizable groups that do not set. Use them to find the North Star.

Of the seven stars that form the Big Dipper (a), the two lowest ones point to the North Star, around four times farther away than the distance between them.

Cassiopeia (b) isW-shaped, on the opposite side of the North Star and the same distance away as the Big Dipper. On clear, dark nights this overlays the MilkyWay. The center star points toward the Big Dipper. A line can be drawn connecting Cassiopeia and the Big Dipper through the North Star. Orion (c) rises above the equator and can be seen in both hemispheres. It rises on its side, due east, and sets due west. It is farther from the North Star than Cassiopeia and the Big Dipper.

Other stars that rise and set can be used to indicate direction. Place 2 stakes in the ground, one shorter than the other. Look along them at any star except for the North Star. From the star's apparent movement you can deduce the direction in which you are facing:

Apparently rising = facing east
Apparently falling = facing west
Looping flatly to the right = facing south
Looping flatly to the left = facing north

These are only approximate directions. They will be
reversed in the southern hemisphere.

THE SOUTHERN SKY: There is no equivalent of the North
Star close to the South celestial pole, but the Southern
Cross—a constellation of five stars—provides a
signpost to south. It can be distinguished from two other
cross-shaped groups by its smaller size and its two
pointer stars. Look along the Milky Way for a dark patch
(the Coal Sack); the Southern Cross is to one side of it.

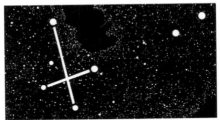

To locate south, project an imaginary line along the
cross and four and a half times longer than it, then drop
it vertically down to the horizon. If you can, fix a
prominent landmark on the horizon or drive two sticks
into the ground, to help you find the position during
the day.

WEATHER SIGNS

Weather is much more localized than climate, and there can be obvious variations between one small area and another.

COASTAL AREAS

A regular pattern of day–night change in wind direction suggests a large body of water—whether that is an ocean, an inland sea, or a lake—in the direction from which the day wind blows (during the day breezes blow from the sea to the land; at night the wind changes and blows off the land).

WINDS

Certain scents—the smell of the sea or of vegetation— carried by the wind can provide information about the place from which they blow.

Study the wind and weather patterns: wind from a certain direction is likely to bring similar weather each time it blows. Where winds maintain their direction, they can be an aid in sticking to a course—but verify your course by other means at regular intervals.

If a wind is strong and dry, the weather should remain constant until the wind drops or veers, then it may rain.

If it is foggy and misty, you may get condensation, but you will not get rain. However, if a wind rises and blows away the fog, it may turn to rain.

On a clear day a noticeable increase in the strength of the wind indicates an imminent weather change (see pp. 370–373).

READING THE SIGNS

CLOUDS

Clouds are the most reliable of the weather signs. There are ten main types of cloud formations. Approximate altitudes are given for each type. The same shapes occur at lower altitudes in polar regions. The higher the clouds, the finer the weather will be. The figures given at the end of the following entries indicate cloud heights.

 CIRROCUMULUS CLOUDS: *These look like rippled sand. An omen of fair weather, they usually follow a storm and dissipate to leave a clear, blue sky.*

 ALTOCUMULUS CLOUDS: *Fair-weather clouds. On a larger scale than cirrocumulus, thicker, not as white, and with shadows in them. These usually appear after a storm.*

 CUMULONIMBUS CLOUDS: *Low thunder clouds. Dark and menacing, with the top flattening out in an anvil shape. These bring hail, a strong wind, thunder, and lightning. False cirrus appear above them and false nimbostratus below.*

 CUMULUS CLOUDS: *Easily recognizable: fluffy, white clouds. These usually indicate fair weather when they are widely separated, but if they are large and many-headed, they are capable of producing sudden heavy showers. When they are seen at sea in an otherwise cloudless sky, they are often an indication that land lies beneath them.*

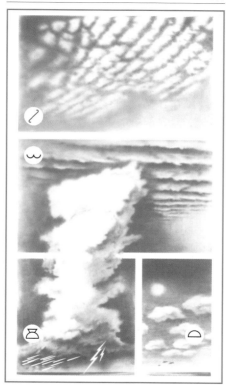

CIRRUS CLOUDS: *High, wispy clouds formed from ice crystals that give them a white appearance. Seen in fine weather. 3.1–5.5 miles (5–9 km).*

CIRROSTRATUS CLOUDS: *These are made up of ice particles and look like white veins. They produce a halo around the sun or moon.*

If a cirrus-filled sky darkens and the clouds change to cirrostratus, it is an indication that rain or snow is on the way. 3.1–5.5 miles (5–9 km).

ALTOSTRATUS CLOUDS: *These form a grayish veil over the sun or moon. If wet weather is approaching, the cloud will darken and thicken, obscuring the sun or moon until it begins to rain. 1.6–3.7 miles (2.5–6 km).*

NIMBOSTRATUS CLOUDS: *These form low, dark blankets, which signal rain or snow within 4–5 hours, usually lasting for several hours. 0.9–3.1 miles (1.5–5 km).*

STRATOCUMULUS CLOUDS: *These form a low, lumpy, rolling mass, usually covering the whole sky, although they are often thin enough for the sun to filter through. Light showers may precipitate from them, but these clouds usually dissipate in the afternoon, leaving a clear night sky. Below 1.6 miles (2.5 km).*

STRATUS CLOUDS: *The lowest clouds. These form a uniform layer like fog in the air—they are often described as hill fog. Although not a normal rain cloud, they can produce drizzle. When they form thickly overnight and cover the morning sky, they will usually be followed by a fine day. Below 1.6 miles (2.5 km).*

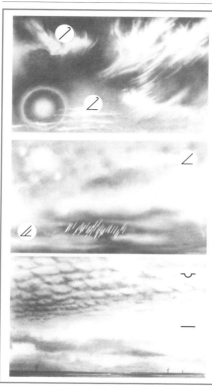

PREDICTING WEATHER

To be caught out in bad weather could be fatal. Before setting out, take notice of the weather. Observe the wind and pressure changes. Keep a record of the weather, the conditions that precede it, and what they develop into.

Animals are sensitive to atmospheric pressure and are good for short-term weather predictions. Insect-eating birds feed higher up in good weather and lower when a storm is approaching. Unusual rodent activity during the day may be a prelude to bad weather.

Humans can sometimes sense a change in the weather, too. Curly-haired people find that their hair becomes tight and unmanageable as bad weather approaches. Those with rheumatism, corns, or similar ailments suffer discomfort in wet weather.

If campfire smoke rises steadily, the weather is likely to remain fine. If it starts swirling or is beaten down after rising a short distance, a storm or a shower is coming.

Sounds carry farther when wet weather is on the way, and the smell of vegetation becomes more distinctive before the arrival of rain.

A red sky at night means that there is little moisture in the atmosphere and that rain is unlikely within the next two hours. A red sky in the morning indicates that a storm is approaching. A gray morning sky heralds a dry day, and a gray evening sky means that rain is imminent.

A *corona*, a colored circle that is visible around the sun or the moon, will enlarge if fair weather lies ahead and shrink if rain is likely. A rainbow in the late afternoon is another sign of good weather.

ON THE MOVE

This section deals with skills that are needed while on the move. It should be read in conjunction with the techniques described in **Climate and Terrain** (p. 37 ff).

THE DECISION TO MOVE

In the short term, unless local dangers or a lack of food and water make it imperative to leave the site of your accident, stay close in the hope of being rescued. If you have injured persons and limited resources, send a party to contact help, while the others stay to care for the sick.

In the long term, if no rescue comes, resources may become exhausted, and there is an increased risk of diseases from staying in one place for too long. Such factors will make a move advisable.

Where to go next will be determined by the information that you have been able to gather, by the fitness and endurance of the group, and by the nature of the terrain. Remember: the most direct route may not be the easiest to travel.

If you have a clear idea of your location, head for the nearest settlement. If you have no idea where you are, follow waterways downstream—they generally lead to populated areas. Move at least three days' journey from the old camp so that fuel, flora, and fauna will be undisturbed in the new location.

Before you abandon camp, leave signs to show that you have moved on (see p. 283) and where you are heading. Rescuers can then follow you.

ON THE MOVE

PREPARATIONS

Stock up preserved food and make water containers.

Make foot coverings and clothing, and packs to carry equipment and supplies. Build a sled or raft or another form of transportation.

Take your signaling gear and shelter materials with you. If shelter can be quickly erected upon arrival, you will then be free to gather food and fuel.

Study the weather patterns. Set off in calm weather.

HUDSON BAY PACK: A comfortable and simple way to carry equipment, this needs strong, waterproof material

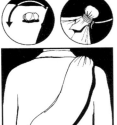

4 inches (9 cm) square, two small stones, and a cord or thong long enough to loop across the body.

Place stones in diagonally opposite corners of the cloth. Fold ends of cloth over stones. Tie cord below stones to secure them in position—they will prevent cord from slipping off. Lay cloth on ground and roll possessions up tightly. Wrap pack around body, either across the back or around the waist.

Carry babies in a papoose on your back or front. Tie lower corners of a rectangle of cloth around your waist, place the baby inside, and tie upper corners around your neck.

Sit small children on a backpack frame. For adults and heavy equipment make a travois (see p. 204) or a sled.

MAKING A SLED

Ideal for snow and ice, sleds may also be used on smooth ground. Use doors and cowlings from a crashed vehicle or plane for construction. Tie lines to the front runners with a bowline to the people hauling it—ideally two at the front and two at the rear. Test it before use.

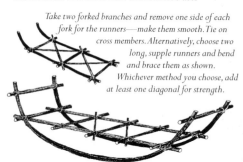

Take two forked branches and remove one side of each fork for the runners—make them smooth. Tie on cross members. Alternatively, choose two long, supple runners and bend and brace them as shown. Whichever method you choose, add at least one diagonal for strength.

PLANNING THE ROUTE

Visibility will often be restricted, and you must guess what lies ahead. Things you can see may be misleading: what looks like an easy slope may prove to be a barrier when you get up close. If you have them, use binoculars.

Climbing a tree may help you see farther, but stay close to the trunk and test each branch before risking your weight on it. This is no time to risk a fall.

ON THE MOVE

FOLLOWING RIVERS

Watercourses offer a route to civilization and a life-support system along the way. Aside from the rare occasions when they suddenly disappear underground, rivers offer a clearly defined route. Where they cut through gorges it may be impossible to follow their banks —go to high ground and cut off the bends.

In tropical conditions vegetation may be the densest by the river and the banks may be hard to negotiate. If the river is wide enough, build a raft from bamboo or fallen trees.

When a river meanders widely on a plain, the inside of loops may be swampy and prone to flooding. Avoid these marshy areas if you can—cut across the loop.

MAINTAINING DIRECTION

Choose a distant landmark and head toward it.

Try to skirt around dense vegetation: orientation is difficult in forests. A compass becomes a valuable asset.

In featureless territory, if in a group of three or more, to maintain a straight line, separate and follow in each other's tracks at intervals. Look back frequently: those behind should be directly behind each other in a straight line. Move in a relay: the one who went ahead can rest while everyone else moves up from the rear.

If traveling alone, align yourself by looking back at your own tracks, if visible, or set up markers (sticks, piles of stones) at intervals in alignment with each other so you can check that you are not deviating from your route.

Once on high ground, stick to it until you are sure that you have found the spur down which will allow you to make the best progress in the desired direction.

ON THE MOVE

MOVING IN GROUPS

Always move in formation. This will make it easy to check that no stragglers have been left behind. Have a briefing before setting out to discuss the route and to designate rallying points at which to regroup.

DIVIDING RESPONSIBILITIES

Appoint a scout to select the best route and find ways to skirt obstacles. A number two should make sure that the scout maintains the correct overall direction. Both will need to be relieved frequently, as it is tiring work.

The others should travel in pairs to ensure that no one drops by the wayside. A head count is vital after negotiating difficult terrain (check equipment regularly too). Nominate prominent landmarks as rallying points so that everyone knows what to head for if separated.

PACE AND PROGRESS

A large group can send an advance party to clear the route and set up camp. A clear trail will make carrying baggage and injured people much easier.

The scout must not go too fast. Frequent rests—a 10-minute break every 30–45 minutes—are vital. After an obstacle wait and allow everyone to catch up and check and adjust your loads.

Try to maintain an even pace. A smooth, pendulum-like movement is the easiest. Keep your arms free to aid with balance. On steep ground the pace should be shortened, on easy ground lengthened. Avoid overstepping on descents. Use ropes to provide handholds on slippery terrain. Attach prusik knots (see p. 222) for extra safety.

ON THE MOVE

WALKING AT NIGHT

Negotiating territory at night can be dangerous, but it may be necessary. Because it is difficult to see clearly, you are easily disorientated. It is always darker among trees, so stay in open spaces if you can. When you are looking at an object at night, look at one side instead of directly at it. It is hard to distinguish anything in a dark mass, but edges show clearly.

It takes 30–40 minutes for the eyes to get accustomed to darkness. Once this is achieved, protect eyes from bright lights, or night vision will be impaired. If a light must be used, cover one eye so that vision in that eye will be retained. A red filter over a flashlight will also help.

Ears are good sensors. The sound of a river indicates how fast it flows. Smells can aid in identification.

Walk slowly. Test each step before putting your weight forward. Use a shuffling step to descend down slopes.

TRAVELING UPLAND

In mountainous country stay on high ground—it makes navigation easier. Rivers in steep-sided gullies are difficult to negotiate on foot: climb up and follow the ridges. Climb down to collect water and seek shelter, but don't go all the way to the valley bottom if you can find what you need along the way. Pockets of cold air get trapped in valley bottoms: you may be warmer and less tired if you choose a sheltered spot higher up. If you carry water and materials for shelter, stay on the high ground and make camp in a sheltered spot. When the river gets larger and the valley opens up, drop down to follow the riverbanks again.

ON THE MOVE

STEEP SLOPES

Traverse slopes in a zigzag. As you change direction, always start with the uphill foot to avoid crossing your legs over and losing your balance. When you are climbing steep slopes, lock your knees together after each step to rest the muscles.

To descend slopes, keep your knees bent and try to go straight down (sit back and dig in your heels if you pick up too much speed). Avoid loose rocks and scree. When your are climbing, test every foothold before putting your weight on it. Avoid stepping on stones or logs that may dislodge.

Jump down loose ground, as long as there are no sudden drops. Keep your feet square and shoulder-width apart, dig in your heels and slide. You will lose control as your speed increases—jump again. Rappel down steep slopes (see p. 47).

JUNGLE TRAVEL

You may have to cut through dense jungles if there is no way around them. Chop downward and as low as possible at the stems on both sides so that they fall away from the path, not across it. Avoid leaving bamboo spikes—they can be lethal if stumbled on. Atap and rattan have thorns like fishhooks at the ends of the leaves. If you get snared, back off and untangle. Rushing only makes it worse.

> Keep feet covered to protect them from sapling spikes, snakes, chigoes (chiggers), and burrowing parasites. Stop frequently to remove any parasites. Chigoes left for more than an hour will cause infections.

WATERWAYS

A wide river will be easier to float on than to walk next to. Long-term survivors should experiment making canoes by burning out the center of a tree trunk or covering a frame made of willow with birch bark or skins.

RAFTS

A raft, even if the structure is not perfect, will not easily capsize.

Use bamboo, uprooted trees that are solid and not rotting, or the tops of the trunks of dead falls. Oil drums or floating objects will support a raft. If there is no supply of timber, a sheet of waterproof material can be used as a person-carrying coracle.

Never take chances. Only a really tough structure will survive in rapids, and on wide waterways you face a long swim to the bank if your raft breaks apart. Test all rafts in safe water near camp before setting off.

Tie all equipment securely to the raft or a safety line. Make sure that nothing trails over the edges—it could snag in the shallows.

Everyone aboard should have a bowline around their waists, securing them to a safety line or to the raft. Lifelines should be long enough to allow free movement, but no so long that they trail in the water. In swift-flowing rivers with rapids and waterfalls it is better not to be tied on. Head for the bank if the raft is out of control.

In shallow water control the raft with two long poles like a punt—one person poling at the front corner and another at the diagonally opposite back corner.

BAMBOO RAFT: Cut thick bamboo in 10 foot (3 m) pieces. Make holes through canes near ends and halfway along them. Pass stakes through holes to connect canes. Tie each cane to the stakes with twine or vines. Make a second layer to fit on top of the first and tie them together.

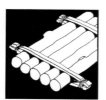

GRIPPER BAR RAFT: Place two thick, pliable stakes on the ground—they should be long enough to overlap the width of the deck. Lay logs over them. Place two stakes on top. Tie each pair of stakes on one side. Then, with a helper standing on top to force the other ends together, tie these so that the logs are gripped between them. Notching the ends of the gripper bars will stop ropes slipping.

STEERING: Make a paddle rudder and mount it on an A-frame near one end of the raft. Secure the A-frame with guys to the corners of the raft. Tie the rudder on so that it does not slip. You may need to notch the raft for the A-frame base.

ON THE MOVE

TRAVELING BY RAFT

A large group will need several rafts. The first should not carry any equipment or provisions, just the most able group members to act as lookouts for hazards.

Waterfalls and rapids are often indicated by spray or mist. They can also be heard from some distance. If you are in doubt, moor the raft and reconnoiter on foot.

Unload the raft when you reach a dangerous stretch. Carry equipment overland and downstream and post someone at the point where the river becomes safe to recover the raft. Then go back and release the raft to drift down. It may need repairs, but you will be safe.

Never raft in the dark. At night secure the raft firmly and make shelter on high ground away from the river.

BOGS, MARSHES, AND QUICKSAND
Avoid crossing a marsh if it is possible. If it is unavoidable, jump from tuft to tuft. If you sink in a bog, swim with a breaststroke to firm ground. Don't try to jump. Spreading your body distributes your weight.

CROSSING RIVERS

River headwaters are narrow and flow swiftly. Find a place where the water is shallow enough to wade across—test for hidden depths with a pole. Look for stepping stones, but be careful not to slip and sprain an ankle.

Estuaries have strong currents and are subject to tides. Avoid crossing there unless you are equipped with a boat or raft. Head upstream to find a safer spot. Do not set off directly across from the point you hope to reach—make allowances for where the current will take you.

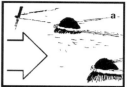

STUDY THE WATER:
Surface movements can indicate what lies beneath. The main flow of the current is evident from a chevron shape of smoother water around any projection (a), the V widening downstream.

Waves that seem to stay in one position (b) are evidence of a boulder on the bottom.

An obstruction close to the surface creates an eddy downstream where surface water appears to run back against the main flow. If a large boulder coincides with a steep drop (c), these eddies can produce a powerful backward pull downstream of the obstruction. They are very dangerous.

ON THE MOVE

 ICE-COLD WATER IS A KILLER
Do not swim or wade through deep water at very low temperatures, it could prove fatal. Make a raft. Only wade if no more than your feet will get wet and dry them vigorously as soon as you reach the other bank.

ON THE MOVE

Wading across

Never underestimate a stretch of water, however shallow. Use a stick to aid balance. Roll your pants up or take them off so they are dry for the other side. Keep boots on—they give a better grip than bare feet. Undo the belt fastening of a backpack so you can slip it off if you get swept over, but don't let go of it: use it to help get yourself up again.

Turn at a slight angle, sideways to your destination. The current will then take you there. Do not stride: shuffle sideways, using the stick to test for depth and trying each foothold before using it.

A group wading across together should line up behind the strongest person, each one holding the person in front at the waist and moving in step. Alternatively, link your arms side-by-side, holding on to a branch or pole to stay in alignment. Cross facing the bank and moving forward. Only the side of the first person opposes the current, and the group provides stability for everyone.

 Look out for submerged branches. You could get tangled up and lose your balance. When you are forced against an obstruction by the current, you feel its full force and may be unable to move.

Crossing with ropes

You need a loop of rope that is three times as long as the width of the stream and at least three people in the party—the most able person crosses, while two control the rope to keep it out of the water as much as possible and stand by to haul the crosser to safety if difficulties are encountered.

ON THE MOVE

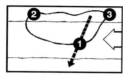

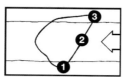

The person crossing is secured around the chest to the loop. The other two are not tied on. They let the rope out as it is needed. The strongest person should cross first.

*When he reaches the bank, **1** unties himself and **2** ties on and crosses, controlled by the others. Any number of people can be sent across this way.*

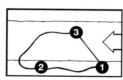

*When **2** has reached the bank, **3** ties on and crosses. **1** takes most of the strain; **2** stands by in case anything goes wrong.*

RIVERS ARE DANGEROUS

Never enter the water unless there is no other way of getting across. Choose a crossing point carefully.

Avoid high banks that are difficult to climb out onto. Avoid obstructions in the water.

The current is likely to be the fastest on the outside of bends, and steep banks may be undercut, making landing impossible.

Look for an even section of the riverbed—shingle is the best surface for wading

Swimming across

If you can't swim, don't try—rely on others and use a float. Even strong swimmers should use flotation aids to save energy and keep equipment dry. Don't swim fully clothed, you need something warm to put on at the other end.

Make sure that your landing point has a beach or something to haul yourself out with. Avoid tangled branches in the water where you might get trapped. Enter far upstream and let the current carry you.

Check the strength of the current by watching floating logs and flotsam. Look for obstructions and eddies. If you hit seaweed in the water, use a crawl stroke to cut through it. Once a strong swimmer has cleared a passage, others may follow in that channel.

FLOTATION AIDS

Use anything that floats: fuel cans, plastic bottles, logs.

Put clothes in a waterproof bag, leaving plenty of air space. Tie the neck of the bag, fold it over, and tie again. Hold on to it, using only your legs to propel yourself.

Pile twigs and straw into the center of a waterproof sheet to create air pockets, then pile your clothes and equipment on top and tie it securely. Do not attempt to sit on the bundles or place your weight on them.

A group should split into fours, each group tying their bags together and using them as a support for an injured person or a nonswimmer.

If no waterproof material is available, make a small raft or coracle to float your things on. Bundle your belongings and, if they are heavy, make the raft with 2 layers so that only the lower layer sinks and your equipment stays dry.

SURVIVAL AT SEA

Four fifths of the earth's surface is open water—the most difficult environment in which to survive. Water and wind rapidly chill the body. Alone in cold water, your chances are not good without equipment. If you know your location, you may be able to predict where the currents will carry you. Warm currents, e.g. the Gulf Stream, are often rich in sea foods, as are coastal waters. Your main problem will most likely be a shortage of freshwater if you have no means of distilling seawater.

ABANDONING SHIP

When you are onboard a ship, a lifeboat drill should be a well-rehearsed procedure. Even in small boats everyone onboard should be acquainted with safety equipment and procedures.

If the signal is given to abandon ship, put on warm—preferably woolen—clothing, including a hat and gloves, and wrap a towel around your neck. Take a flashlight, chocolates, and hard candy if you can. Don't panic. An orderly embarkation will be faster and establish a calmer attitude. Take whatever equipment you can with you. A life jacket will make it easier to float.

Don't inflate your life jacket until you leave the ship. On small boats life jackets should be worn all the time. If you have to jump overboard, first throw something that floats and then jump close to it. Without a life jacket or safety belt, air trapped in clothing will aid buoyancy—a good reason to keep your clothes on despite the frequent advice to take them off before entering the water.

SURVIVAL AT SEA

If you are swept overboard, stay afloat and try to attract attention. Sound travels well over water—shout and splash. Wave with one arm above the water (not both, you will go under). Movement makes you more noticeable. Most life jackets are equipped with a whistle and light.

IN THE WATER

Swim slowly and steadily. If you are abandoning a sinking boat or aircraft, move upwind and stay clear of it. Stay away from any fuel spills. If you are forced to swim through flames, jump in feet first and upwind. Swim into the wind using the breaststroke. Splash any flames away from your head to make breathing holes. Swim underwater until you are away from danger. If an underwater explosion is likely, reduce the risk of injuries by swimming on your back.

If you are within sight of land, relax and float until the ebb turns and helps carry you to land.

1 In rough seas float upright and take a deep breath. 2 Lower your face into the water (keeping your mouth closed) and bring arms forwards to rest at water level. 3 Relax in this position until you need to take in more air. 4 Raise your head above the surface, tread water, and exhale. Take a breath and return to the relaxed position.

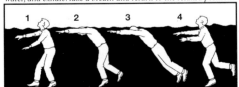

FLOTATION "BAGS": Improvise a short-term float out of a pair of pants. Knot the bottoms of the legs, sweep them over the head to fill with air, then hold the waist below the water to trap in the air, making the legs into water wings.

IMMEDIATE ACTION: Once clear of the wreck, inflate your dinghy. If there is no dinghy, grab as much flotsam as possible to use as a raft. Tie it together with belts, shoelaces, and spare clothing. Salvage any floating equipment.

Inflating a dinghy

Many dinghies are self-inflating. If they are not, a pump is provided. Dinghies are built in sections, so there are several inflation points.

BOARDING AN INFLATABLE DINGHY: If you are already in the water, move to the end (not the side) of the dinghy, place one leg over the edge, and roll into the vessel. Do not jump in from above, as you may damage it. Large dinghies have a righting line attached to one side. Grab it from the opposite side, brace your feet against the dinghy, and pull. The dinghy should rise up and over,  momentarily pulling you out of the water. In rough seas or high winds this can be very difficult.

To haul someone else aboard, hold their shoulders and lift one leg over the end, then roll them in. Discourage them from putting their arms around your neck—they could pull you into the water. Tie yourself and others to the dinghy.

Ensure that the dinghy is fully inflated. It should be firm, but not rock-hard. If it is not, inflate it with your own breath or a pump. The valves are one-way, and air will not escape when you take off the protective cap.

Check for leaks. Escaping air causes bubbles under the water and a hissing sound above water. Seal any holes with screw-in conical plugs in the dinghy equipment. There should also be a supply of rubber patches and adhesive.

Make daily checks for inflation and leaks. To repair a leak on the underside, swim underneath and insert a plug.

SURVIVAL AFLOAT

Rafts, boats, and dinghies are built to carry a limited number of people. This should not be exceeded.

Place infants and injured people aboard, and as many able-bodied people as can be accommodated. The rest must hang on in the water, frequently swapping places with able-bodied survivors in the raft.

Stow gear in stowage places and tie it securely. Check that no sharp objects will damage the raft. Put any items that will spoil if they get wet in a waterproof container.

Check signaling equipment: heliographs, flares, etc.

If distress signals have been sent out giving your position, try to maintain your location. A sea anchor streamed out from the boat will keep it into the weather and slow down any drift. Improvise a sea anchor from any weighted object that is securely tied to a line. Use clothing tied to a paddle with reef knots.

If you can see the shore, head toward it.

SURVIVAL AT SEA

SURVIVAL PRIORITIES:
PROTECTION against weather and effects of exposure.
LOCATION Try to establish where you are and the best
way of attracting rescue.
WATER Take stock. Ration it at once. Collect rain.
FOOD Don't eat unless you have sufficient water.
Check all rations, stow them securely. Start fishing.

PROTECTION

Keep a log: record names of survivors; date, time, and
position of accident; weather conditions; equipment
salvaged. Record any sightings and circumstances daily.

IN A COLD CLIMATE: Get out of cold water as soon as
possible. Keep the dinghy as dry as you can. Bail out any
water. If it doesn't have a built-in shelter, rig up a spray
shield and windbreak using any material that is available .
    Dry all wet clothing. If there is no dry clothing,
squeeze out as much water as possible and put it back on.
Maintain your body heat by wrapping up in any available
material, e.g. a parachute or canvas. If you are in a group,
huddle together. To keep your circulation going, do gentle
exercises, but do not disturb the balance of the raft.

IN A HOT CLIMATE: Stay covered up in strong sun. Cover
your head and neck to avoid sunstroke. Protect your eyes
from glare (see p. 60). Dampen any clothes to cool your
body, but make sure you are dry by the evening, as nights
can be very cold, and darkness comes quickly in the
tropics. Prolonged contact with seawater causes sores.
    Air expands with heat, so if it is very hot, let some air
out of an inflatable. Reinflate in the cool of the evening.

SURVIVAL AT SEA

TRAVELING

If an SOS has been sent out, or you are in or near regular shipping lanes, stay in the same vicinity for 72 hours. If none of these circumstances apply, move on immediately to take advantage of initial energy. Assess the nearest shipping lane and head in that direction. Your craft will move with the wind and current—rarely more than 6–8 miles (9–13 km) per day. Pull in the sea anchor. Use a paddle as a rudder. If the wind is against your chosen direction, stream sea anchor along to maintain position.

> **Take these factors into consideration when making your decision whether to stay or travel:**
> Has an SOS been sent? Is your position known to rescuers? Do you know it? Is the weather favorable for a search? Are other vessels likely to pass you? How many days' supply of food and water do you have?

TO USE THE WIND: Inflate the dinghy fully and sit up high. Improvise a sail if necessary. Do not secure its lower edges. Hold lower lines or bottom of sail, then release them in sudden gusts of wind so that the raft does not capsize.

IN ROUGH WATER: Stream your sea anchor out from the bow to keep it into the wind and prevent capsizing. Stay low. Do not sit on the sides, stand up, or make sudden movements. Tie several rafts or dinghies together.

> Assign lookouts, even in darkness, to watch out for shipping, aircraft, signs of land, seaweed, fish, birds, and flotsam. They should also inspect the raft for signs of leakage or chafing. Watches should be kept short to avoid exhaustion and lack of concentration.

SURVIVAL AT SEA

INDICATIONS OF LAND CLOSEBY

Cumulus clouds in an otherwise clear sky are likely to form over land. In tropical waters the reflection of sunlight from shallow water over coral reefs produces a green tint on the underside of the cloud.

Lone birds may have been blown off course by rough weather, but very few seabirds sleep over water or fly more than 100 miles (62 km) from land. Their direction of flight is usually outward from land before noon and inward in the late afternoon. The continuous sound of bird cries is usually an indication that land is closeby.

Drifting vegetation, e.g. coconuts, may be a sign of land (but they can be carried all the way across an ocean).

A change in the sea's direction may be caused by the tide pattern around an island. A constant wind with a decreasing swell suggests land to windward.

Water that is muddy with silt is likely to have come from the mouth of a large river.

SIGNALING AT SEA

Use flares, dye markers, and movement of any kind to attract attention while at sea.

If you have no signaling equipment, wave clothing or tarpaulins and churn the water if it is still. At night or in fog use a whistle to maintain contact with other survivors.

If a radio transmitter is part of the equipment onboard a life raft, the instructions for its operation will be found on its side (see p. 271).

Sea markers that release dye are only of use in the daytime. They are usually conspicuous for three hours.

SURVIVAL AT SEA

Pyrotechnic equipment must be kept secure and dry. Read the instructions and beware of fire hazards. When firing flares, do not point them downward or toward yourself or anyone else. Use flares only when you are certain that they will be seen. Fire when a plane is flying toward you, not when it has flown past (see pp. 281-282).

HEALTH

Exposure and severe hydration are major problems.

Constipation and difficulty urinating or concentrated urine are not unusual. Do not attempt to treat them, or you could force further loss of liquid.

If you feel sick, try not to vomit. Never induce vomiting.

Continued exposure to saltwater can cause boils. Do not prick or squeeze them. Do not dampen yourself too often with saltwater. Stop dampening yourself with seawater if there is any soreness.

Protect your eyes from glare. If eyes are sore, moisten a cloth with seawater and place it over the eyes and rest them. Do not do this for long, it can make skin sore.

Trenchfoot (see p.328) can occur when it is awash with water. Exercise will help protect you from it and from frostbite and exposure. Keep it well covered when resting and, when on watch, gently exercise the limbs.

WATER

Even if you have a good water supply, ration it immediately. Do not relax the ration until there has been a final rescue or until you can replenish it, as you have no idea how long you will have to last.

WATER RATIONS
DAY 1: No water. The body is a reservoir.
DAYS 2–4: 14 ounces (400 cc) if available.
DAY 5 onward: 2-8 ounces (55-225 cc) daily,
depending on the climate and water available.
**When you are drinking, moisten your lips, tongue,
and throat before swallowing. Sip slowly—
gulping will make you vomit.**

REDUCING WATER NEEDS: Reduce sweating. Make use of
breezes and seawater to cool the body. If it is very hot and
the waters are safe, take a dip over the side—but first check
your safety line. You should always be tied on. Beware of
dangerous fish and be sure that you can get back aboard.

Take antisickness pills, if they are available, as soon as
you feel queasy, as vomiting will lose valuable fluids.

If you are low on water, do not eat (see p. 27).

GATHERING FRESHWATER: Collect rainwater night and day
—rig up a catchment out of canvas or plastic. At night rig
the canvas with the edges folded to catch dew. Stow as
much in containers as you can. Drink up the puddles in the
boat first. But be careful in heavy seas as the water will be
contaminated with salt.

Sea ice can produce drinking water (see p. 32). In the
summer pools on old sea ice may be drinkable (if they are
not wave splashes). Taste it carefully before drinking.

You can also get water from fish (see p. 35).

TREATMENT OF SEAWATER: Life-raft equipment may include
solar stills and desalination kits (see p. 32). Set the solar
stills out immediately but only use desalination tablets

when the weather is unfavorable for the stills and dew or rain catchment is ineffective.

> DO NOT drink seawater
> DO NOT drink urine
> DO NOT drink alcohol
> DO NOT smoke
> DO NOT eat unless water is available

Sleep and rest are the best ways of enduring periods of reduced water and food—but make sure that you have adequate shade during the day. If the sea is rough, tie yourself to the raft, close any cover, and ride out the storm as best you can. Try to relax.

FOOD

Conserve emergency food supplies until needed. Try to live off sea life. There are dangerous fish (see p. 350 ff), but in the open sea fish are generally safe to eat. Near the shore there are dangerous and poisonous species.

FISHING

Never wrap fishing line around bare hands or tie it to an inflatable dinghy. Salt gives it a sharp cutting edge.

Wear gloves if available or use a cloth to handle fish to avoid injuries from sharp fins and gill covers.

Fish and turtles attracted to the shelter of a dinghy will swim under it. Pass a net under the keel from one end to the other (it takes two people to hold the ends).

Improvise hooks (see p. 147). If you are using a metal spoon or spinner, keep it moving by paying out and reeling in. Let the "bait" sink and then retrieve it.

Fish flesh spoils easily and must be eaten fresh, unless the air is dry when it can be dried in the sun for future meals. Clean and gut it before drying.

BIRDS: Will be attracted to a raft as a potential perching place. Stay still until they settle, and try to grab them.

Wrap a diamond-shaped tin gorge with fish and trail it to attract birds. When it is seized by a bird, the gorge should lodge across its throat.

SEAWEED: Occurs on shorelines and in floating forms. Raw seaweeds are tough, salty, and hard to digest. They absorb fluids—do not eat them when water is scarce.

Seaweeds also provide food in the form of small fish, crabs, and shrimps living on them. These decapods are not easy to see, since they are mottled brown, like seaweed.

Make a grapple hook by tying pieces of wood or metal wreckage together to form a multiple hook. Attach it to a line and trail it or throw it out to rake in seaweed. Use it for gathering drifting wreckage to consolidate a raft.

SURVIVAL AT SEA

DANGEROUS FISH

POISONOUS FISH: Many reef fish have toxic flesh (avoid the liver, intestines, and eggs). No amount of cooking neutralizes the poison. They are tasteless, so standard edibility tests are useless. Do not assume that because a bird can eat a fish, it is nontoxic. Cats and birds are less susceptible to the toxins than human beings.

Symptoms of poisoning include numbness of the lips, tongue, and extremities, severe itching, and a reversal of temperature sensations: cold things seem hot, and hot things seem cold. Nausea, vomiting, loss of speech, dizziness, and paralysis may follow. They can be fatal.

AGGRESSIVE FISH: These include barracudas, which charge at lights or shiny objects at night; huge sea bass; and moray eels. Sea snakes are venomous.

SHARKS

The survivor out at sea is vulnerable to shark attacks. Ocean sharks are usually not ferocious when food is plentiful. Most are cowards and can be scared away by the jab of a stick, especially on their noses. However, making a commotion may attract sharks.

Sharks feed off the ocean bottom, but hungry sharks will follow fish to the surface and into shallow water; their hunger at these times makes them dangerous.

Sharks feed at night, dusk, and dawn, locating prey by smell and vibrations. They seek easy prey (wounded fish and stragglers) and are attracted to blood, bodily wastes, and garbage (they will scavenge refuse thrown overboard). Weak movements draw attention. Strong, regular movements and loud noises repel them. Human appearance is strange to a shark, and clothing produces a confusing shape. A group of clothed humans bunched up together will be safer than a lone individual. If a shark keeps its distance, it is only curious. If it circles inward and makes sudden movements, it is likely to attack.

PROTECTION AGAINST SHARKS: IN THE WATER

Avoid passing body wastes. If you must urinate, do it in short spurts and allow it to dissipate between spurts. Collect feces and throw it faraway. Try to hold vomit in the mouth and reswallow it (or throw it faraway). If you must swim, use strong strokes; avoid schools of fish.

Sharks cannot stop or turn quickly. A good swimmer can evade a single shark by rapid changes in direction.

If you are in a group, bunch up together and face outward. Kick and punch with a stiff arm using the heel of your hand. Slap the water with cupped hands. Put your head underwater and shout. If you have a knife, let the shark take it in the snout or go for the gills and eyes.

PROTECTION AGAINST SHARKS: ON A BOAT

Don't fish when sharks are around. Don't throw waste overboard. Let go of baited hooks. Do not trail your arms or legs in the water. To deter a shark from attacking, jab its snout with a paddle or pole. Beware: a large shark could take a bite out of a boat.

If you catch a small shark, haul it to the side of the craft, pull the head out, and club it hard before approaching and finishing it off with more blows. Don't try this with a large shark. It could injure you and your craft. Cut your line and sacrifice part of it—the shark's threshing will soon attract its fellow sharks.

SURVIVAL AT SEA

MAKING A LANDFALL

When you are approaching land, select a landing point where it will be easy to beach or swim ashore. Take the sail down; the sea anchor will keep you pointing at the shore and will slow down your progress. Steer away from any rocks. Try not to land with the sun in your eyes.

A sloping beach with a small surf is ideal. Try to ride the back of a breaker. To avoid being swamped by an oncoming wave, paddle hard, but do not overshoot a breaker that is carrying you along. In heavy surf point the vessel seaward and paddle into an approaching wave.

Notice the lie of the land: high ground, vegetation, and watercourses. If you are with companions, choose a rendezvous point in case you are separated. Do not try to land at night—it is too dangerous. Wait until the morning.

If you float into an estuary, try to reach a bank. The turning tide could carry you back out to sea. Pull in the sea anchor and make the boat as light as possible. Bail out an inflatable and inflate it to its maximum to make the most of the incoming tide. If you are being swept back out to sea by the ebb, ballast the dinghy by partially-filling it with water and streaming the sea anchor.

> Tie yourself to the raft. Even if it is overturned or damaged and you are rendered unconscious, you stand a chance of surviving, whereas alone in the water and dashed on the rocks, you will be killed.

If swimming ashore in a heavy sea, keep on clothing, shoes, and life jacket. Raise your legs, knees bent, and take the shock of impact of the rocks on the soles of your feet.

RESCUE

The first requirement for rescue is to let others know of
your situation and your location. Once contact has been
made, you can pass on other information.

SIGNALING

SOS (Save Our Souls) is an internationally recognized
distress signal. Mayday (from *m'aidez:* French for *help
me*) is the signal used in radio-telecommunications.

Almost any signal repeated three times will serve as a
distress signal: three fires or columns of smoke; three
whistles, shots, or flashes of light. If you are using noises
or lights, wait one minute between each group of three.

TRANSMITTERS: Dinghies, life rafts, and life jackets are
often equipped with transmitters that indicate position
over a short range. To avoid wasting batteries, hold this in
reserve until there is a chance of their signals getting
picked up. With long-range transmitters, send distress
signals at regular intervals. Frequencies are usually
preset at 121.5 and 243 megacycles, and the range is
about 20 miles (32 km). Portable VHF transceivers can
only communicate with stations in a direct line of sight
and without any intervening obstruction (although a
relay station may be established on a high point). Such
sets are usually tuned to a mountain rescue frequency,
but procedures should be established before departure.

If you have a transmitter, check the batteries. Can an
engine be used to generate electricity or recharge the
batteries? Conserve fuel and plan your transmissions to
a pattern rather than attempting long periods on air.

RESCUE

   The International Mountain Distress Signal is six whistles per minute (or six waves, light flashes, etc.) followed by a minute's silence, then repeated.

Siting signals

Take account of the terrain. Choose high points for light signals. Erect an unusual silhouette on a ridge to attract attention.

   Planes fly over hilly territory from the lower to the higher ridges. Thus slopes behind ridges may be hidden as the plane approaches. Signals near the tops of ridges should be seen from any direction. Lay out marks on level ground or on slopes that are not likely to be overlooked.

VEHICLE OR AIRCRAFT WRECKAGE: A stranded vehicle or downed aircraft provides useful signaling aids. Fuel, oil, and hydraulic fluid can be burned. Tires and electrical insulation generate smoke. Glass and chrome make good reflectors. Life jackets, dinghies, and parachutes are eye-catching. Arrange colorful, shiny objects in a visible spot to attract attention to your location.

   Turn lights on at night. If your batteries are low, keep them in reserve to flash headlights and honk the horn.

FIRE AND SMOKE: Establish signal fires once immediate needs for treatment of injuries and provisions for shelter have been met. Gather fuel for camp and signal fires.

   Place three fires in a triangle at equal distances apart. If this is not possible, a group of clearly separated fires will work. If fuel is scarce, only use your campfire.

   Signal fires should be kept dry and maintained, ready to be lit to attract the attention of passing aircraft. Use tinder to get them going rapidly (see p. 173ff).

RESCUE

Gasoline can be used as a fire lighter but don't pour it on. Lay a piece of gasoline-soaked rag among the tinder. Don't light it right away. Carry the fuel canister away to a safe distance. Wait a few seconds, then light the wick. If a fire does not light first time, pull tinder apart and check for sparks or embers, before adding extra gasoline.

Keep a supply of green boughs, oil, or rubber closeby to create smoke if it is needed.

Among vegetation or close to trees build an earth wall around each fire to contain it.

Do not build fires among trees where the canopy will block out the signal. Place them in a clearing.

If you are by a lake or river, build rafts to place your fires on and securely anchor or tether them into position. The arrow indicates the direction of the current.

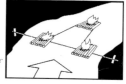

TORCH THE TREES: Use small, isolated trees for fire signals. Build a fire between the boughs, using dry twigs or old bird's nests. This will ignite the foliage, producing lots of smoke. Fires at the base of dead trees burn for a long time, but don't risk starting a forest fire. Aside from the damage that this will cause, your life is in jeopardy.

LUMINOUS CONE FIRES: On a clear, open site make a tripod with a platform to support a fire. Use evergreen boughs as cover to keep the cone dry; they will burn

RESCUE

brightly and give off smoke. Cover the cone with brightly-colored material, e.g. a parachute, which will be noticeable during the day. Whip it off when you ignite the fire—you may not attract attention the first time.

Keep tripods well maintained, ensuring that the wood is dry. Drive pole ends into the ground to prevent them from tipping in strong winds. A flaming cone fire is visible for miles. In exposed locations make a tepee of fabric with a smoke and heat outlet at the top to keep fire under control. Add fuel from side so as not to mask firelight.

USE WRECKAGE TO HELP WITH FIRE SIGNALING: Stand a fire on a piece of metal. When it is hot it increases convection and makes the fire burn brightly. If it is polished, it will act as a reflector, intensifying the brightness.

SMOKE INDICATORS

During the day smoke is a good locator. Have a supply of smoke-producing materials ready to put on the fires. Smoke not only helps rescue aircraft find you, it also shows surface wind direction. Make sure that smoke is downwind of landing site and of any panel codes you have laid so it does not obscure them.

Light smoke stands out against dark earth or forest. Use green grass, leaves, mosses, and ferns. Wet materials produce a good smudge fire, e.g. damp seat covers smolder for a long time. The smoke also keeps insects at bay.

Dark smoke shows up the best against snow or desert sand. Use rubber or oil to produce it. If atmospheric conditions make the smoke hang in layers along the ground, build up the fire to increase its height. Thermal currents will then take the smoke to a good height.

BE IMAGINATIVE: On a river a noticeable floating object carrying a message may attract attention, e.g. a small raft with a bright sail labeled SOS, for instance.

> If rescue is unlikely and you start finding your own way back, leave clear signs so that searchers have an indication of the route that you have taken. Stay close to regular flight routes or stay in open territory.

CODES

GROUND-TO-AIR SIGNALING

Attract attention during daylight, even if you are asleep or injured with the following signals. Make them as large and as noticeable as possible. A recommended size is 40 x 10 feet (10 x 3 m) for each symbol, with 10 feet (3 m) between signals.

Lay panel codes out in the open; avoid steep gullies or ravines and do not make them on reverse slopes. Use the marker panels from your survival pouch (see p. 22) or improvise. Lay out wreckage or dig a shallow trench: banked up earth increases the depth of the shadow. Use rocks or boughs to accentuate it. On snow trampled-out codes will show clearly until the next snowfall.

RESCUE

GROUND-TO-AIR CODE

I Serious injury—immediate CASEVAC
(casualty evacuation—can also mean "need doctor")

II Need medical supplies

F Need food and water

N Negative *(No)*

A Affirmative *(Yes)*—*(Y will also be understood)*

LL All is well

X Unable to move on

→ Am moving on this way

K Indicate direction to proceed

⌐L Do not understand

□ Need compass and map

△ Think it is safe to land here
(Broken at angles, means "attempting takeoff")

! Need radio/signal lamp/battery

⌐⌐ Aircraft badly damaged

RESCUE

Once contact has been made, a message signaled by the aircraft can be answered with A or Y (affirmative) and N (negative) signals, morse code, or body signals.

NIGHT SIGNALS: Use inflammable substances to make signals which will work at night. Dig or scrape an SOS (or any symbol) in the earth, sand or snow and, when the signal is needed, pour petrol into it and ignite it.

MESSAGE SIGNALING

International morse code can be transmitted by flashing lights on and off, by a heliograph, or by waving a flag or a shirt tied to a stick. Always carry a copy of the code.

HELIOGRAPH: Use the sun and a reflector to flash light signals. Any shiny object will do—polished tin, glass, a piece of foil—but a hand mirror is the best. Long flashes are dashes, and quick ones are dots. If you do not know morse code, random flashes should attract attention. At least learn the code for SOS. A flash can be seen at a great distance and requires little energy. Sweep the horizon during the day. If a plane approaches, make intermittent flashes so that you do not dazzle the pilot. Once you have been seen, stop signaling.

With an improvised single-sided reflector, pick up sunlight to get an image on the ground or some other surface and lead it in the direction of the aircraft.

RESCUE

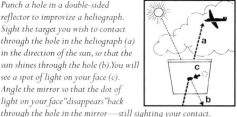

Punch a hole in a double-sided reflector to improvise a heliograph. Sight the target you wish to contact through the hole in the heliograph (a) in the direction of the sun, so that the sun shines through the hole (b).You will see a spot of light on your face (c). Angle the mirror so that the dot of light on your face "disappears" back through the hole in the mirror—still sighting your contact.

If your attempts are unsuccessful, bring the mirror close to your eyes with a hand lined up between you and the contact. Angle the mirror to flash onto your hand, then move your hand away.

Practice this form of signaling, but unless you are in a survival situation, do not signal aircraft or transmit messages that could cause alarm or danger to others.

RAG SIGNALS: Tie a flag or a piece of brightly-colored clothing to a pole. Move it left for dashes and right for dots. Exaggerate with a figure eight movement.

For a "dot" swing it to the right and make a figure eight; for a "dash" swing it to the left and make a figure eight.

At close range this may work without figure eight movements.

Keep "dash" pauses on the left, slightly longer than the "dot" movements to the right.

RESCUE

MORSE CODE

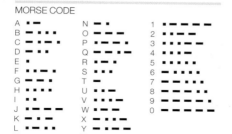

SENDING SIGNALS   (* SEND AS ONE WORD WITH NO PAUSES)

AAAAA* etc.—Call sign. *I have a message.*
AAA*—End of sentence. *More follows.*
Pause—End of word. *More follows.*
EEEEE* etc.—Error. *Start from last correct word.*
AR—End of message.

RECEIVING SIGNALS

TTTTT* etc.—*I am receiving you.*
K—I am ready. *Start message.*
T—Word received.
IMI*—Repeat sign. *I do not understand.*
R—Message received.

USEFUL WORDS

RESCUE

BODY SIGNALS

Use these to signal to airmen. Make all signals in a clear and exaggerated manner. Notice the changes from frontal to sideways positions and the use of leg and body posture, as well as hand movements. Use a cloth in the hand to emphasize YES and NO signals.

Pick us up

Need mechanical help

Land here

Yes

No

All is well

Can proceed shortly

Have radio

Do not attempt to land here

Need medical assistance

Drop a message

RESCUE

Pilots will respond to body signals as follows:

Message received and understood

In daylight: tipping the plane's wings from side to side

At night: flashing green lights

Message received but not understood

In daylight: flying the plane in a right-handed circle

At night: flashing red lights

MOUNTAIN RESCUE CODE

* Repeat after 1 minute interval

Message: SOS

    Flare signal: Red

    Sound signal: 3 short blasts, 3 long, 3 short*

    Light signal: 3 short flashes, 3 long, 3 short*

Message: HELP NEEDED

    Flare signal: Red

    Sound signal: 6 blasts in quick succession*

    Light signal: 6 flashes in quick succession*

Message: MESSAGE UNDERSTOOD

    Flare signal: White

    Sound signal: 3 flashes in quick succession*

    Light signal: 3 flashes in quick succession*

Message: RETURN TO BASE

    Flare signal: Green

    Sound signal: Prolonged succession of blasts

    Light signal: Prolonged succession of flashes

FLARES

Any flare will be investigated in a search, but choose the one that is the most suitable to the location. In densely-wooded country green does not stand out but red does. Over snow white merges—green and red are the best.

RESCUE

Make sure that you understand the instructions, as some flares eject a white-hot ball of magnesium that will burn a hole in anything that it hits—your chest or a dinghy.

Some flares are handheld and reversible. One end produces smoke for daytime, and the other end is a flare for nighttime. The higher these are held, the easier they are to see. Flares fired into the air can be seen from faraway.

Keep the flares dry and away from naked flames and heat sources. Ensure that safety pins are in position and secure, but they may be easily removed when necessary.

HANDLING FLARES: Handheld flares are cylindrical tubes with a cap at each end. The top cap is often embossed so that it can be identified by touch. Remove it first. Then remove base cap, exposing a short string and safety pin or other safety device. Point flare upward and away from you and anyone else. Remove pin or turn it to the fire position. Hold flare at arm's length, shoulder-height, pointing up. Tug firing string vertically downward. Brace yourself for the kickback. Some flares have a spring-mechanism trigger.

To fire a Very light, load, point skyward, cock the hammer, and squeeze the trigger. Miniflares are lighter than Very lights but as effective. Handle with care. To use, screw a flare of the selected color into the end of the discharger, aim it skyward, pull back the striker, and fire!

 Handheld flares get hot. When they burn down, do not drop them into the bottom of a boat, where they could start a fire or burn straight through an inflatable.

INFORMATION SIGNALS

If you abandon camp, leave clear direction markers to indicate your route. Continue to make them, not only for people to follow, but to establish your own route as a guide if you start going back on your trail.

RESCUE

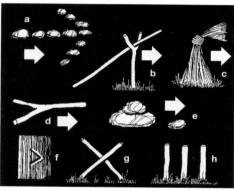

Place rocks or debris in an arrow shape (a) to be visible from the air. Ground level signs include: stick in a crooked support, with the top indicating the direction being followed (b); grasses tied in an overhand knot with the end hanging in the direction being followed (c); forked branches laid with the fork pointing in direction being followed (d); small rocks on larger rocks, with a small rock beside (e), indicating a turn, or arrow notches cut in tree trunks (f). A cross of sticks or stones (g) means "not this way." Signal danger or emergency with 3 rocks, sticks, or clumps of grass.

RESCUE

SEARCH

A search will start from the last known location and sweep along the proposed route. An assessment will be made of the probable strategy that was adopted. The search will then be extended to cover the whole area. Ideally this will be done from the air, but severe weather may mean that it has to be done on foot.

Aerial search patterns will cover both sides of the intended flight path of missing aircraft or your known route. If weather conditions permit, a night search will be made, as lights will be visible from a great height and a wider area can be covered.

If you are signaling to an aircraft and it turns away, keep watching. It may be following a search pattern, and you will be able to anticipate when to signal again. Most aerial searches involve parallel sweeps toward and away from the sun, so any reflection from a missing aircraft or other wreckage and signals will be seen.

At sea combined sea-and-air searches allow aircraft to locate survivors so that ships can pick them up.

HELICOPTER RESCUE

Helicopters are frequently used to carry out rescues. Where it is possible, the pilot will land to pick up survivors and fly them out. Survivors should check out suitable landing sites and create a site if it is necessary.

A helicopter requires an obstruction-free approach and exit path, both into the prevailing winds. The ground should be level—a slope of no more than 7 ° (a gradient of 1 in 10) is acceptable. The touchdown surface must be firm and free of loose materials—no leaves, etc.

SELECTING AND PREPARING A LANDING SITE

Find a natural clearing at least 80 feet (26 m) in diameter. A further 15 feet (5 m) should be cleared to a height of 2 feet (60 cm). It must have a clear approach path into the prevailing wind with no obstructions within an angle of 15° of the landing pad (LP). In dense country, seek a riverbank on a large bend. On level high ground fell trees so that they fall downhill, clear of approach and exit paths. Don't attempt to cut an LP on flat ground.

Mark the touchdown point with an H made out of rocks (keep the surface smooth), or securely anchored clothing. Stamp snow down firmly to stop it swirling. Water dry surfaces to keep down the dust. In mountains updrafts and downdrafts can be considerable. Select a site that gives maximum lift in the direction of take-off.

Use smoke to indicate the direction and strength of the wind, but make sure that it doesn't obscure the touchdown area. If a fire is not practical, make a T sign from contrasting materials and place it at the downwind edge of the LP, with horizontal bar of T placed upwind. Or stand on far downwind side of the LP with your arms outstretched and back to the wind to signal. Don't do this too soon and then only in the correct position. It is similar to the body signal of "need help."

For a night rescue use flares and fires to indicate your position. If using flashlights or other beams, shine them skyward to attract attention, then shine them onto the touchdown or winching area. Don't dazzle the pilot.

When the helicopter touches down, do not approach it from the rear. This is a blind spot for the crew, and the tail rotor is unprotected. On sloping ground always approach up a slope, never down a slope.

RESCUE

Do not carry anything that could foul the main rotor. Keep sharp objects away from body panels of the helicopter. Sit in seat allocated to you by the crewmen, fasten seat belt, and keep fastened until told otherwise. Do not try to alight until engine has been shut off after you have landed—even then wait for directions.

NONLANDING RESCUE: If an LP is impossible, you can be winched up while the helicopter hovers.

If survivors are being lifted from a ship, place the deck at 40 ° to the right of the eye of the wind. Try to give a wind speed over the deck of around 18 mph (29 kph).

WINCHING TECHNIQUES

Double lift: A crewman is lowered on the winch with another strop for the survivor. During the lift, the crewman supports the survivor with his legs and hands. After the strop has been put in place and tightened, keep your arms down by your sides and do not lift them.

Single lift: Place yourself into the strop. When you have placed it under your armpits and securely tightened the grommet, give the "thumbs up" sign. Make no more signals until you are onboard. When you reach the cabin doorway, do exactly as the winchman directs.

If you are on a raft, disconnect yourself from the lifeline. Fold down cover and lower sails. Stream the sea anchor to assist pilot in trapping the raft under rotor downwash.

Aircraft build up static electricity. This is discharged when the aircraft, or the cable, touches the ground. Allow winch sling or cable to touch down before you approach it, or you will get a substantial electric shock.

HEALTH

Take precautions to avoid sickness and injuries, but make sure that in the event that medical problems do arise, everyone in the group knows first aid. If there is no hope of expert help, the survivor may have to take drastic measures to save a life. Some of the advice given in this section is intended for such circumstances only.

FIRST AID

PRIORITIES

Where there are many casualties, first treat those with multiple injuries, bleeding, breathing, and heart trouble. Assess the injuries and handle in this sequence:

1 **Restore and maintain breathing/heartbeat**
2 **Stop bleeding**
3 **Protect wounds and burns**
4 **Immobilize fractures**
5 **Treat shock**

 The possibility of an AIDS infection demands care when dealing with blood and wounds. Cover your hands with gloves or plastic bags.

REDUCING DANGER

Before approaching a casualty, check for danger from falling debris, gas, traffic, etc. Switch off the current before touching electrocution victims (see p. 292).

If it is possible, examine the patient before moving them, but if there is danger, move patient to safety. Those with spinal injuries are at risk when moved (see p. 315).

HEALTH

UNCONSCIOUS CASUALTIES

Check whether they are breathing and begin artificial respiration immediately if necessary. Check for external bleeding and injuries. Establish cause of unconsciousness.

Unconscious but still breathing

Check that there are no spinal injuries, clear out obstructions in the mouth, deal with any serious bleeding, and place them in recovery position. Turn patient on one side (by grasping clothing at hip). Loosen tight clothing.

Move the arm and leg on one side outward to stop patient lying flat. Bend the elbow and knee. Turn the head in the same direction. Lay the other arm along the other side of the patient. Allow the other leg to bend slightly to produce a stable position. Check that the airway is clear.

> Do not place a casualty with a suspected spinal injury in the recovery position. Use an artificial airway if it is available to maintain respiration.

BREATHING AND PULSE

Loud breathing, froth around the nose or lips, blueness of the lips and ears all indicate breathing difficulties. Check breathing often: listen near the nose and mouth. Remove obstructions. If breathing stops, give artificial respiration (see p. 293).
Check at the neck or wrist for a pulse (see p. 296).

HEALTH

CESSATION OF BREATHING

This dire emergency may be caused by:

Choking or blockage of air passages (see below)

Drowning or electric shock (see pp. 291–292)

Inhalation of smoke, gases, or flame (see p. 291)

Lack of oxygen (see p. 291)

Compression of the chest (see p. 291)

CHOKING AND BLOCKAGES

If breathing has stopped, remove any obstructions in the airway, sweep out the mouth with a finger, and ensure that the tongue has not fallen back. Give artificial respiration.

If a person can inhale and cough, encourage them to cough out the blockage. If they cannot clear the airway, use the Heimlich maneuver on adults (see p. 290 for methods to use on infants and other special cases).

HEIMLICH MANEUVER: Stand behind a conscious casualty, with arms around them. Make a fist with one hand and press it, thumb inward, above the navel but below the sternum. Clasp your other hand around the fist. Pull sharply upward and inward four times.

If this does not work, give 4 sharp blows to the back between the shoulder blades and repeat the maneuver. Check to see if the blockage is dislodged. Repeat—do not give up.

HEALTH

Place the unconscious casualty on his or her back, with their head tilted back. Kneel astride or alongside them, place your hands, one on top of the other, with the heels of your hands resting above the navel. Keep your fingers clear. With your arm straight, make quick thrusts upward and inward as if to the center of rib cage. Thrusts must be strong enough to dislodge the blockage. If you are

unsuccessful, roll the patient onto their side and strike four times between shoulder blades. Repeat abdominal thrust as necessary.

Self-help
If alone, use the Heimlich maneuver by pulling or pushing against a blunt projection (e.g. a tree or chair back).

CHOKING: SPECIAL CASES

Children: Hold the child upside down by their heels and strike 4 blows with the heel of your hand between the shoulder blades. Alternatively, lay the child over your lap, head-down, supporting the child under their chest. Slap the back with the heel of your hand. If the blockage is not dislodged, apply Heimlich maneuver with one hand. Use less pressure than for an adult, but it must be sufficient to clear the blockage.

Babies: Use much less pressure for back slaps. If the blockage is not dislodged, put 2 fingers of one or both hands between the navel and bottom of the sternum. Press down and forward quickly, repeat 4 times.

Pregnant women: Position your fists against the middle of sternum and thrust upward and inward.

HEALTH

PREVENTING ASPHYXIATION

Pressure on the chest can cause asphyxiation. In an avalanche or landslide crouch with your arms bent and elbows tucked in to protect the chest. A climber who slips and is suspended by a rope around his chest will find it hard to breathe. Pass a loop down to relieve the pressure.

If the wreckage cannot be lifted off a trapped person, use a lever to raise it and prop it up securely.

Smoke and gas can be prevented from entering lungs by placing a fine mesh over nose and mouth. Casualties must have fresh air. Get upwind or use a respirator.

Lack of oxygen is a danger in shelters with no ventilation. A fire adds the risk of carbon monoxide poisoning. Casualties need fresh air.

Carbon monoxide poisoning is deadly in confined spaces, but it is hard to detect. Symptoms resemble an alcohol overdose: impaired memory and judgment, and a disregard for danger.

Ensure adequate ventilation when using stoves. To test whether there is sufficient oxygen, light a candle: if the flame gets longer and higher, there is a severe lack of oxygen: ventilate. Casualties must have fresh air.

NOT BREATHING AND NO PULSE
DROWNING

Symptoms: This can occur through fluid blockages, but the patient is often immersed. The face, especially the lips and ears, are livid and congested; fine froth at the mouth and nostrils.   (cont. over)

HEALTH

Treatment: Do not attempt to remove liquid from the lungs. Begin artificial respiration (see p. 295) as soon as possible. If victim is still in the water, support body and begin mouth-to-mouth after removing any obstructions.

ELECTROCUTION

Symptoms: The heart may stop; muscle spasms may throw the victim some distance. Electrical burns will be much deeper than they appear.

Treatment: Do not touch them until current is off. It may be possible to break contact by pulling on an insulated cable to disengage. But beware—liquids will conduct current (victims may urinate). Give artificial respiration and treat for cardiac arrest (see p. 297), then treat burns.

LIGHTNING

Symptoms: Victim is usually stunned or unconscious. Clothing may catch fire. Electrical burns will be the most severe where metal objects (jewelry, etc.) are worn.

Treatment: Give artificial respiration (see p. 293) if it is required and treat burns (see pp. 304–305). Prolonged resuscitation may be needed. Recovery is often delayed.

POISONING

Symptoms: Poisons that enter the lungs or attack the nervous system can cause asphyxia (see pp. 320–321).

HEART ATTACK

Symptoms: Severe chest pain, shortness of breath, giddiness, collapse, anxiety, heavy sweating, irregular pulse, blueness of the lips or skin.

Treatment: If breathing fails give artificial respiration and cardiac compression (see p. 297) if pulse stops.

ARTIFICIAL RESPIRATION (A.R.)

HEALTH

With any form of resuscitation, the first 5 minutes are the most critical, but if breathing does not start, keep artificial respiration up for at least an hour. In a group take turns. Don't give up!

Mouth-to-mouth ("Kiss of life")

The fastest and most effective method. Begin as soon as airway is cleared. If face is injured, or poison or chemical burns are likely, use the Silvester method (see p. 294).

Lie patient on their back, tilt head back, hold jaw open and nostrils closed. Check mouth and throat are clear. Loosen tight clothing. Take a deep breath, place your mouth over patient's mouth, and blow.

Watch for the chest to rise (if it does not, the airway may be blocked: treat for choking, see p. 289). Remove your mouth, and the chest will fall. Repeat quickly 6 times, then continue at a rate of 12–16 inflations per minute until breathing is restored.

FOR A CHILD: Seal your mouth around the baby's or child's mouth and nostrils. Don't tilt the baby's head back too far. Breathe gently into the lungs, 20 inflations per minute. Check the pulse after two inflations.

HEALTH

> AIDS: The danger of infection is small, but if you feel at risk, place a clean handkerchief or a thin polyethylene bag with a small slit in it between your mouth and that of the victim. Blow through the slit or handkerchief.

Silvester method

Use this when poisoning or facial injuries prevent mouth-to-mouth, and when patient needs cardiac compression.

Lie victim on their back, raise the shoulders with a pad of folded material. Kneel astride victim's head, place your hands flat over lower ribs and rock forward to press steadily downward. Lift victim's arms upward and outward as far as possible.

Repeat this rhythmically 12 times per minute for adults. If there is no improvement, treat for choking to clear the blocked airway, then resume artificial respiration treatment.

AFTER BREATHING HAS BEEN RESTORED: Place the patient in the recovery position—after all forms of resuscitation, but not in cases of spinal injuries.

HEALTH

Holger Nielson method

Use this to resuscitate a drowning victim if mouth-to-mouth is not possible. Face-down position allows liquids to flow freely from mouth without choking the patient.

Lay victim face-down, with head turned to one side, arms bent, forehead resting on hands. Loosen tight garments, clear their mouth of seaweed, mud, etc., and ensure tongue is brought forward. Kneel at head, facing casualty. Place your hands over their shoulder blades, thumbs touching, and fingers spread. Perform the following procedure to a count of 8:
1-2-3 Rock forward with arms straight, producing gentle, even, increasing pressure (around 2 seconds).
4 Rock back, sliding your hands to grasp victim's upper arms (½–1 second).
5-6-7 Pull and raise victim's arms gently by rocking farther backward (2 seconds). Avoid raising the torso or disturbing the head too much.
8 Lower victim's arms to the ground and slide your hands back to initial position (½–1 second).
Repeat 12 times per minute

If victim's arms are injured, place a folded garment under their forehead, and lift under the armpits. This is impracticable if the ribs or shoulders are badly damaged.

HEALTH

IS THE HEART BEATING?

Taking a pulse at wrist
Rest your fingers lightly at front of wrist, around 0.3 inches (1 cm) from thumb side at ower end of forearm.

Taking a pulse at neck
Turn face to one side. Slide your fingers from Adam's apple into groove alongside it and press gently.

In a relaxed adult the normal pulse rate is 60–80 beats per minute (average is 72); in young children 90–140 per minute. The rate increases with excitement.

Count the beats in 30 seconds and multiply this by 2. Use a watch with a second hand to keep the timing accurate; make a note of the result.

> If you cannot feel a pulse and the pupils of the eyes are much larger than normal, start cardiac compression while artificial respiration is continued. Mouth-to-mouth and the Silvester method allow both activities to be carried out at the same time.

CARDIAC COMPRESSION

Regardless of which method of resuscitation is used, if there is no pulse and no improvement after 10–12 breaths, cardiac compression (external heart massage) should be started.

HEALTH

Cardiac compression

Lay casualty on their back on a firm surface and kneel alongside. Place the heel of one hand on lower half of their sternum, around 1 inch (2.5cm) above where the ribs meet, not on the end of the sternum or below it. Place the heel of the other hand on top. Keep your fingers off the casualty's chest. With your arms straight, rock forward and press down around 1.5 inches (4cm) 15 times. Repeat this around 80 times per minute—more than once per second. Press smoothly and firmly. Erratic or rough pressure could cause injury.

INFANTS AND CHILDREN: Use less pressure and more compressions. For a baby or toddler light pressure with two fingers is enough at 100 compressions per minute. Depress the chest only 1 inch (2.5 cm). For children up to 10 years old, use the heel of one hand only and push lightly 90–100 times per minute to a depth of 1.5 inches (3.5 cm). Give 5 compressions to one lung inflation.

 Compression should only be carried out by a trained first aid person. Never give compressions if the heart is beating—even if only a faint pulse can be felt. You could stop the heart.

HEALTH

A.R. WITH COMPRESSION

If you are alone, use mouth-to-mouth or the Silvester method of resuscitation, give 2 lung inflations, 15 compressions, and repeat. Check for a pulse after 1 minute, and then at 3-minute intervals. Don't give up.

If 2 first aid persons are present, give 5 compressions, followed by 1 deep inflation on the upstroke of fifth compression. Repeat. The first aid person giving the inflations should also check the pulse and pupils.

As soon as a pulse is detected, stop the compressions but continue the inflations until the casualty is breathing unaided. Place the victim in the recovery position.

SEVERE BLEEDING

An adult has up to 11 pints (6 L) of circulating blood. The loss of 1 pint (0.5 L) causes mild faintness, 2 pints (1 L) causes faintness, an increased pulse rate, and shallow breathing. 3 pints (1.5 L) leads to collapse, and more than 4 pints (2.25 L) can be fatal. Immediate steps must be taken to stop the flow of blood. Internal bleeding may not be apparent. If it is severe, it often leads to shock and can kill.

> When bleeding is coupled with cessation of breathing, treat both at the same time as a double emergency.

Bleeding from veins and capillaries can be stemmed by simple pressure over the bleeding point, with or without a dressing. Pressure must be kept up for at least 5–15 minutes to let the clotting take effect. Ideally the wound should be covered with a sterile dressing, but preventing loss of blood is the priority, so use any clean, nonfluffy cloth. If no dressing is available, use your hand. Squeeze the edges of a gaping wound together. If the wound is on a limb, raise it above level of the heart—lay victim down and prop up the head or limbs. If you are wounded and alone, use a free hand to apply direct pressure to the wound.

If anything is embedded in the wound, do not try to remove it. Apply pressure beside the fragment.

Arterial bleeding

Speed is vital in stopping the blood spurting from an artery. Compress the artery at pressure points where it flows near the surface over a bone. Watch the wound: if blood flow does not lessen, move your fingers until it does. The figures and captions below and overleaf show where to apply pressure to stanch arterial bleeding.

Temple or scalp (a):
Forward of or above the ear
Face below eyes (b):
Side of the jaw

Shoulder or upper arm (c):
Above the clavicle
Elbow (d):
Underside of the upper arm

Lower arm (e):
Crook of the elbow
Hand (f):
Front of the wrist

HEALTH

Thigh (g): *Midway on the groin / top of the thigh*
Lower leg (h): *Upper sides of the knee*
Foot (i): *Front of the ankle*

Do not apply pressure for more than 15 minutes.
You will cut off the blood supply to the tissue.

When the bleeding is under control, apply a sterile
dressing and bandage securely, but not so tight that it cuts
off circulation. Do not lift up the dressing—if a clot is
disturbed, the bleeding will get worse.

 After bandaging a limb, check the circulation
often. Loosen a dressing if the toes or fingers
are blue, cold, or numb; there is a risk of gangrene if dressings are too tight. Never use a tourniquet.

Lesser bleeding

Clean the wound carefully and apply a sterile dressing. To
avoid the risk of an infection, do not touch the wound or
allow nonsterile materials to touch it. Only replace the
dressing when it becomes very dirty.

For a nosebleed, sit the patient up with their head
slightly forward and pinch the soft part of the nostrils for
10 minutes. The patient must breathe through their mouth
and not sniff or blow their nose. Loosen tight clothing.

HEALTH

Internal bleeding

This serious condition is common after a violent blow, broken bones, or penetrating wounds. It is hard to detect.

SYMPTOMS

Victim feels light-headed, restless, and faint; looks pale; skin cold and clammy; pulse weak but very fast.

Red/wine-colored urine (injuries to kidney/bladder)

Blood passed with feces (lower bowel injuries)

Blood vomited (stomach injuries)

Blood coughed up as red froth (damage to lungs)

Lie the patient flat with the legs slightly elevated. Keep the patient warm but do not overheat them. Serious internal bleeding requires expert medical care.

WOUNDS AND DRESSINGS

Open wounds are at risk from infections, especially from tetanus—immunization is essential for adventurers.

Foreign bodies must be extracted with sterile tweezers. Other than in a survival situation, this should be left to trained medics. Cut away clothing, clean the area, and irrigate wounds to wash out the dirt. Clean any wound from the center out, do not swab it from the outside in. Dry it and apply a clean dressing. Immobilize the wound in a position that is comfortable. Dressings should be changed if they get wet, give off a bad smell, or if the pain increases and throbs, indicating an infection.

Treat a local infection by soaking it in hot salty water or applying poultices to draw out any pus. Anything that

HEALTH

can be mashed can be used as poultice: rice, potatoes, shredded tree bark, clay, etc. Boil and wrap them in a cloth. Apply this to the infected area as hot as can be tolerated. Don't scald them. Applied heat, e.g. a warm rock wrapped in cloth, can also aid with healing.

> Soap is antiseptic: use it to wash wounds. Wash your hands in boiled water before cleaning a wound. Wash the wound in boiled water or, if none is available, use urine, which is sterile and will not cause an infection.

Stitching up wounds

Minor wounds, e.g. knife wounds, can be closed up by suturing. Clean the wound thoroughly, then stitch across it or use butterfly sutures from your survival kit.

STITCHES: Use a sterilized needle and thread or gut. Make each stitch individually, beginning across the midpoint of the wound. Pull edges together and tie off thread, then work outward.

ADHESIVE SUTURES: Use butterfly sutures or Band-Aids™ cut in a butterfly shape. Pull the edges of wound together. Apply a Band-Aid™ to one side, close it up as much as possible, and press down on the other side.

If the wound becomes infected—red, swollen, or tense—remove some or all of the stitches to let the pus out. Leave it to drain.

HEALTH

Open treatment

The safest way to manage most survival wounds is to cover them with a dressing but not to suture. If unable to clean it thoroughly, the wound must be left to heal from the inside.

You may need to drain a deep wound or open an abcess and insert sterilized loose packing of a bandage. Leave a tail hanging out. Allow the wound to drain for a few days. Reduce the packing as healing progresses, until you are able to remove it all and apply a dressing. If you are lancing or reopening a wound, sterilize the blade first. Do not use antiseptic on deep wounds as there is a risk of tissue damage. Wash the wound with boiled water.

Chest wounds: Place the palm of your hand over sucking wounds (where the chest cavity has been penetrated) to stop any air from entering. Lay casualty down, head and shoulders supported, inclining toward injured side. Plug the wound with a large, loose, wet dressing or cover it with plastic film or aluminum foil (ideally coated with petroleum jelly) and bandage firmly.

Abdominal wounds: No solids or liquids may be given. Relieve thirst with a damp cloth to moisten lips and tongue. If the gut is extruded, cover and keep it damp. Do not try to push it back in place. If no organs extrude, dress and bandage firmly.

Head injuries: Ensure airway is clear and tongue is forward. Remove dentures. Control bleeding. As long as there are no spinal injuries, place in recovery position.

Traumatic amputation: Examine the wound and tie off any exposed arteries with sterile thread.

HEALTH

BURNS

Extinguish burning clothing without fanning the flames.
Get the victim down on the ground and roll them over,
covering them with a blanket. Remove smoldering clothes
(which retain heat) and tight garments, jewelry, etc.

Reduce the temperature by drenching burned tissues
with water to cool them—hold under slow-running cold
water for at least 10 minutes. Do not apply antiseptic, butter,
or ointments. Continue cooling until withdrawal from water
does not lead to increase in pain. Leave burns except to apply
a dry, sterile dressing. Put dressings between burned fingers
and toes to prevent them from sticking to each other. Later,
hardwood barks (e.g. oak or beech) can be boiled in water and
applied to burned flesh when cool to soothe the wound.

Give the patient plenty of fluids in the form of small cold
drinks with a ½ teaspoon of salt or bicarbonate of soda per
pint of water.

Types of burns

Deep burns are charred or white, and bones or muscles may
be visible. Superficial burns are much more painful. Blisters
should never be burst deliberately. If the face and neck are
burned, ensure that the airway is clear. Scalds are caused by
liquids—treat as you would for burns.

Mouth and throat burns are caused by hot gases, hot
liquids, or corrosive chemicals. Give sips of cold water to
cool. Swelling in the throat may affect breathing. Give
artificial respiration (Silvester method, see p.294) if
necessary. With eye burns, hold the eyelid open and pour
plenty of water over the eye to wash out chemicals. Tilt head
so that the chemical is not washed into mouth or nose.

Use lots of water to dilute or wash off corrosive chemicals and remove clothing. Do not try to neutralize acid with alkali or vice versa. Treat as you would for a burn. For electrical and lightning burns see the treatment on p. 292. Treat as you would for heat burns.

> Most burns will result in shock. Flooding extensive burns with cold water may increase shock, but that must be weighed against reducing tissue damage. Keep cooling for at least 10 minutes.

FRACTURES

Examine for broken bones before swelling complicates the task of locating the fracture and before touching or moving the casualty. Treat urgent injuries, such as asphyxia and bleeding, first. Immobilize before moving them, and finish treatment later.

There are two types of fractures: open (wound is open to fracture, or bone pushes through skin) and closed. In open fractures infection can gain access to bone. If limb is distorted, it must be straightened before splinting. It will hurt, so if the patient is unconscious do it right away.

SYMPTOMS
Severe pain, aggravated by movement of injured part.
Tenderness, even with only gentle pressure.
Swelling, with subsequent discoloration or bruising.
Deformity: apparent shortening of a limb, irregularity, unnatural movement—compare with unharmed limb.
A grating sound when the limbs are moved (do not move limbs deliberately to check for this).

HEALTH

If no medical help is expected, reduce closed fractures as soon as possible after an injury by applying traction (a slow, strong pull until the edges of a fractured bone are brought together), then splint and immobilize the whole length of the limb. Splints can be (pieces of wood, rolls of newspaper, ski poles, etc.) Separate the hard splint material from the skin with padding (moss is ideal), or pressure sores may develop.

If no splint is available, strap the injured limb to the body. Insert padding in natural hollows to keep it in position. Secure it above and below the fracture and below nearest joints. Tie with soft materials , using reef knots. Do not tie splints directly over injury or let knots press against limb. Check the circulation periodically.

Types of fractures

FRACTURE OF ARM BELOW ELBOW, OF HAND, OR OF FINGERS: Place the sling (e.g. long-sleeved sweater) between the arm and body. Immobilize from elbow to mid-fingers with padded splint. Take one arm of shirt behind head. Tie to other on opposite side to injury. Knot below the elbow to prevent slipping. This way the arm is elevated to prevent swelling.

FRACTURE AT THE ELBOW: *If the elbow is bent, support it in a narrow sling. Bind it across upper arm and chest. Check the pulse to ensure that the artery is not trapped. If there is no pulse, straighten the arm a little, and if there is still no pulse, urgent medical aid is required.*

If the elbow is straight, do not bend it. Place a pad in the armpit and strap the arm to the body or place padded splints on either side of the arm.

FRACTURE OF THE UPPER ARM: *Place a pad in the armpit, with a splint from shoulder to elbow on the outside of the arm and a narrow sling at the wrist. Bind the arm.*

FRACTURE OF THE SHOULDER BLADE OR CLAVICLE: *Make a sling to take the weight off the injured part and immobilize it with bandage across the arm and body.*

For fractures of the thigh or lower leg, apply a figure eight bandage, binding the feet and ankles of both legs.

FRACTURE OF THE HIP OR UPPER LEG: *Place a splint on the inside of the leg and another from the ankle to the armpit. Use a stick to push the tying bands under the hollows of the leg. If no splints are available, pad a folded blanket between the legs and tie the broken leg to the healthy leg.*

FRACTURE TO THE KNEE:
If the leg is straight, place the splint behind the leg. Apply a cold compress to the knee.

If the leg is bent, bring both legs together, place padding between calves and thighs, and strap it in those places. This is a temporary measure only. If rescue is unlikely, the leg must be made as straight as possible.

FRACTURE TO THE LOWER LEG: *Splint from above the knee to beyond the heel or pad between the legs and tie them both together (see fracture of the hip or upper leg, above).*

HEALTH

FRACTURE OF THE ANKLE OR FOOT:
A splint is not normally used. Elevate the foot to reduce swelling and immobilize it with a folded blanket strapped twice at the ankle and once under the foot. If it is a closed fracture, a shoe or boot will provide stability. Do not put weight on the foot.

FRACTURE OF THE PELVIS: Symptoms are pain in groin or lower abdomen. Pad between the thighs and tie at the knees and ankles. Place a pillow support below bent legs and strap the patient to a flat support (e.g. a door, stretcher) at shoulder, waist, and ankle. Alternatively, place the padding between the legs and bandage around feet, ankles, and knees, with two overlapping bandages over the pelvis.

FRACTURE OF THE SKULL: Symptoms include blood or watery fluid seeping from the ear or nose. Lay the victim in the recovery position, with the leaking side down. Lightly cover the ear with a sterile dressing and check breathing and the pulse. Immobilize.

FRACTURE OF THE SPINE: Symptoms include pain in the back and loss of sensation in the lower limbs. Ask casualty to move their fingers and toes and gently test for feeling. The patient must be immobilized—place soft, solid objects around the patient to prevent movement of the head or body.

HEALTH

FRACTURE OF THE NECK:
Immobilization is essential. Use a
cervical collar of rolled-up paper or a
towel folded to 4–5.5 inches
(10–14cm) wide to fit from top of
the sternum to jaw. Fold the edges to
make them narrower at the back than

the front. Overlap raound the neck and secure with a belt or tie.

SPRAINS

The tearing of tissues connected to a joint. Symptoms:
pain, swelling. Bathe with cold water, support with a
bandage (not too tight), elevate limb, and rest. Do not put
under painful stress, or you risk permanent damage. If you
must walk on a sprained ankle, keep boot on for support. If
in doubt whether a sprain or a break, treat as a fracture.

DISLOCATIONS

Symptoms: pain and obvious deformity, but no grating
sound. Muscle spasms fix thebone in position.

Types of dislocations

For a dislocated shoulder, take off your shoe, put your
foot in the casualty's armpit, and pull on the arm.

     A dislocated finger should be pulled then gently
released so that the bone slips back. Be very gentle with
the thumb. If it does not work the first time, leave it alone.

     If the jaw is dislocated, place a pad of cloth over the
lower teeth. Rest the head on a firm support and press
down on pads with your thumbs, rotating the dislocated
side of jaw backward and upward. It should snap into place.
Bandage around head and under jaw. Feed them soft foods.

HEALTH

SHOCK

Shock can kill. Act quickly to prevent it. Symptoms are:

Cold and clammy skin

Casualty is weak, dizzy, or faint

Shallow and rapid pulse

Casualty may be thirsty

Vomiting or unconsciousness

Skin is paler than normal, often grayish

Loss of color in the lips

Severe bleeding, loss of body fluids from severe burns, or prolonged vomiting or diarrhea commonly lead to shock. Other causes are electrocution and heart attacks.

Reassure the casualty and do not excite or move them more than is necessary. If they are conscious, lay them flat, with their legs elevated about 1 foot (30 cm). Loosen tight clothing. The priority is to encourage the supply of blood to the vital organs. Do not give them anything to eat or drink. Cover them to keep them warm, but do not add heat. Check breathing and pulse and treat injuries. If there is loss of consciousness, impaired breathing, or signs that vomiting may occur, place the casualty in the recovery position.

Stand by to give mouth-to-mouth resuscitation and cardiac compression. Shock can take a long time to pass. Encourage rest and do not move them unnecessarily. If you appear calm and in control, the patient will feel cared for and will respond. Never leave a shock victim on their own.

BANDAGING

A triangular bandage, with short sides not less than 3 feet (1 m) is a versatile dressing for slings and bandages.

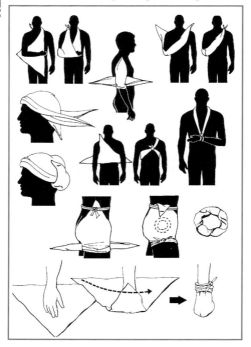

HEALTH

Bandages should be applied firmly enough to stop slipping, but not so tight that they cut into the flesh or interfere with circulation. Crepe bandages are the best, but any fabric will do. Keep bandages rolled up; unrolling them as you apply helps keep bandages smooth and even.

After applying a dressing (a pad of cotton wool covered with gauze in a sterile wrapping—if you must improvise, use very clean, nonfluffy material—and do not touch the pad when applying it), begin bandaging with a firm, oblique turn to anchor it. Each turn should overlap the previous one by two thirds, with the edges parallel. Tuck in the ends below the last layer and secure it with a safety pin or adhesive tape or tie it in a reef knot away from the wound.

> Never connect bandages with knots. Anchor separate strips by binding over a previously applied layer. Tie finishing knots over uninjured side or limb. Use knots that are easily untied and easily accessible.

MINOR AILMENTS

Even minor ailments can get bad if they are left untreated. Wash friction blisters, sterilize a needle, and pierce near the blister's edge. Gently press out any fluid, cover with a dressing and bandage. Earaches can be relieved by pouring drops of warmed, edible oil into the ear and plugging it with cotton wool. Toothaches are usually caused by an exposed nerve. Plug the cavity with pine tree resin: scar the tree trunk, soak up the gum that oozes out on cotton wool, and plug the hole in the tooth with it.

HEALTH

MOVING AN INJURED PERSON

Improvize a stretcher by passing two poles through pieces of sacking, heavy plastic, or clothing or use a door or tabletop. If no poles are available, roll in the sides of a blanket and use these rolls to get a grip. Test out an improvized stretcher before using it.

Loading a stretcher

A patient on a blanket can be lifted using the blanket. Other methods of lifting depend on the number of helpers. Agree on signals for synchronized movements.

WITH 4 PERSONS: C supports head and shoulders, D hooks their fingers with adjoining hands of B and C to aid with the lift. A, B, and C support, while D places stretcher in position. D helps lower the patient.

WITH 3 PERSONS: Place the stretcher at patient's head. C lifts at knees, A and B lock their fingers under shoulders and hips. Move casualty from the foot of the stretcher over it.

WITH 2 PERSONS: Both stand astride casualty. B links their arms beneath shoulders, A lifts with one hand under thighs, the other under knees. Both move forward to above the stretcher.

HEALTH

CASUALTIES WITH SPINAL INJURIES
Move only if in danger. Need three or four people. Do
not bend or twist. One person supports head and
neck, another holds shoulders. In the absence of a
stretcher, roll onto a blanket. Support head and torso.
If working alone, do not twist or turn casualty over. Pull
by shoulders if face down, by ankles if face up, in the
direction in which body is lying. On rough ground drag
from behind, pulling them by shoulders and resting the
casualty's head on your forearms.

Lifting on your own

Choose a method that you can sustain without dropping
the casualty. Lift a light casualty by the cradle method:
one arm under the thighs, the other under the armpit.
Alternatively, as long as the casualty's arms are not hurt,
use the crutch method: place and hold one of their arms
around your neck; put your arm around their waist,
grasping their clothing at the hip.

The fireman's lift can be used with an unconscious or
conscious casualty, but it is not suitable if the victim is
heavy.

*UNCONSCIOUS CASUALTY: Place them face down. Kneel at
head. Slide your hands under shoulders. Lift under the armpits
into a kneeling position, then to upright. Raise their right arm
with your left hand. Continue as for
conscious casualty (overleaf).*

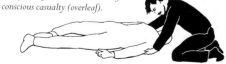

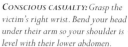

CONSCIOUS CASUALTY: *Grasp the victim's right wrist. Bend your head under their arm so your shoulder is level with their lower abdomen.*

Bend your knees, allowing the weight to fall across your shoulders. Place your right arm between or around

their legs.

Transfer their right wrist to your right hand and lift, taking the weight on your right shoulder.

Stand up and adjust the weight across your shoulders. The casualty is head-down—this is not suitable for facial or head injuries.

LIFTING WITH A SLING: *The best one-man-carry method for long distances.*

Make a continuous loop to act as a sling, wide enough not to cut into the casualty and long enough to go over your shoulders and twice across the victim's back. Place the sling beneath the victim's thighs and lower back so that the two loops protrude. Lie between the victim's legs and put your arms through the loops. Tighten the slack. Grasp the victim's hand and leg on the injured side.

Turn away from the injured side, rolling so that the victim lies on top. Adjust the sling to make the load comfortable and rise to a kneeling position (if the belt is loose or the load is insecure, return to the previous position and adjust). You should be able to proceed with both hands free.

HEALTH

EMERGENCY CHILDBIRTH

Labor can be precipitated by stress. Signs include lower backache, regular contractions, and a discharge of blood-stained mucus. This stage may last several hours; the second stage begins when contractions grow stronger and more frequent. Water may break at any time. Sterilize scissors or a knife and three 9 inch (20 cm) lengths of thread. Have plenty of hot water available. Helpers must be healthy (free of colds, infections, or sores) and should scrub their hands thoroughly for 4 minutes.

In the second stage the mother should adopt the most natural position, e.g. a supported squat, but she should not lie down. She should keep her knees pulled up, pulling them up farther as she bears down during contractions. If a bowel movement occurs, wipe her clean from front to back. She must stop pushing and pant the when baby's head appears. Tear any membrane that is covering the face. If the umbilical cord is around the baby's neck, ease it over the head or loop it over the shoulder. Support baby's head in palm of your hands; as shoulders appear, support body under armpits and lift toward mother's abdomen. Be prepared for the baby to be *very* slippery. Ensuring that no tension is put on the cord, place baby between or by mother's legs, head lower than body. If baby does not appear headfirst and delivery is held up for more than 3 minutes after shoulders emerge, pull very gently.

Clear the baby's mouth with a clean swab. Do not smack it. If it does not cry and isn't breathing, begin very gentle mouth-to-mouth resuscitation. When the baby cries, lay it by its mother's breast.

HEALTH

The third stage of labor is the delivery of the placenta (10–30 minutes after birth). When it is expelled and cord has stopped pulsating, the blood should flow out of the cord, into the baby. The cord will turn from blue to white. Tie a piece of sterile thread around it 6 inches (15 cm) from the baby's navel, then another at 8 inches (20 cm). First check that the tie is secure, or baby may lose blood. Sever cord between two ties with sterile scissors. Place a sterile dressing over the cut end. Leave for 10 minutes, then check there has been no bleeding. Tie a further thread 4 inches (10 cm) from baby. Wash the mother.

BITES

MAMMAL BITES: Danger from infections is the main risk. Antitetanus shots and rabies vaccines should be obtained before traveling. Rabies is not treatable without a vaccine and almost always fatal. Symptoms: irritability, dislike of light, violent aversion to water, and paralysis. Ensure that the victim does not transmit the disease to anyone else.

Clean all bites, washing for at least 5 minutes to remove any saliva. Then tend to bleeding, dress, and bandage it. Even if the bite heals, report it when you are rescued. You should be examined by a doctor.

SNAKE BITES: Most species inject venom very deeply. Do not consider sucking or cutting the wound. To prevent the poison from spreading, make the victim relax, apply pressure at the wound site, and immobilize affected part. Apply a bandage—not a tourniquet—above the bite and bandage down over the bite (e.g. for an ankle bite, start bandaging at the knee). This should apply a firm pressure,

HEALTH

but the limb should not darken or swell up. A splint will prevent flexing. If the bite is on the torso, apply pressure with wad of fabric. Put the wound in cool water, e.g. a stream, or use ice to cool it. Try not to move the victim. Check the pulse and breathing, stand by to give artificial respiration. (See also p. 342 ff.)

SPIDER BITES: Treat as you would for snakebites. A cold compress helps reduce pain (ice wrapped in cloth is ideal).

STINGS: Scorpions inject a powerful venom. Bee, wasp, and hornet stings may cause severe allergic reactions, especially if there are multiple stings. Bee stingers should be removed from the skin as quickly as possible by stroking the stinger with the side of a needle then extracting it with tweezers. Do not squeeze the poison sac as this will release more venom. Apply a cold compress.

GENERAL POISONING

Do not induce vomiting—it can do more harm than good. It is only suitable if poisonous berries have very recently been swallowed: gently put a finger to the back of the victim's throat. Never induce vomiting if corrosive substances, gasoline, or solvents are involved.

   Try to find out what has been swallowed. Burns around the mouth indicate that a caustic substance is involved. You must learn in advance the properties of chemicals to which you are exposed and appropriate remedies in cases of accidents. Keep the airway open: place the victim in the recovery position. Be prepared for vomiting, fits, or convulsions. If breathing stops, give artificial respiration, but avoid any traces of poison around the mouth.

HEALTH

Mix tea and charcoal—with milk of magnesia, if it is available. This antidote absorbs the poison in the system.

Some plants, e.g. poison ivy, poison sumac, and poison oak, cause skin irritations. Skin that has been in contact with the plant should be washed thoroughly with soap and water. Remove and wash clothing. Use alcohol to neutralize the oil left on the skin.

 If handling a plant produces a severe reaction, do not put your hand to your face or touch other parts of your body until it has been washed well. Rashes and swellings can interfere with breathing, vision, and urination.

GENERAL DISORDERS

Small digestive upsets are relatively insignificant, but symptoms that suggest more serious conditions should not be ignored. If food is adequate, the best treatment is to fast for a day and rest. Drink plenty of fluids.

Treat fevers with rest and aspirin and find its causes.

More serious, pneumonia is indicated by inflammation of the lungs with chills and fever, breathlessness, a cough with green-yellow phlegm or blood, and pain when breathing. Keep the patient warm and give them frequent sips of hot water.

DISEASES

Infectious diseases are caused by bacteria (e.g. cholera, dysentery, tuberculosis), viruses (colds, flu, measles), and rickettsias (e.g. typhus). Such contagious diseases are unlikely to occur unless you have brought them with you or catch them from humans that you encounter.

HEALTH

The survivor is more likely to be exposed to waterborne diseases or those carried by insects and animals. Tropical diseases are less familiar and will therefore be dealt with here in more detail. Where drugs are not available, treatment is mostly a matter of dealing with symptoms and making the patient comfortable.

Prevention is better than treatment. To avoid diseases:

Get all suitable immunization before traveling

Purify drinking water

Clean the hands when preparing or eating food

Wash and peel fruits

Sterilize eating utensils

Cover the body to reduce the risk of insect bites

Wash and smoke louse-ridden clothes

Wash the body, but avoid swallowing water

Bury excreta

Protect food and drink from flies and vermin

Isolate outbreaks of infectious diseases. Maintain contact with other members of the group to a minimum; boil all utensils used by the patient; cover cuts and sores against exposure to infectionz. Wash thoroughly after treating the patient. Avoid mucus from coughs and sneezes. Take extra care in disposing of the patient's feces where they cannot spread the infection or be disturbed.

Boil all water, even for brushing teeth. Cover wounds and avoid standing in water in areas that are at risk.

Worldwide diseases

LEPTOSPIROSIS: Spread by rodents and infected water. Causes a serious form of jaundice. Gains entry through cuts or sores or in contaminated drinking water.
Symptoms: *Jaundiced appearance, lethargy, fever.*
Treatment: *Procane penicillin and tetracycline.*

INFECTIOUS HEPATITIS: Passed on through infected feces or urine. Enters via contaminated water and through cuts in the skin.
Symptoms: *Nausea, loss of appetite, abdominal pain. Skin usually turns yellowish.*
Treatment: *Rest and good nursing are the only treatment.*

POLIOMYELITIS: Spread by contaminated drinking water.
Symptoms: *Paralysis.*
Treatment: *Hot packs on the muscles and good nursing.*

BACILLARY DYSENTERY: Spread by flies, contaminated water, and contact with feces containing the bacillus.
Symptoms: *Blood-streaked feces, sudden high temperature.*
Treatment: *Antibiotics, rest, and plenty of fluids to counter risk of dehydration due to the loss of body fluids.*

TYPHOID (ENTERIC) FEVER: Caused by a salmonella bacillus.
Symptoms: *Similar to dysentery, with headaches, abdominal pains, fever, loss of appetite, pains in the limbs, and delirium.*
Treatment: *Antibiotics. Innoculation will prevent it.*

CHOLERA: A threat anywhere in insanitary conditions.
Symptoms: *Vomiting, loss of pulse at the wrist, cold, clammy skin, and muscle cramps.*
Protection: *Can be obtained by regular innoculation with the cholera vaccine.*

HEALTH

WARM CLIMATE DISEASES

Waterborne diseases

SCHISTOSOMIASIS: Disease of the bowel or bladder caused by a microscopic worm endemic in parts of Africa, Arabia, China, Japan, and S. America. Enters the body through drinking infected water or through broken skin.
Symptoms: Irritation of the urinary tract.
Treatment: Niridazole in recommended doses.

HOOKWORMS: Gain entry through infected drinking water or penetrate bare skin (usually the feet). Larvae may cause pneumonia. Hookworms live in the intestine.
Symptoms: Anemia and general lethargy.
Treatment: Alcapar and Mintezol in recommended doses. A decoction of bracken is a powerful dewormer.

AMOEBIC DYSENTERY: Transmitted in contaminated water and uncooked food.
Symptoms: Fatigue, listlessness. May produce a higher temperature. Feces may be solid but will smell foul and carry blood and jellylike red mucus.
Treatment: Plenty of fluids, rest, and treatment with Flagyl.

Insectborne diseases

To reduce any risk, keep the skin covered, sleep under a mosquito net, use insect repellents, and do not camp near swamps or stagnant water. A course of tablets, begun before exposure, can protect against malaria.

MALARIA: Not restricted to the tropics. Transmitted through saliva of female anopheles mosquitoes. It kills over one million people per year in Africa alone.

HEALTH

Symptoms: A recurrent fever. Although they are sweating, patient feels intensely chilled and shivers violently. There are various strains with severe headaches, malaise, and vomiting accompanying the fever, leaving the patient weak and exhausted.

Treatment: A number of antimalarial drugs are available, including Larium, Paludrine, and now Malarone. Ask your doctor about which drug is most appropriate for your situation.

DENGUE (BREAKBONE FEVER): Spread by mosquitoes.

Symptoms: Rashes, headaches, fever, and extreme muscle and joint pains. Full recovery may take several weeks.

Treatment: Rest. There is no vaccine or cure.

YELLOW FEVER: Prevalent in Africa, South America.

Symptoms: Headaches, nosebleeds, nausea, and fever. Heartbeat may be slow. In severe cases: pain in the legs, back, and neck. Rapid liver damage may lead to jaundice and kidney failure.

Treatment: Rest and nursing. There is no effective drug. Obtain the vaccination before traveling.

TYPHUS: A group of infectious diseases that is usually spread by insects such as fleas, mites, and ticks.

Symptoms: Headaches, constipation, collapse, back pains, and coughing, followed by fever, mild delirium, and a rash of small red spots. There may also be a weak heartbeat.

Treatment: Antibiotics. There is also a vaccine available.

Small parasites that burrow benath the skin, e.g. larvae of warble fly, or the chigoe, should be removed before they can open up a route for further infections. Chigoes penetrate the skin of the feet or lower leg leaving red pinpricks in the skin. Remove creatures with a needle and apply antiseptic ointment to the affected area.

HEALTH

WARM CLIMATE AILMENTS

PRICKLY HEAT: Heavy sweating paired with rubbing by clothing produces blockages in the sweat glands.
Symptoms: *Uncomfortable skin irritation.*
Treatment: *Remove clothing, wash the body with cool water, and put on dry clothes. Drinking more liquid may make it worse. Antihistamines relieve discomfort.*

HEAT CRAMPS: Often first warning of heat exhaustion.
Symptoms: *Shallow breathing, vomiting, and dizziness.*
Treatment: *Rest in shade. Drink water with a pinch of salt.*

HEAT EXHAUSTION: Caused by exposure to heat and humidity. Can occur without direct exposure to the sun.
Symptoms: *Pale face, cold, clammy skin, weak pulse; with weakness, dizziness and perhaps cramps. Delirium or unconsciousness may follow.*
Treatment: *Treat as you would for cramps.*

HEATSTROKE: The most serious result of heat exposure.
Symptoms: *Hot, dry skin; flushed, feverish face, but sweating stops. Temperature rises, pulse is rapid and strong. Severe headache, often with vomiting. Unconsciousness may follow.*
Treatment: *Lay in shade, head and shoulders slightly raised. Remove outer clothing. Cool body by wetting underclothes with tepid (not cold) water and fanning. Do not fully immerse in water—sprinkle it over patient. Lay in a well-ventilated hollow. When consciousness returns, administer water to sip. When temperature returns to normal, replace clothing and keep warm.*
    Immersion in cold water is very dangerous, but in extreme cases where risk of death or brain damage outweighs shock, use this after initial cooling takes effect, lowering slowly into water.

Massage extremities to increase blood flow. Remove them from the water as soon as temperature falls. Cover patient if it plummets. You may need to cool and cover them several times before their temperature stabilizes.

COLD CLIMATE HAZARDS

Prolonged exposure to the cold is dangerous anywhere.

HYPOTHERMIA: Loss of temperature due to exposure. Brought on by exhaustion, inadequate clothing or shelter, lack of food, and lack of knowledge and preparation. Wet clothing or immersion in cold water will aggravate it, so will anxiety, stress, and injuries that immobilize.

Symptoms: Irrational behavior: sudden bursts of energy followed by lethargy. Slowing down of responses, sudden, uncontrolled fits of shivering. Loss of coordination. Headaches, blurred vision, and abdominal pains. Collapse or unconsciousness.

Treatment: Prevent further heat loss. Shelter from the elements. Replace wet garments with dry ones, one item at a time. Apply warmth (other bodies, warm rocks). Place warmth in pit of stomach, small of back, armpits, back of neck, wrists, and between thighs. Give warm fluids and sugary foods, but only if fully conscious. Do not administer alcohol. The patient is not cured when temperature returns to normal: recovery takes time.

If heat is lost rapidly—rewarm rapidly
If heat is lost slowly—rewarm slowly

FROSTBITE: Occurs when the skin and flesh freeze. Affects all exposed parts of the body and the regions farthest from the heart: hands, feet, and face. The first sign is often a prickly feeling, then waxy patches on the skin that feel numb (later turning hard, pebbly), and

HEALTH

HEALTH

painful, swelling, reddening, and blistering before
deadening and dropping off in the final stage.
*Prevention: Keep a constant lookout for signs: act at the first
appearance of waxy skin. Grimace to exercise the face, flex hands,
stamp feet. Never go out without adequate clothing. Avoid getting
wet. Never touch metal with your bare hands. Avoid spilling
gasoline on bare flesh in subzero temperatures.*
*Treatment: Frostnip only affects the skin: warm the affected
part (it will be painful when it is thawed out). Deep frostbite
should be gradually thawed out with warm water at around the
temperature that your elbow can comfortably bear. Do not rub it
with snow or expose it to an open fire. Protect the affected area
from further injuries. Advanced frostbite may form blisters that can
turn into ulcers. Do not burst the blisters and never rub the
affected part. Use "animal warmth" to warm gradually; severe pain
indicates that it has been warmed up too quickly.*

SNOW BLINDNESS: Temporary blindness. Can even occur in
bright, overcast periods with no direct sunlight.
*Symptoms: Eyes become sensitive to glare;s blinking and
squinting begins. Vision takes on a pink/red hue. Eyes feel gritty.*
*Treatment: Move into a dark place and blindfold the eyes. Apply
a cool, damp cloth to the forehead. The condition corrects itself.*

TRENCH FOOT: Occurs when feet are immersed or are
damp and cold for long periods. **Prevention:** *Keep the feet
dry, wear well-fitting boots, exercise the feet and legs.*
*Symptoms: Pins and needles, then numbness interspersed with
sharp pains. The feet appear purple with swelling and blisters.*
*Treatment: Dry the feet, but do not rub or damage the blisters.
Elevate the feet and keep them warm. Do not apply artificial heat.
Do not massage them. Rest and warmth are the cure.*

NATURAL MEDICINE

Natural remedies can be used when medical supplies are exhausted or to supplement your supply. Urine can be used as an antiseptic to wash out wounds. Maggots will keep a wound open and clean until better treatment can be given (make sure that they do not devour good tissues).

PLANT PREPARATIONS

Many modern drugs are derived from plants, but the processes are complex, and attempts to use such plants in treatments could be very dangerous. What follows is a list of plants and medical uses to which they can be put in simple preparations. Identify the plants carefully. As a general rule, plants are the most potent when they are in flower. Different parts may have different uses. Larger or stronger doses may do more harm than good.

TO MAKE AN INFUSION: Cut and crush a herb, pour boiling water over it, stir it, and leave to cool. There is no need to strain—herbs will sink to the bottom. If you can't boil water, use half the amount of cold water and stand vessel in the sun. Use a small handful of herbs 1 ounce (30g) to 1 pint (0.5 L) of water. If there is no sun or water, suck or chew leaves to extract the juices, then spit out the pulp.

TO MAKE A DECOCTION: Cut, scrape, and mash the roots. Soak in water (handful to 1.5 pints/85cc) for half an hour. Bring to a boil, simmer until liquid reduces by one third.

TO MAKE A POULTICE: Mash up the vroots, leaves, or the entire plant and make it into a flat pad. Add water if it is too dry. Apply to the affected part (stiff joints, sprains, abcesses) and cover with a large leaf. Bind it into position.

HEALTH

EXPRESSED JUICE: Reduce stem and leaves to a juicy mush by crushing it with your hands, rocks, or sticks. Squeeze the juice only into a wound and spread pulp around the infected area. Keep in place with a large leaf and bind it.

REMEDIES

STOPPING BLEEDING:

> **Puffball fungus**: *Packed as a poultice*
> **Plantain**: *Pounded leaves as a poultice*

CLEANING RASHES / SORES / WOUNDS: Use this externally to bathe 2 or 3 times a day or, if indicated, as a poultice

> **Burdock**: *Decoction of the roots; crushed raw roots and salt for animal bites*
> **Chickweed**: *Expressed juice of the leaves*
> **Comfrey**: *Decoction of the roots as a poultice*
> **Deadnettle**: *Infusion of the flowers and shoots*
> **Dock**: *Crushed leaves*
> **Elder**: *Expressed juice of the leaves.*
> **Oak**: *Decoction of the bark*
> **Scurvey grass**: *Crushed leaves*
> **Shepherd's purse**: *Infusion of whole plant, except roots, as poultice*
> **Silverweed**: *Infusion of the whole plant, except the roots*
> **Sorrel**: *Crushed leaves*
> **Tansy**: *Crushed leaves*
> **Watercress**: *Expressed juice*

FEVERS: These plants will induce perspiration to break a fever.

> **Elder**: *Infusion of the flowers and fruits*
> **Lime**: *Infusion of the flowers*

ACHES / PAINS / BRUISES: Use externally where indicated.

> **Birch**: *Infusion of the leaves*
> **Borage**: *Infusion of the whole plant, except the roots*
> **Burdock**: *Decoction of the roots*
> **Chickweed**: *Infusion of the whole plant, except the roots*

HEALTH

Comfrey: Decoction of the roots applied to swellings
Dock: Crushed leaves (bruises)
Mountain cranberry: Infusion of the leaves and fruits
Poplar: Infusion of the leaf buds
Sorrel: Crushed leaves applied to bruises
Tansy: Crushed leaves applied to bruises
Willow: Decoction of bark (headaches)

COLDS / SORE THROATS / RESPIRATORY COMPLAINTS:

Angelica: Decoction of the roots
Bilberry: Infusion of the leaves and fruits
Borage: Infusion of the whole plant, except the roots
Burdock: Decoction of the roots
Comfrey: Infusion of the whole plant
Horseradish: Raw roots
Lime: Infusion of the flowers
Nettle: Infusion of the leaves
Oak: Decoction of the bark; use to gargle
Plantain: Infusion of the leaves and stems
Poplar: Infusion of the leaf buds
Rose: Decoction of the rose hips
Willow: Decoction of the bark

STOMACHACHES:

Bilberry: Decoction of the fruits
Bracken: Infusion of the leaves
Bramble: Infusion of the leaves
Dandelion: Decoction of the whole plant
Horseradish: Infusion of the roots
Mint: Infusion of the whole plant, except the roots, with crushed charcoal

DIARRHEA: Take 2–3 times daily until the symptoms subside.

Bilberry: Decoction of the fruits
Bistort: Infusion of the whole plant, except the roots
Bramble: Infusion of the leaves or decoction of the fruits
Great burnet: Infusion of the leaves and shoots
Hazel: Infusion of the leaves

HEALTH

Mint: Infusion of the whole plant, except the roots
Mountain cranberry: Decoction of the fruits
Oak: Decoction of the bark
Plantain: Infusion of the leaves and stems
Silverweed: Infusion of whole plant, except roots

CONSTIPATION:

Barberry: Expressed juice of the fruits
Couch grass: Decoction of the root
Dandelion: Decoction of the whole plant
Elder: Expressed juice of the fruits
Rowan: Expressed juice of the fruits
Rose: Decoction of the rose hips
Walnut: Decoction of the bark

HEMORRHOIDS: Apply externally, 2—3 times a day.

Bilberry: Expressed juice of the fruits
Oak: Decoction of the bark
Plantain: Expressed juice
Poplar: Decoction of the leaf buds
Silverweed: Infusion of the whole plant, except the roots

EXPELLING WORMS:

Bracken: Infusion of the roots
Tansy: Infusion of the leaves and flowers, use sparingly in small amounts

SOME USEFUL HERBAL PREPARATIONS
Headaches: Willow leaves and bark make a decoction containing salicin, a constituent of aspirin.
Healing: The expressed juice of comfrey leaves aids tissue regrowth.
Strawberry roots contain a descaler to clean teeth.
Delphinium seeds can be crushed to treat head lice.
Birch bark can be distilled to produce a tar oil that soothes skin irritations.

TROPICAL MEDICINAL PLANTS

The following are a few of the plants that may be of use, but lacking accurate data on medicinal plants, you would do better to take medicines with you. Never experiment with plants that you cannot positively identify.

Key

● Habitat   ◆ Leaves   ▲ Height   ❖ Flowers

Copperleaf ● India, S.E. Asia ▲ 6.5–10 feet (2–3 m). ◆ Heart-shaped, often variegated: red, pink, and green. A decoction of the roots and leaves of this shrub is a laxative and restorative.

Alstonia ● India, Philippines, Indonesia, Australia. Boil the bark in water for a tonic to reduce fevers, relieve diabetes, and kill internal parasitic worms.

China bark (red bark). ● Tropics. ◆ Large trees, reddish-brown trunk. Decoction of quinine-containing bark for malaria.

Horseradish tree ● Tropics. Use the expressed juice of the roots and leaves to treat skin eruptions and inflammations.

Kibatalia arborea ● Asia. Tree. The bark, when cut, yields a latexlike sap. Use this sap, in small amounts, to treat worms.

Sida cordifolia ● India to Taiwan. An erect, downy annual. ▲ Up to 3 feet (1 m) tall. ◆ Oblong, toothed. ❖ Yellowish. Use an infusion of leaves for coughs/fevers. Seeds are mildly laxative.

Pergularia extensa ● Tropical Africa. Stems have stiff, spreading hairs. ◆ Broadly oval, up to 5 inches (15 cm) long. ❖ Small, greenish-white. Use tender leaves and shoots as a potherb or in a strong infusion to treat tapeworm and diarrhea. Use a poultice of the leaves on boils, abscesses, and wounds.

Baobab (see p.112). Use the leaves to encourage sweating to relieve colds, fevers, and asthma, and a decoction of the bark to suppress malaria.

Acacia (see p.112). Scrape the gum off the bark. Use this to treat worms and diarrhea.

HEALTH

MEDICINAL PLANTS

Key
● Habitat ◆ Leaves
▲ Height ❖ Flowers

General and antiseptics

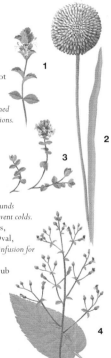

1 **Eyebright** ● Grassy places,
mountains in Eurasia. ▲ Up to 1 foot
(30 cm) ◆ Oval, often downy.
❖ White, tinged violet, or purple
veined with yellow spots. *Use a strained
infusion of the whole plant for eye infections.
Also eases hay fever, catarrh, and nasal
congestion.*

2 **Garlic** ● Temperate and tropical
parts. ◆ Long, straplike. ❖ Small,
pink or white, on top of tall stems.
The smell will lead you to them.
*The bulb is antiseptic. Use externally as
expressed juice diluted with water for wounds
and swellings. Eat garlic to treat and prevent colds.*

3 **Wild thyme** ● Dry, grassy places,
western Eurasia. Mat-forming. ◆ Oval,
small. ❖ Reddish-purple. *Use as an infusion for
coughs and colds or as potherb.*

4 **Figwort** ● Woods, clearings, scrub
in Eurasia. ▲ Up to 3 feet (90 cm).
◆ Pointed oval. ❖ Reddish-brown.
Square stems. *Apply as a decoction to
reduce swellings, sprains, and boils, to
dissipate blood clots, and to treat
hemorrhoids.*

HEALTH

Bleeding

1 **Self-heal** ● Dry, grassy waste places in Eurasia. Downy creeping plant. ◆ Pointed oval. ❖ Violet. *Use the expressed juice to stanch bleeding or as an infusion for internal hemorrhaging.*

2 **Geranium or cranesbill** ● Dry grassy wasteland. ◆ Deeply lobed. Hairy stem. ❖ Small, pink, 5-petaled. *Use expressed juice to stanch bleeding or as a decoction for internal hemorrhaging.*

3 **Marsh woundwort** ● Damp places, woods, and shady wasteland. ▲ Up to 3 feet (90 cm). Strong-smelling, hairy. ◆ Toothed, heart-shaped. ❖ White-blotched, dark pink to purple spikes. Similar species occur by woodland edges and shady waste places. *Use the expressed juice to stanch bleeding or as an infusion to bathe aches, sprains, and wounds.*

4 **Sanicle** ● Woodland in Eurasia. ▲ Up to 20 inches (50 cm) ◆ Hand-shaped, deeply lobed. ❖ Tiny, white or pink. *Use the expressed juice to stanch bleeding or as an infusion for internal hemorrhaging.*

5 **Myrtle or periwinkle** ● Woods, scrubland and rocky areas in Eurasia. ▲ Up to 20 inches (50 cm) ◆ Broad, spear-shaped. ❖ Large, blue-violet. *Use the expressed juice externally to stanch bleeding.*

HEALTH

Intestinal problems

1 **Mountain avens** ● Mountainous rocky, and northern arctic areas. Resembles a creeping wild strawberry ◆ Well-lobed, paler below. ❖ Large, white, with yellow stamens. *Use an infusion of the stems, leaves, and flowers for diarrhea or to gargle.*

2 **Balm** ● Grassy areas in warmer parts of Eurasia. ▲ Up to 2 feet (60 cm). ◆ Toothed, oval, green-yellow. ❖ Small, white, occurring at leaf bases. *Use an infusion of whole plant for fevers and nausea. Can also be used to ease painful menstruation.*

3 **Water mint** ● Near freshwater. ▲ Up to 32 inches (80 cm). ◆ Aromatic, hairy, toothed, pointed oval. ❖ Clusters, pink. *Use an infusion of the leaves for diarrhea, and use it heated to induce perspiration in fevers. If it is too strong, the infusion becomes emetic. Similar mints are also effective.*

4 **Elm** Tall trees ◆ Large, oval, toothed. Green, disk-shaped fruits. Often suckers at the base of the trunk. *Use decoction of bark for diarrhea and skin eruptions.*

HEALTH

5 **Cleavers** or **yard grass**
● Widespread on moist, woody, and waste lands. Straggling with long, prickly stems. ◆ Narrow, prickly.
❖ Small, white. *Use an infusion to ease constipation. Give frequent doses, mixed with marshmallow for cystitis.*

6 **Agrimony** ● Dry, grassy places. ▲ Up to 3 feet (90 cm). Downy stem. ◆ Toothed, spear-shaped leaflets. ❖ Yellow, on a tall spike. *Use an infusion of the whole plant for constipation and an acidic stomach. Frequent small doses for cystitis.*

7 **Lesser celandine**
● Wet woodland, damp areas.
▲ Up to 8 inches (20 cm). ◆ Shiny, dark green, heart-shaped.
❖ Yellow. *Apply the expressed juice externally for hemorrhoids; do not confuse with its poisonous relative, the buttercup.*

8 **Solomon's seal** ● Woods or scrubland. Small, patch-forming, with arching stems. ❖ Tube-shaped, green-white. *Use a decoction of the roots externally for hemorrhoids and bruises. Infusion for nausea. When boiled, roots set hard as a makeshift splinting agent. An infusion or poultice of the powdered roots eases bruising. Berries are poisonous.*

HEALTH

Fevers, coughs, and colds

1 **Camomile** ● Grassy places in Eurasia. Aromatic, creeping. ◆ Finely dissected ❖ Daisylike. *Use an infusion of whole plant for fevers, headaches, migraines, and colds or an expressed juice of the flowers for aches and strains. Has a calming influence.*

2 **Coltsfoot** ● Bare or waste ground from the late winter. ◆ Heart-shaped. ❖ Large, yellow, dandelion-like. Asparagus-like stems. *Use an infusion of the leaves for colds and coughs.*

3 **Lungwort** ● Mixed woods and scrub in Eurasia. ▲ Up to 1 foot (30 cm). ◆ Downy, pale-spotted, spear-shaped. ❖ Bell-shaped, pink or purplish-blue. *Use an infusion of the whole plant for chest complaints and diarrhea. For coughs use it with equal parts of coltsfoot.*

4 **Horehound** ● Dry scrubland in Eurasia. Thyme-scented, downy; squarish stems. ▲ Up to 20 inches (50 cm) ◆ Roundish, crinkly, greenish-white. ❖ White, in whorls. *Use an infusion of whole plant for chills and respiratory disorders; oil expressed from the leaves soothes earaches. A good cough remedy for infants. In large doses it is a laxative.*

5 **Yarrow** ● Grassy places. Downy, aromatic. ▲ Up to 2 feet (60 cm). ◆ Dissected, feathery, dark green. ❖ White or pink, tiny. *Use an infusion of the whole plant, but not the roots, for colds and fevers. Hastens the clotting of blood in an injury and reduces blood pressure and bleeding in hemorrhoids.*

6 **Musk mallow** ● Grassy, scrubby places. ▲ Hairy stem up to 2 feet (60 cm). ◆ Deeply divided. ❖ Large, pink, 5-petaled. Widespread, many varieties. *Use as marshmallow (below).*

7 **Tree mallow** ● Rocky coastal areas Europe to Asia Minor. ▲ Up to 9 feet (3 m). Hairy stem, woody at the base. ◆ Ivy-shaped. ❖ Pink-purple, streaked with darker purple. *Use as marshmallow (below).*

8 **Marshmallow** ▲ Up to 3 feet (90 cm). Downy gray. ◆ Large lobed. ❖ Pale pink. *Use an infusion of whole plant for chest complaints or one of roots to relieve giddiness from loss of blood and to clean wounds. Rub insect bites with bruised leaves; boil leaves as a poultice for skin eruptions.*

9 **Great mullein** ● Dry, warm grassy places. ▲ Up to 6 feet (2 m). Covered in pale, woolly down. ◆ Large, spear-shaped. ❖ Yellow, 5-petaled, in a dense spike. *Use an infusion of flowers and leaves for coughs and chest complaints or a decoction of roots to gargle. Powder the flowers for a pain-relieving tea.*

10 **Saint-John's-wort** ● Open woods, grassland. ▲ Up to 2 feet (60 cm). ◆ Small, oblong, translucently spotted. ❖ Golden-yellow flower that exudes a red juice when crushed. *Use an infusion of whole plant for colds and chest complaints.*

HEALTH

BITES AND STINGS

*These creatures are not a major
problem, but they should be
treated with respect.*

1 **Scorpion** ● Tropical/subtropical
regions. Lives under tree bark,
rocks, etc. Color varies from yellow to
brown or black. Most are nocturnal.
Cornered or crushed scorpions may
sting repeatedly. *The venom is neuro-
toxic, causing respiratory or cardiac
problems. It is rarely fatal in adults.*

2 **Brown recluse** or **fiddleback spider**
● Asia, U.S., S. America, Europe.
Brown with a "violin" mark on center of
its midsection. *Bite causes a burning sensation
at first, then pain increases, and the wound turns
red and blisters. May be fatal if the kidneys
are affected. Can lead to amputation
if it is untreated.*

3 **Black widow spider**
● Warm areas, worldwide. Small, dark,
recognizable by its red, yellow, or white
hourglass-shaped markings on its
abdomen. *Bites cause dull pain in the
limbs, chest, and abdomen. Nausea,
cramps, and vomiting follow. Fatal in children.*

4 **Funnel–web spider** ● Australia. Small, black
spider. Spins funnel-shaped web. *Fangs
can penetrate through clothing. A bite can
kill an adult in 90 minutes.*

5 **Tarantula** Large, hairy spider.
Despite its menacing appearance,
the poison is mild and only causes skin irritation.

6 **Centipede** ● Worldwide, under
stones, in piles of wood, and damp
places. Most are small and harmless, but
some tropical and desert kinds may
reach up to 1 foot (30 cm). Their feet have
sharp claws that can puncture skin
and cause infections. Some species'
bites cause swellings and infections.
*Do not swat them with bare hands. Brush them
off in the direction they are moving.*

7 **Hornet** ● Swarms guard their nests ferociously.
Very aggressive; the killing of a single worker
can disturb the whole colony. They will chase you
over great distances, inflicting numerous stings.
Avoid them. *Painful sting—several at once
could be fatal.*

8 **Tick** ● Common in tropics. Flat-
bodied and round. *Do not pull them off: the head will
remain and cause an infection. Use heat, gasoline, alcohol
or hot water to make it drop off.*

9 **Leech** ● Jungles and moist areas.
Blood-sucking, wormlike creature.
It waits, threadlike, on vegetation before
attaching itself to a victim. *Do not pull them off:
remove them with fire or a pinch of salt.
Leeches often carry infections.*

10 **Vampire bat** ● Central and
S. America. Small, nocturnal, sucks
the blood of sleeping victims. *Bites may
carry rabies. Stay covered up at night in these areas.*

HEALTH

POISONOUS SNAKES: SAFETY RULES

Do not approach, provoke, or handle snakes—even if they seem to be dead. Some only move to strike when prey is closeby—and they can strike faster than you can!

Watch where you step: after eating and when they are shedding skin, snakes are sluggish, and a well camouflaged snake can be easily stepped on.

Look closely before parting bushes or picking fruits. Some snakes are arboreal.

Stay calm: do not move suddenly or corner a snake. Back off slowly. Most snakes will be eager to escape.

Do not put hands or feet in places you can't see. Use tools or sticks, not hands, to turn over logs and rocks.

Wear solid boots.

Check your bedding, clothes, and backpacks before putting them on—snakes may use them as shelter.

If you have to kill a snake, use a long stick to make a single, chopping blow to the back of its head. Make it effective the first time—a wounded snake is very dangerous.

Not every snake is poisonous, nor do poisonous species always inject venom when they bite. The effects of bites vary depending on age, health, and fitness of victim. Most bites are on the arms or unprotected legs.

Spitting snakes: A few cobras spit poison as well as bite. This is not dangerous, unless the poison reaches an open cut or the eyes. If it does, wash it out immediately with water or, in an emergency, with urine.

What to do if you are bitten by a snake: see pp.319–320

HEALTH

POISONOUS SNAKES

North and South America

1 **Rattlesnake** Chunky body, wide head. The rattle at end of tail is usually, but not always, sounded as a warning. Widespread in U.S. and Mexico. The largest are the various diamondbacks, with distinctive blotches. 18 inches–7 feet (4.5–21 m). *Very dangerous.*

2 **Copperhead** Stout body, buff or orange-brown with rich brown bands and a coppery-red head. Mostly in eastern U.S. 24–36 inches (60–90 cm) long. Fairly timid, it vibrates its tail if it is angry. *Bites are rarely fatal.*

3 **Water moccasin (cottonmouth)** Thick, brown or brown-olive body, yellowish belly, sometimes blotched. The inside of its mouth is white. 24–54 inches (60–130 cm) long. Aquatic, found in or by freshwater in the southern U.S. *Belligerent—do not annoy it! Victims may suffer tissue damage that necessitates amputation.*

4 **Cascabel** or **tropical rattlesnake** Diamond-shaped marks, two dark stripes on the neck, and rattle on the tail. 5–6 feet (1.5–2 m) long. Nocturnal. Dry areas; S. and Central America. *Aggressive, one of the world's most dangerous snakes.*

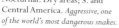

HEALTH

5 **Fer-de-lance** Brown with paler geometric markings. 4–6 feet (1.25–2 m) long. Various related species in S. and Central America. Some are arboreal. *The cause of many deaths. They tend to loop their bodies before striking.*

6 **Bushmaster** Large-headed, pink-brown with dark brown triangles. 6–8 feet (2–2.6 m) long. Nocturnal. Lowland forests in Central and S. America. Often found in burrows. *Vicious when cornered, they are one of the most feared of all New World snakes.*

7 **Coral snake** Slender, strikingly colored with bands of black and red, yellow and white. Southern U.S. to S. America. Similar species in S.E. Asia. 18–35 inches (45–90 cm) long. *Small-mouthed and reluctant to bite, but deadly.*

Europe

1 **Adder** The only poisonous snake of N. Europe. Found on heaths, moors, and in open areas. Olive-gray to reddish-brown with a zigzag pattern. 12–30 inches (30–75 cm) long. *Timid, but will strike quickly and repeatedly if alarmed. Bite is rarely fatal.*

Africa and Asia

1 **Puff adder** Thick-bodied, large-headed, and short-tailed. 35–51 inches (90–130 cm) long. Straw-colored with darker markings. Found in savannas and semiarid areas, often near water, Africa and Arabian Peninsula. *Very poisonous —bite causes extensive internal bleeding.*

2 **Saw-scaled viper** Rough-scaled, pale reddish to sandy-brown with darker markings and light blotches. 16–26 inches (40–55 cm) long; in arid areas from North Africa to India. *Vicious; causes many fatalities.*

3. **Russell's viper** Brownish, with three rows of spots formed of white-bordered black rings with a reddish-brown center. 40–50 inches (1–1.25 m). Found in most areas from Pakistan east to Taiwan. *Responsible for the majority of viper bites in the area. Highly venomous.*

4 **Malay pit viper** Fawny, reddish, or gray marked with geometric patterns, the belly is yellowish or spotted greenish-brown. 24–32 inches (60–80 cm) long. S.E. Asia and Indonesia. *Bites are common. This snake has many relatives in the area, so avoid any that resemble it.*

1 ☠
2 ☠
3 ☠
4 ☠

HEALTH

5 **Cobra** When it is alarmed, it is recognizable by its raised head and spreading hood. Common, especially in rocky and semiarid areas of Asia andMiddle East to Far East. 5–6 feet (1.5–2 m) long. *Highly toxic venom.*

6 **Mamba** Small-headed, very slender, usually with large green or grayish scales. 5–7 feet (1.5–2.1 m) long; in Africa south of the Sahara, usually in trees. The large black mamba is mostly terrestrial. *Often quick to strike, black mambas deliver large doses of venom that affect the brain and heart. Bites are fatal in almost all untreated cases.*

7 **Boomslang** Very slender, varying from green to brown or black. 4–5 feet (1.3–1.5 m) long. Hard to spot, lives in trees in the savannas of Africa, south of the Sahara. *Highly venomous; it inflates its throat when it is alarmed.*

8 **Krait** Small-headed, some have black and white or black and yellow bands. 3–5 feet (90–150 cm) long. In open and forest areas, from India to Indonesia. Nocturnal. *Slow to strike, but its venom is especially powerful. Bite is almost painless. Symptoms may take several hours to develop, by which time it may be too late. Can be fatal.* Its ocean-dwelling relative, the banded sea krait, is found in the Bay of Bengal, off Japan, and around the coasts of Australia and New Zealand. The venom is twice as toxic as that of a cobra.

HEALTH

Australasia

Of the 23 most poisonous snakes in the world, 20 are Australian, including all of the top ten.

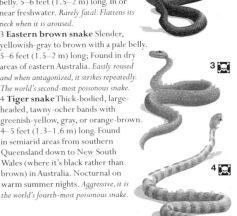

1 **Death adder** Thick-bodied, brownish, reddish, or gray with darker banding. 18–24 inches (45–60 cm) long. In sandy areas of much of Australia, Papua New Guinea, and some nearby islands. Well camouflaged. *Highly venomous.*

2 **Australian blacksnake** Slender, blue-back with a bright red belly. 5–6 feet (1.5–2 m) long. In or near freshwater. *Rarely fatal. Flattens its neck when it is aroused.*

3 **Eastern brown snake** Slender, yellowish-gray to brown with a pale belly. 5–6 feet (1.5–2 m) long; Found in dry areas of eastern Australia. *Easily roused and when antagonized, it strikes repeatedly. The world's second-most poisonous snake.*

4 **Tiger snake** Thick-bodied, large-headed, tawny-ocher bands with greenish-yellow, gray, or orange-brown. 4–5 feet (1.3–1.6 m) long. Found in semiarid areas from southern Queensland down to New South Wales (where it's black rather than brown) in Australia. Nocturnal on warm summer nights. *Aggressive, it is the world's fourth-most poisonous snake.*

HEALTH

5 **Taipan** Uniformly light to dark brown with yellowish-brown on its sides and belly. Found from the Kimberley Plateau through Arubaland to Queensland. Up to 11 feet (3.5 m) long. *Ferocious when provoked. The world's third-most poisonous snake.* Its relative, the western taipan or small-scaled snake, is considered to be the most lethal land snake in the world.

6 **Yellow-bellied sea snake** One of the most widely distributed of all sea snakes, it averages 28–35 inches (72–88 cm) long. Like most other sea snakes, it is found in the Indian and Pacific oceans. Some sea snakes are partially terrestrial, living in estuaries and coastal swamps. *The highly toxic venom of the yellow-bellied sea snake causes respiratory paralysis. Can be fatal.*

LIZARDS

1 **Gila monster** Large, rounded head, thick, chunky body, short, stumpy tail and brightly patterned in yellow. Found in the deserts of Arizona, Mexico, and nearby areas. 15–18 inches (37–45 cm) long. *The bite is poisonous but only likely when it is handled.*

2 **Beaded lizard** Resembles the Gila monster, but it is darker and larger, with a narower tail and spots rather than a mottling of color; in a few arid parts of Mexico and Central America. *Docile, but the bite is poisonous. Do not handle.*

CROCODILES AND ALLIGATORS

HEALTH

Crocodiles and alligators are amphibious, living on the banks of lakes, streams, and swamps. Not all species are considered dangerous, but don't take any chances.

Most float almost submerged with only their eyes and nostrils breaking the surface of the water. They are lazy creatures, but they will attack large mammals, including humans, pulling their prey beneath the surface to drown them. On land, despite their short legs, they are capable of considerable speed over short distances. They mostly hunt at night, sunning themselves during the day.

Do not swim, especially at night, in crocodile or alligator areas and never during the rainy season (when most documented attacks have occured).

When in crocodile country, stick to "safe" areas. Do not allow children to go near the water or roam unsupervised, do not clean fish near the water, and do not go near nests or groups of baby crocodiles—the mother may not be faraway.

American alligator Southeastern U.S. (Florida and Louisiana). Average length: 13 feet (4 m).

African crocodile Throughout tropical Africa (including offshore islands) in saltwater and freshwater. Up to 16 feet (5 m).

Saltwater crocodile or **estuarine crocodile** India, Malay Archipelago, Australia, in coastal rivers and swamps as well as in saltwater. Grows up to 23 feet (7 m). An infamous man-eater.

Mugger (Marsh crocodile) St ill common in parts of India (and considered sacred). Up to 10 feet (3 m) in length.

Black caiman Amazon and Orinoco basins. Largest of the caimans, it is big enough to pose a threat to humans.

HEALTH

DANGEROUS WATER CREATURES

Rivers

1 **Electric eel** Native to the Orinoco and Amazon river systems of S. America. 7 feet (2 m) long and 8 inches (20 cm) thick. Rounded body, olive to black, pale belly. Often prefers shallow water. *The shock from a large one can be 500 volts, enough to knock a person off their feet and pose a threat to swimmers.*

2 **Piranha** Orinoco, Amazon, and Paraguay river systems of S. America. Vary in size, up to 20 inches (50 cm) long. All are deep-bodied and thickset, with large jaws and razor-sharp, interlocking teeth. *Can be very dangerous, especially in the dry season when the water levels are low.*

Seas and rivers

3 **Stingray** A danger in shallow waters worldwide. Very variable, but all have the distinctive ray shape. *Venomous spines in the tail can inflict severe injuries. Amputation or death may result.*

Saltwater

4 **Rabbitfish** or **spinefoot** Mostly found on reefs in the Indian and Pacific oceans. 10–12 inches (25–30 cm) long. Edible, but with sharp spines in most fins. *Venomous. Handle with care.*

HEALTH

1 **Tang** or **surgeonfish** Found in all tropical waters, where they often form large schools. 8–10 inches (20–25 cm) long. Deep-bodied, small-mouthed, colorful. *Small venom glands in the dorsal spines, but danger comes from the razor-sharp tail, which in some species open like a switchblade*

2 **Toadfish** Found in tropical, subtropical, and temperate waters. 2.75–4 inches (7–10 cm) long. Dull-colored and large-mouthed. Lie buried in sand. *Sharp, very poisonous spines on side of head.*

3 **Scorpion fish** or **zebrafish** Found on reefs in the tropical Indian and Pacific oceans. 4–8 inches (10–20 cm) long. Very variable, but usually reddish with long, wavy fin rays and spines. *A sting is intensively painful. Heart failure may result.*

4 **Stonefish** Found in tropical Indo-Pacific waters. 16 inches (40 cm) long. Their drab colors and lumpy shape make them difficult to see. *When stepped on, their dorsal spines inject venom that is agonizingly painful, causing convulsions and paralysis. Recovery may take months, and stings are sometimes fatal.*

HEALTH

*The sharks shown here account for most human casualties
(see pp. 268–269).*

1 **Great white shark** Cold temperate to tropical waters;
common off southern Africa, N. America and southern Australia
and New Zealand. Up to 23 feet (7 m) long, gray above, white
below, thick-bodied; black eyes, a stubby conical snout.
2 **Mako shark** Common in the temperate seas of Australia, New
Zealand, and South Africa. Up to 13 feet (4 m) long; sturdy body;
gray to blue-black with a white belly.
A fast swimmer, it is capable of leaping 18 feet (6 m) out of the water.

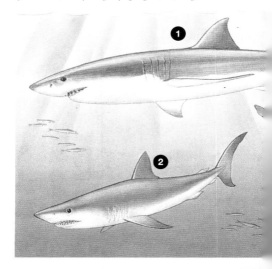

3 **Tiger shark** Common in tropical and subtropical oceans. 10–16 feet (3–5 m) long; short snout, long tail; grayish-brown back, cream belly. *Powerful and aggressive.*

4 **Hammerhead shark** Tropical and subtropical waters. 13–20 feet (4–6 m) long; distinctive hammer-shaped head. *Generally timid, but unprovoked attacks have occurred in shallow waters.*

PROTECTION AGAINST SHARKS: If you have shark repellent, follow the manufacturer's instructions. It may not be fully effective, but even so, only use it if the situation is very grave. Repellent soon dissipates in the water and becomes ineffective. Choose your moment well, since you can only use it once.

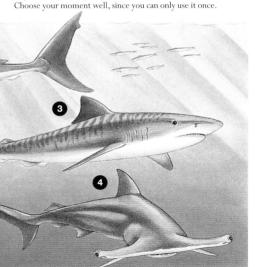

HEALTH

OTHER SEA CREATURES

1 **Portuguese man-of-war** Mostly subtropical, it is common in the Gulf Stream. Especially common in waters with high salinity, e.g. those around Australia and Florida. Floating bladder may only be 6 inches (15 cm) long, but the tentacles with their nematocysts can stream out for 40 feet (15 m). *Stings are very painful and may cause breathing and swimming difficulties. Even dead ones can sting.*

2 **Blue-ringed octopus** Small, sometimes only fist-sized. Found in shallow waters and pools off Australia. Venom causes swelling, dizzine,s and respiratory paralysis. *Apply artificial respiration. Treat all tropical reef octopuses with caution.*

3 **Cone snail (conidae)** Subtropical and tropical gastropod with a venomous, harpoonlike barb that pokes through the narrow end of the shell. Varying shell patterns. *Do not touch! Can cause temporary paralysis and breathing difficulties, leading to death within 6 hours.*

4 **Auger** or **terebra** Found in temperate and tropical seas, it has a stinging barb, much thinner and longer than that of the cone snail. *The sting is not as serious as the cone snail's, but do not eat it.*

HEALTH

5 **Weeverfish** Tapered, dull-colored,
1 foot (30 cm) long. Lies buried in
the shallow, sandy bays along the
coasts of Europe south to west Africa
and the Mediterranean. *Venomous
spines on the back and gills cause disabling
pain. Soothe it by applying very
hot water. Possible risk of secondary infections
and gangrene. Can be fatal.*

Poisonous to eat

1 **Porcupine fish** Found in
all shallow, tropical waters.
20–24 inches (50–60 cm) long.
Varieties differ somewhat in appearance,
but when they are alarmed, they all inflate
into a spiny ball. *The flesh is poisonous.*

2 **Puffer fish** Found in tropical
and warmer temperate waters,
a few types found in rivers in S.E.
Asia and tropical Africa. Stout-
bodied, rounded, 6–30 inches
(15–75 cm) long. Most types have
spines; when alarmed, they puff
into a ball. *Their blood, liver, and
gonads are poisonous; even a tiny
quantity of the poison can kill.*

3 **Triggerfish** Found in huge
varieties, mostly in shallow,
tropical seas. Deep-bodied,
compressed, usually under
24 inches (60 cm), with very
large, stout dorsal spines.
*Many types are poisonous to eat.
Avoid them all.*

HEALTH

SOME OTHER DANGEROUS SEA CREATURES

The sea wasp (box jellyfish)—a cube-shaped jellyfish 10 inches (25 cm) across—has clusters of tentacles at the corners up to 30 feet (9 m) long. Venom can be fatal. Avoid all jellyfish streamers, even when they are washed up on the beach.

Many fish with dangerously sharp spines are hard to detect, except close up. The spines usually occur on the back, but they may also be on fins on the side of the fish. Even a small spine can inflict a bad prick with the consequent risk of an infection. Large spines—and some spiny catfish grow as large as a man—are as effective as stiletto knives. Wade/step with caution.

Sea urchins can also inflict painful injuries, and sea anemones can sting.

Toadfish, stonefish, and scorpion fish (see p. 351) are edible. If you catch one, strike it on the head and only handle it when it is dead, and then with great care.

POISONOUS TO EAT

Many inshore fish, living in reefs and lagoons, are poisonous to eat. Most of these are confined to the tropics, but wherever you are be wary of eating any fish that you cannot positively identify.

Some fish that are otherwise good to eat are inedible when they are taken from reefs and lagoons, where they will have absorbed poisonous substances.

The most poisonous types, such as puffer fish, usually have rounded bodies with hard, shell-like skins that are covered in bony plates and spines. They also commonly have parrotlike mouths, small gill openings, and either lack pelvic fins or only have a small one.

DISASTER STRATEGIES

Accidents and isolation are not the only causes of a survival situation. Many natural and man-made forces can produce disasters in which your survival skills and strategies will come into use.

PREDICTING DISASTERS

Meteorological stations around the world study weather conditions 24 hours a day and play a major role in warning about disasters. Monitor weather broadcasts for advance warnings of severe weather conditions and disasters such as flooding, hurricanes, volcanic eruptions, and earthquakes.

DROUGHT

In temperate regions, if rainfall drops much below the average, periodic drought may be produced. The resulting death of vegetation causes deprivation all the way through the food chains that are based upon it. If the drought becomes severe, dead and dying animals may pollute what waterever supplies still remain.

Risk of fires

The corpses of dead animals should be buried in deep graves. Dry ground can be very hard, but burying is the best way to remove these possible sources of infections. The bodies could be burned, but since drought leaves everything tinder-dry, a fire could easily get out of hand and, without any water to check the flames, fire spreads rapidly. If you must have a fire, dig down to bare earth and keep the fire small and attended at all times.

DISASTER STRATEGIES

Hygiene

Lack of water for washing and sanitation poses a health risk. Sweating will help keep pores open and free of dirt, but even when you need all available water for drinking, try to clean your hands after defecation and before preparing food. Make a latrine near camp (see pp. 195–196).

Store and conserve water

If a monsoon does not come, or a hot, dry summer causes parching of the earth, take precautions by storing as much water as possible and using it wisely. Keep it covered and shaded to avoid evaporation.

Dig a pit for a storage cistern in a shady spot, avoiding tree roots. Line it with a polyethylene sheet or with cement if it is available (but don't fill it up until the cement has had a chance to dry thoroughly). If there is clay in the area, dig a pit and line it with clay. If the clay or concrete is built into a partial dome, it will help keep the contents cool and leave a smaller opening to keep covered.

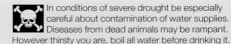
In conditions of severe drought be especially careful about contamination of water supplies. Diseases from dead animals may be rampant. However thirsty you are, boil all water before drinking it.

Never waste water. Water that is used for cooking can later be used for washing.

Boil all drinking water. If a well runs dry, you may gain more water by digging deeper, but the farther you dig, the more you deplete the water stored in the earth.

Try to eat foods with a high moisture content (such as fruit) and which require little preparation or clean up afterward.

Flies may be a serious problem—ensure that all foodstuffs are covered. Protect your supplies from dust, which may become a hazard as the topsoil is blown away.

 When nature is disturbed by a severe drought, animals act abnormally. Crazed by thirst, normally docile creatures may attack you.

FIRE

The best protection from a fire is prevention. Many fires are caused by carelessness with lit cigarettes and burning matches. The sun shining through a piece of glass can start a blaze in a dry season.

FOREST FIRES

If you are present where a fire starts (or where a campfire accidentally spreads) in woodland, heath, or grassland, your first action should be to smother it.

The first sign of an approaching forest fire will be the smell of smoke. Then you will probably hear the fire before you see the flames. You may notice unusual animal behavior before you realize the cause.

Escape route

If you are caught in an area where a fire is raging, and when it is too late to put it out yourself, do not immediately flee—unless the fire is so close that there is no choice.

DISASTER STRATEGIES

Even though you may feel that clothing hampers your movement, do not discard it, as it will shield you from the full force of the radiated heat.

Smoke will indicate the direction of the wind—the fire will be traveling the fastest in that direction. If the wind is blowing away from you, toward the fire, move into the wind. Head for any natural firebreak—such as a swathe through the trees, where the flames should be stopped. A river is the best break—even if the flames can leap it, you will be reasonably safe in the water. In forestry plantations look for the firebreaks.

> Do not run wildly. Stop and think. Choose your escape route. Check the surrounding terrain and the wind direction to assess the possible spread of the fire.

If the wind is blowing toward you, the fire is likely to travel quicker—and the flames can leap a larger gap. Fire travels faster uphill, so do not head for high ground. Try to go around the fire if you can, but some forest fires burn on a front that is several miles wide, making it impossible. If you cannot either skirt or outdistance the blaze, take refuge in a large clearing, deep ravine, watercourse, or gully.

Going to the earth

If you can partially immerse yourself in a creek, that's the best bet. However, if there is no natural break or gully in which to shelter and the fire is too deep to think of running through it, you may have to seek the protection of the earth itself.

People have survived fires by digging themselves in and covering themselves with earth, allowing the fire to burn over the top of them. The risk is great, not just from heat, but from suffocation: fire burns up oxygen.

Scrape out as much of a hollow as you can, clearing away grass and foliage and throwing the earth on to a coat or cloth if you have one. Lie face down and pull the cloth over you with its earth covering. Cup your hands over your mouth and nose and breathe through them. This won't increase the amount of oxygen, but it will cool down and filter the very hot air and sparks, which can damage the respiratory system. Try to hold your breath as the fire passes over you.

STAY IN A VEHICLE

Don't try to drive through thick smoke. If you are caught in a fire while in a vehicle, park in a clear area. Pull off the road, but don't risk getting stuck. Turn on the headlights and stay inside the car. Wind the windows tightly shut. Turn off the ventilation system and seal the air vents. The car will give you some protection from the radiant heat. It is possible to survive by staying in a vehicle until the glass begins to melt, by which time the fire will have moved beyond you. There is the danger of a gas tank exploding but, if the fire is intense, your chances are much better inside the vehicle than outside of it.

Fighting a forest fire

In forestry plantations you should see racks of fire-beating equipment at intervals along the main routes. This consists of bundles of twigs tied in a broom and spade-shaped beaters with rubber blades. They can be effective in putting out the beginnings of a blaze.

DISASTER STRATEGIES

Despite their name, do not beat rapidly with them. The aim is to smother the fire by bringing the beater down over the flames to extinguish them.

If no equipment is available, use a coat or blanket to smother the fire, or use a leafy branch to beat it out.

Fighting fire with fire

As long as it is still some distance away, it may be possible to use fire to create protection when there is no way of getting out of the path of a forest fire or going through it.

The technique is to burn a patch of the ground before the main fire reaches it. With nothing left to ignite, the flames cannot advance, giving you a place of refuge. The main fire must be far enough away for your fire to burn a space it cannot jump before it arrives.

Light your own fire along as wide a line as possible, at least 30 feet (10 m) wide, but 300 feet (100 m) would be better. It will burn in the same direction as the main fire, creating a break that you can move into. Make sure you determine the wind direction correctly.

BEWARE: Winds may be swirling, and fires create their own drafts, so you may still have to make a dash through your own flames. The main fire must be far enough away for your own fire to burn and pass. Do not underestimate the speed at which flames travel—they may be approaching faster than you can run. Do not light another fire unless you are desperate and fairly certain of the outcome.

Escaping through fire

Sometimes the best escape route may be to run
through the flames. This is impossible if they are very
intense and the area that is covered by the fire is great.
In a large clearing or on a heath, however, it may be
possible to run through less dense fires to refuge on the
already burned-out land.

Thick vegetation burns fiercely—so choose the
spot for your breakthrough carefully. Make your mind
up, then do not delay. Dampen a piece of cloth to cover
your nose and mouth. Cover as much exposed skin as
you can (including your head) with a blanket, curtain,
or overcoat. If water is available, dump some over you
to dampen down clothing, hair, and any flesh you have
not been able to cover. Take a deep breath. Cover your
nose and mouth to keep the smoke out and run.

If your clothes catch alight, do not stay on your feet
when you are out of the fire. Flames and smoke will
travel up your body, over your face, and into your lungs.

 Do not run if your clothes are ablaze—this
will only fan the flames. Roll on the ground
and try to wrap yourself up in something
that will smother the flames—a mat, blanket, or
overcoat.

If someone else comes running out of a fire with
their clothes alight, push them to the ground and use
the same methods of restricting oxygen to the flames.
Do not hug them to you, or your clothes may catch
fire.

DISASTER STRATEGIES

DISASTER STRATEGIES

FIRES IN BUILDINGS

Block gaps around doors and windows. Close all blinds and curtains. Stay away from outside walls and don't get panicked into running out of the house when the fire reaches it.

Once the fire has passed, avoid excessive smoke inhalation but go outside and put out any small fires.

VEHICLE FIRES

The greatest danger with cars is the risk of the gas tank being ignited. The aim is to control the fire before it can reach the tank. Everything has a flash point, and a gas tank is more at risk than most things. Usually a fuel line (if i is not armored) will catch fire first, acting as a fuse that eventually ignites the tank.

If a car catches fire in a confined space, smoke and toxic fumes will soon build up. Try to put the fire out first—but if that is not practicable, remove the car from the building before it further endangers any lives or property. Do not get into the car. You can do everything from the outside, including steering. If possible, push or pull the car out. If your car has a starter button, select a low gear or reverse and use the starter to bounce the car out. With a conventional ignition, turn the key in short bursts. Be prepared for the car to jerk forward violently.

In a crashed car doors may jam. If it catches fire, get out through any window or kick the windshield out. If the fire is inside the car, use the extinguisher or smother it with a rug or coat. Synthetic materials that are used in the upholstery in many cars burn rapidly and give off thick smoke and toxic gases. These will persist even when the flames are extinguished, so get out into the open as soon as possible.

> KEEP YOU FIRE EXTINGUISHER HANDY!
> Don't keep your fire extinguisher in the trunk—keep it where you can get to it immediately. Impact could distort the trunk and prevent you from opening it.

FIRES IN THE AIR

Airplanes are equipped with automatic extinguishers for engine fires and handheld extinguishers in the cabin. Action should be taken immediately. On civil airlines summon a flight attendant immediately if you suspect fire—the staff know where the equipment is and how to use it. Avoid creating panic among other passengers. If you see smoldering or flames, smother it with an airline blanket or clothing.

The main fire dangers are before takeoff, when there is volatile fuel and vapor around the plane, and especially when landing under difficult circumstances when fuel tanks could be ruptured and electrical or friction sparks could ignite the aviation spirit. Every safety precaution is taken to ensure that fire is not a hazard. You can help. Do not smoke when you are told not to smoke. Do not smoke and doze at the same time.

FLOOD

Flooding can occur for many reasons. It may be caused by the overflowing of rivers, lakes, and reservoirs, caused by heavy rains (not necessarily rainfall at the place where the

DISASTER STRATEGIES

flood occurs); by the buildup of seawater or lake water, due to the effects of submarine earthquakes, hurricanes, and freak hightides and winds; or by the collapse or dams or dykes.

Heavy rain can rapidly produce torrents, where there had been a dry riverbed, or a build up in a narrow channel or behind a barrier that then gives way to a rushing wall of water enveloping everything in its path.

Persistent rainfall over a long period after a dry spell and heavy storms should alert you to stay clear of water channels and low-lying ground, but a flood can affect much wider areas. It is always safer to camp on a spur. If the water is rising, move to higher ground. In hilly areas stay out of valley bottoms that are especially prone to flash floods.

Food is not likely to be a problem, at least at first, as animals will also head for high ground. Both predators and prey are likely to concentrate on getting to safety— but beware of injuries from panic-stricken animals in the water.

Drinking water may be difficult to obtain, as the water swirling around you may be contaminated. Collect rainwater to drink and boil any other water before you use it.

Flooded buildings

If you are in a building when the water begins to rise, stay where you are. You will be less at risk than if you try to evacuate on foot. Turn off the gas and electricity and prepare emergency food supplies, warm clothing, and drinking water in well-sealed containers. Collect a flashlight, whistle, mirror, and brightly-colored cloths for signaling, and add them to your gear, along with a camp stove, candles, and matches.

Move to an upper floor or onto the roof in a single-story building. If you are forced to occupy the roof, erect a shelter. If it is a sloping roof, tie everyone to a chimneystack or other solid structure. If the water continues to rise, prepare some type of raft. If you have no ropes, use bedsheets. Unless the water rises so high that you are forced to evacuate, stay until it stops rising.

Evacuation

Seek shelter on higher ground. You don't have to be at the bottom of a hill to be on low ground!

When you are walking or driving to a safer location remember that a small drop in the level of the roadway down a hill can make a difference to the water depth.

If your car stalls, abandon it. You and your vehicle could be swept away.

Do not attempt to cross a pool or stream unless you are certain that the water will not be higher than the center of the car's wheels or your knees. If you must cross, use river-crossing techniques (see pp. 252–256). If crossing bridges that are underwater, take extra care if thenflood has already swept part of the bridge away.

Flash floods

In a sudden, heavy rainfall stay out of valley bottoms and streambeds both during and after the rainfall. You don't have to be at the bottom of a hill to be caught by water rushing down it carrying mud and debris.

DISASTER STRATEGIES

DISASTER STRATEGIES

Coastal flooding

This is usually a combination of high tides and winds that make them even higher. Flood warnings will usually be given, and evacuation is the best course of action.

Flood aftermath

Do not go outside until you know that it is safe. More storms could be on the way.

As floodwaters recede, they leave a scene of devastation littered with debris and the bodies of flood victims. With decay and the pollution of the water comes the risk of diseases. Take extra precautions: burn all animal corpses—do not risk eating them—and thoroughly boil all water before using it. Some crops may still be available after the floodwaters recede, and birds that have escaped the flood will be safe and good to eat.

TSUNAMI

A tsunami, or tidal wave, is linked to an earthquake beneath the ocean, creating a series of waves that can reach more than 100 feet (30 m) high and travel vast distances, causing damage along the coasts. Not all earthquakes cause tsunamis, but any earthquake could.

Stay away from the shores and head to higher ground when there are tremors. Do not go look for a tsunami— if you are close enough to see one, you are too close to escape it, unless you are high above its level. There is no defense against a moving wall of water. Evacuate.

A tsunami is not one wave but a series of waves. Do not return to the danger area after the first wave, as you may be killed by the onslaught of a second or third wave.

AVALANCHE

There are several types of avalanches.

SOFT-SLAB AVALANCHE

Snow falling on lee slopes, often below a cornice, fails to settle and compact like the snow below. A gap forms behind it. It may feel hard and safe, but any disturbance or loud noise can set the whole slab in motion.

AIRBORNE AVALANCHE

This is frequently the result of new snow falling on an already hard crust or in cold, dry conditions. This may begin as a slab avalanche, but it gathers momentum and more powdered snow to reach very high speeds. Cover the nose and mouth to stand a chance of survival—death is caused by drowning from inhaling the snow.

WET-SNOW AVALANCHE

More common in times of thaw, these often follow a rapid temperature rise after a snowfall. It moves more slowly than an airborne avalanche, picking up trees and rocks in its path. When it stops, it freezes solid almost instantly, making rescue very difficult.

Lay flat and use the crawl stroke to stay on top of the slide (the debris can form a very deep layer). Get rid of your backpack and other encumbrances. Cover nose and mouth to avoid swallowing snow. When you come to rest, make as big a cavity around you as you can before the snow freezes and try to reach the surface. Slip off any undiscarded gear—it will hamper your extraction. Save your energy to shout when you hear people.

DISASTER STRATEGIES

HURRICANE

A hurricane is a wind of high speed—above force 12 on the Beaufort scale—that brings torrential rain and can destroy any flimsy structures. It is a tropical form of a cyclone, which in more temperate latitudes would be prevented from developing in the upper levels of the air by the prevailing westerly winds.

Hurricanes are known by various names around the world:
Hurricane: Caribbean and north Atlantic, eastern north Pacific, western south Pacific.
Cyclone: Arabian Sea, Bay of Bengal, southern Indian Ocean.
Typhoon: China Sea, western north Pacific.
Willy-willy: Northwest Australia.

Hurricanes develop over the ocean when the sea temperatures are at their highest, especially in the late summer. Warm air creates a low pressure core around which winds may rotate at speeds of up to 200 mph (300 kph) or more, circling counterclockwise in the northern hemisphere, clockwise in the southern. The strongest winds are usually 10–12 miles (16–19 km) from the center of the hurricane. but the center, or eye, brings a temporary calm. The eye may be up to 300 miles (500 km) in diameter. Hurricanes can occur at any time of the year: in the northern hemisphere the main season is June to November, and in the southern it is November to April (especially January and February). Hurricanes are not a feature of the south Atlantic.

DISASTER STRATEGIES

Pattern of the hurricane

Out at sea hurricanes will build up force and begin to veer toward the pole, the wind speed usually being at its greatest on the poleward side of the eye.

Hurricane warnings

Satellite surveillance enables meteorologists to track hurricanes and to warn of their approach. Some move very erratically, so monitor forecasts in hurricane areas.

Without a radio to alert you, the growth of swells can indicate a hurricane, especially when it is paired with other conditions such as highly-colorful sunsets or sunrises; dense banners of cirrus clouds converging toward the vortex of the approaching storm; and abnormal rises in barometric pressure followed by an equally rapid drop.

PRECAUTIONS

Get out of the hurricane's path if you can. Hurricane warnings are usually issued when one is expected within 24 hours and will give you plenty of time to evacuate its path, if you are prepared.

Stay away from the coast and from riverbanks.

Board up the windows and secure any objects outdoors that might be blown away.

At sea take down the canvas, batten down the hatches, and stow all your gear.

If you are in a solid building and on high ground, stay where you are—travel in a hurricane is extremely dangerous. The safest place is usually in a cellar or under the stairs. Do not shelter near an internal chimney breast— the chimney may collapse.

DISASTER STRATEGIES

Store drinking water—water and power supplies may be cut off by the storm—and have a battery-operated radio to listen to for any instructions.

If you are not in a sturdy structure, evacuate to a hurricane shelter. Shut off power supplies before you leave

> Do not drive in a hurricane. Cars offer no protection from high winds and flying debris.

Seeking shelter

Outdoors a cave will offer the best protection. A ditch will be the next best option. If you are unable to escape, lie flat on the ground, where you will be less of a target for flying debris. Crawl to the leeside of any really solid shelter such as a stable, rocky outcrop or a wide belt of large trees. Beware of small trees and fences that could be uprooted.

> Stay where you are when the hurricane appears to have passed—there will usually be less than an hour of calm as the eye passes, and then the winds will resume in the opposite direction. If you are sheltering outdoors, move to the other side of your windbreak in preparation, or move to better shelter if it is closeby.

TORNADO

Tornadoes are the most violent of all atmospheric phenomena and the most destructive over a small area. Wind speeds have been estimated at 400 mph (620 kph).

The diameter of the twister at ground level is usually only 80 feet (25–50 m) but, within it, the destruction is enormous. Everything in its path, except the most solid structures, is sucked up into the air. The difference in pressure outside and inside a building is often the cause of its collapse. Tornadoes can sound like a spinning top or engine and have been heard from up to 25 miles (40 km) away. They travel at 30–40 mph (50–65 kph).

TORNADO PRECAUTIONS

Take shelter in the most solid structure available, ideally in a storm cellar or cave. In a cellar stay close to an outside wall or in a specially reinforced section. If there is no basement, go to the center of the lowest floor, into a small room, or shelter under sturdy furniture—but not where there is heavy furniture on the floor above you. Stay far away from windows.

Close all the doors and windows on the side facing the oncoming whirlwind and open those on the opposite side. This will prevent the wind from getting in and lifting the roof off as it approaches and equalize the pressure to prevent the house from "exploding."

Do not stay in a caravan or car, it could be pulled up into the storm. Outdoors you are vulnerable to flying debris and being lifted up. You can see and hear a tornado coming. Get out of the way. Move at right angles to its apparent path. Take shelter in a ditch or depression, lie flat, and cover your head with your arms.

LIGHTNING

Lightning can be especially dangerous on high ground or when you are the tallest object. In a lightning storm stay away from hill brows, tall trees, and lone boulders. Head for low, level ground and lie flat.

DISASTER STRATEGIES

Insulation

If you cannot get away from tall objects, sit on dry material that will provide insulation. A dry coil of climbing rope makes good insulation. Do not sit on anything wet. Bend your head down and hug your knees to your chest, lifting your feet off the ground and drawing in all your extremities. Do not reach down to the ground with your hands, that could create a contact to conduct the lightning. If you have nothing to insulate you from the ground, lie as flat as you can.

Stay low

You can sometimes sense that a lightning strike is imminent by a tingling in your skin and the sensation of your hair standing on end. If you are standing up, drop to the ground immediately, first going to the knees with the hands touching the ground. If you should be struck, the charge may take the easiest route to the earth through your arms—missing the torso and possibly saving you from heart failure or asphyxiation. *Quickly lie flat.*

Do not hold metal objects when there is lightning around and stay away from metal structures and fences. However, do not jettison equipment if you will lose it completely (when you are climbing, for instance). A dry ax with a wooden handle may spark at the tip, but it is well insulated.

Proximity to large, metal objects can be dangerous, even without contact, because the shockwave caused by the heated air—as the lightning passes—can cause damage to the lungs.

DISASTER STRATEGIES

Shelter

One of the best places to shelter in a lightning storm is at least 10 feet (3 m) inside a deep cave with a minimum of 4 feet (1 m) space on either side of you.

Do not shelter in the mouth of a cave or under an overhang of rock in mountainous country. Lightning can spark across the gap. Small openings in the rock are frequently the ends of fissures that are also drainage routes and automatic lightning channels.

EARTHQUAKE

Earthquakes come suddenly, and with little warning. Minor earth tremors can happen anywhere, but major earthquakes are confined to known earthquake belts.

With monitoring by seismologists, earthquakes can be predicted, and evacuation may be possible. Animals become very alert, tense, and ready to run.

A succession of preliminary tremors, known as fore-shocks, often followed by a seismically quiet period, usually precede a major earthquake, which they can actually trigger. Initial tremors may not be noticeable.

DOMESTIC EARTHQUAKE PRECAUTIONS

Stay tuned to a local radio station for up-to-date reports and advice if you have a warning of a possible earthquake.

Turn off gas, electricity, and water if advised to do so.

Remove large and heavy objects from high shelves.

Have ready in case it is needed: freshwater and emergency food, a flashlight, first aid materials, and a fire extinguisher.

DISASTER STRATEGIES

EARTHQUAKE PRECAUTIONS

In a building

Stay indoors. Douse fires. Stay away from glass, including mirrors, and especially from large windows. An inside corner of the house, or a well-supported interior doorway, are good places to shelter. A lower floor or a cellar gives the best chance for survival. Make sure that there are plenty of exits. Get under a table or large piece of furniture that will give both protection and an air space. In a store stay away from large displays of goods. In high-rise offices never go into an elevator. Staircases may attract panicking people. Get under a desk.

In a car

Stop as quickly as you can, but stay in the car—it will offer some protection from falling objects. Crouch down below seat level, and you will be further protected if anything falls on the car. When the tremors cease, keep watch for any obstructions and hazards such as broken cables and undermined roadways or bridges that could give out.

Outdoors

Lie flat on the ground. Do not try to run. You will be thrown around and could be swallowed up in a fissure. Stay away from tall buildings and trees. Do not deliberately go underground or into a tunnel where you could be trapped by a collapse. If you have managed to get to an open space, do not move back into buildings—for if minor tremors follow, they could collapse any structure left unstable by the first earthquake.

On a hillside it is safer to get to the top. Slopes are liable to landslide, and there would be little chance of survival. People have been known to survive by rolling into a tight ball on the ground.

Beaches—as long as they are not below cliffs—are initially fairly safe but, since tidal waves often follow an earthquake you should move off the beach to high, open ground as soon as the tremor has finished. Further tremors are unlikely to be as dangerous as a tsunami.

Be calm and think fast: speed is essential if an earthquake strikes. There is little time to organize others. Use force if necessary to get them to safety or pull them to the ground.

AFTER THE EARTHQUAKE

Check yourself and others for injuries. Apply first aid if it is necessary.

The rupture of sewage systems, contamination of water, and the hazards of the bodies trapped in the wreckage can all make the risk of diseases as deadly as the earthquake itself. Bury all corpses, animal and human. Take extra precautions over sanitation and personal hygiene. Filter and boil all water. Check that the sewage services are intact before using toilets.

Do not shelter in damaged buildings or ruins. Build a shelter from debris. Be prepared for aftershocks. Open up cupboards carefully, objects may tumble out. Clean up spilled household chemicals and potentially harmful substances. Do not strike matches or lighters or use electrical appliances, if there is any chance of a gas leak. Sparks ignite gas.

DISASTER STRATEGIES

DISASTER STRATEGIES

VOLCANO

Active volcanoes are found in the areas of the world that are also most prone to earthquakes.

ERUPTION HAZARDS

Although it is possible to outrun most basaltic lava flows, they continue relentlessly until they reach a valley bottom or eventually cool off. They crush and bury anything in their path. Lava flows are probably the least hazardous to life, since the able-bodied can escape them. Other hazards are more dangerous.

Missiles

Volcanic missiles, ranging from pebble-sized fragments to lumps of rock and hot lava, can be scattered over vast distances. Volcanic ash can cover an even greater area.

If you are evacuating from close to the volcano, hard helmets offer some protection. Over a wider area evacuation may not be necessary, but protection should be worn against the ash and any accompanying rain.

Ash

Volcanic ash is pulverized rock that has been forced out in a cloud of steam and gases. Abrasive, irritant, and heavy, its weight can cause roofs to collapse. It smothers crops, blocks transportation routes and watercourses and, combined with toxic gases, it can cause lung damage to the very young, the elderly, and those with respiratory problems. Only very close to an eruption are gases concentrated enough to poison healthy people. However, when ash is combined with rain, sulfuric acid (and other acids) are produced in concentrations that can burn skin, eyes, and mucous membranes. Wear goggles that seal the area around the eyes (not sunglases, which will offer no protection). Use a damp cloth over the mouth and nose, or, even better, industrial dust masks. Upon reaching shelter, remove your clothing, thoroughly wash exposed skin, and flush eyes with clean water.

Gas balls

A ball of red-hot gas and dust may roll down the side of a volcano at speeds of more than 100 mph (160 kph). Unless there is an underground shelter nearby, the only chance of survival is to submerge yourself underwater and hold your breath for the half-minute or so it will take to pass.

Mudflows

The volcano may melt ice and snow and cause a glacial flood or—combined with earth—create a mudflow, known as a lahar. This can move at up to 60 mph (100 kph) with devastating effects. In a narrow valley a lahar can be as much as 100 feet (30 m) high. They are a danger long after the major eruption is over and are a risk even when the volcano is dormant if it generates enough heat to produce meltwater retained by ice barriers. Heavy rains may cause it to breach the ice.

Volcanoes usually show increased activity before a major eruption. Sulfurous smells from rivers, stinging acidic rain, loud rumblings, or plumes of steam from the volcano are all warning signs.

DISASTER STRATEGIES

Remember, if you are evacuating by car: ash may make roads slippery, even if it does not block them. Avoid valley routes that could become the path of the lahar.

VEHICLES

Transportation has an important role to play in disaster strategy. Make sure that you know how to get the best use out of your vehicle in any situation.

BEFORE SETTING OFF

For desert travel fit long-range gas tanks and make provisions for storing drinking water. Carry further supplies of both in jerricans. A jack is of no use in soft sand, and an air bag should be carried that is inflated by the exhaust. Extra filters will be needed in the fuel line and air intake. Sand tires must be fitted and sand channels carried to get you moving again when you get bogged down in loose sands.

For high altitudes adjust the carburetor. In scrub country thorn gaiters will reduce puncture risks. Antifreeze and suitable wheels and chains are needed for snow and ice. The engine will need special tuning to match climatic conditions, as well as its own spares. Carry a spare wheel and a good toolbox.

IN HOT CLIMATES

OVERHEATING: Stop and allow the engine to cool down. If you are driving a particularly tricky stretch of road and stopping is out of the question, switch on the heater. This will give greater volume to the cooling water and, although the inside of the car will get even hotter, the engine will cool down. When it is convenient, stop and open up the hood. Do not undo the radiator cap until the temperature drops. Check the radiator and all hoses for leaks. If the radiator is leaking, adding the white of an egg will seal up small holes. If there is a large hole, squeeze the section of the copper piping flat to seal it off. It will reduce the size of the cooling area but, if you drive very steadily, you will be able to keep going.

METAL GETS HOT: Be careful! All metal parts of a car can get hot enough to cause blisters.

 Never leave an injured person or an animal in a closed car in a hot climate—or even on a sunny day in temperate regions. Always leave windows open to ensure ventilation. Heat exhaustion kills even in the shade, since the sun will move.

BE CAREFUL IN SANDY CONDITIONS: When you are adding fuel, sand and dust can get into the tank. Rig up a filter over or just inside the inlet to the tank.

IN COLD CLIMATES

If you are trapped in a blizzard, stay in the car. If you are on a regular traffic route, you will probably be rescued soon. Going for help could be too risky.

Run the engine for heat if you have fuel. Cover the engine so that as little heat as possible is lost, but make sure that the exhaust is clear. Do not risk exhaust fumes coming into the car. If you feel drowsy, stop the engine and open a window. Do not go to sleep with the engine running. Switch off the heater as soon as you have taken

DISASTER STRATEGIES

the chill out, starting it again when the temperature drops. If there is no fuel, wrap up in any spare clothing, rugs, etc. and keep moving around inside the car.

If you have to leave the car to go a short distance, e.g. if you know help is very close, rig up a signpost— a bright scarf on a stick will help you find the car again.

When the blizzard stops, if it is daylight (otherwise wait until the morning), it is worth walking out if there is a clear guide to the route (such as telegraph poles).

If you are miles from anywhere and the snow is building up to bury the car, get out and build yourself a snow cave. When the blizzard stops, scrape large signs in the snow and use other signals to attract attention.

STARTING: Always try to park on a gradient so that you can use a bump start to back up the starter. Once you get the engine going, keep it running, but check that the hand brake is firmly on and never leave children or animals in an unattended vehicle with the engine running.

DEMISTING: Don't try to drive looking through a small clear patch on a misty windshield. Rub an onion or raw potato on the inside to stop it from misting up.

Cover the outside of the windshield and windows with newspaper to prevent frost from building up on them. If it is damp, however, the paper will stick.

COVER THE ENGINE: Wrap a blanket around the engine to help stop it from freezing up, but remember to remove it before you start the engine. Cover the lower part of the radiator with cardboard or wood, so that it does not freeze as you go along. If it is very cold, leave it covered. Otherwise remove it to prevent overheating.

COVER METAL: Don't touch any metal with bare hands. Your fingers could freeze to it and tear off the skin. Where handling metal components with gloves is awkward, wrap fingers with adhesive tape. Treat radiator cap and dipstick in this way to ease your daily checks.

DIESEL ENGINES: Diesel contains water and freezes solid at low temperatures. Always cover front of engine, but check it for overheating. Wrap engine at night or when left standing. Some drivers light small fires under frozen tanks. Only you can judge if this risk is worth taking.

GENERAL

CLUTCH SLIP: This is often caused by oil or grease getting onto the clutch plates. To degrease use the fire extinguisher. Squirt it through the license plate opening.

BROKEN FAN BELT: Improvize with tights, a tie, or string.

HIGH TENSION CABLES: If a high tension cable breaks, you may be able to replace it with a willow twig. Any plant stem with water content will carry a current from the coil to the distributor. Spit on the ends and insert them into push-fit contacts. When you switch it on, there is a deadly current of around 1300 volts: do not touch it. Replace the twig frequently as it dries out.

DEAD BATTERY: Set the vehicle moving by a tow, a push, or letting it run downhill. Put it in second gear and release the clutch to bump start it.

CREDITS & ACKNOWLEDGMENTS

This book was edited and designed by
Anne O'Brien and Stephen Kirk

Sharks painted by Craig Austin
All color illustrations by Norman Arlott
Other illustrations were drawn by
Steve Cross, Chris Lyon,
Andrew Mawson, Tony Spalding

The editors would also like to thank
the following for their assistance:
Belinda Bouchard, Ronald Clark, Mark Crean,
Johnny Pinfold, William Spalding

Department of Community Affairs,
Florida, U.S.

Department of Emergency Management,
Washington, D.C., U.S.

Federal Emergency Management Agency,
Washington, D.C., U.S.

Greater London Council Fire Brigade Department,
London, U.K.

Health and Safety Commission, U.K.

Office of Emergency Services,
California, U.S.